T0329117

ELSEVIER
ASIAN STUDIES SERIES

Series Editor: Professor Chris Rowley,
Cass Business School, City University, London, UK;
Institute of Hallyu Convergence Research, Korea University, Korea
Griffith Business School, Griffith University, Australia
(email: c.rowley@city.ac.uk)

Elsevier is pleased to publish this major Series of books entitled Asian Studies: Contemporary Issues and Trends. The Series Editor is Professor Chris Rowley of Cass Business School, City University, London, UK and Department of International Business and Asian Studies, Griffith University, Australia.

Asia has clearly undergone some major transformations in recent years and books in the Series examine this transformation from a number of perspectives: economic, management, social, political and cultural. We seek authors from a broad range of areas and disciplinary interests covering, for example, business/management, political science, social science, history, sociology, gender studies, ethnography, economics and international relations, etc.

Importantly, the Series examines both current developments and possible future trends. The Series is aimed at an international market of academics and professionals working in the area. The books have been specially commissioned from leading authors. The objective is to provide the reader with an authoritative view of current thinking.

New authors: we would be delighted to hear from you if you have an idea for a book. We are interested in both shorter, practically orientated publications (45,000 + words) and longer, theoretical monographs (75,000−100,000 words). Our books can be single, joint or multi-author volumes. If you have an idea for a book, please contact the publishers or Professor Chris Rowley, the Series Editor.

Dr Glyn Jones   Professor Chris Rowley
Email: g.jones.2@elsevier.com   Email: c.rowley@city.ac.uk

Achieving Inclusive Growth in China Through Vertical Specialization

Achieving Inclusive Growth in China Through Vertical Specialization

Wang Wei

AMSTERDAM • BOSTON • HEIDELBERG • LONDON
NEW YORK • OXFORD • PARIS • SAN DIEGO
SAN FRANCISCO • SINGAPORE • SYDNEY • TOKYO

Chandos Publishing is an imprint of Elsevier

Chandos Publishing is an imprint of Elsevier
50 Hampshire Street, 5th Floor, Cambridge, MA 02139, USA
The Boulevard, Langford Lane, Kidlington, OX5 1GB, UK

Notices
Knowledge and best practice in this field are constantly changing. As new research and experience
broaden our understanding, changes in research methods, professional practices, or medical treatment
may become necessary.

Practitioners and researchers must always rely on their own experience and knowledge in evaluating and
using any information, methods, compounds, or experiments described herein. In using such information
or methods they should be mindful of their own safety and the safety of others, including parties for
whom they have a professional responsibility.

To the fullest extent of the law, neither the Publisher nor the authors, contributors, or editors, assume any
liability for any injury and/or damage to persons or property as a matter of products liability, negligence
or otherwise, or from any use or operation of any methods, products, instructions, or ideas contained in
the material herein.

British Library Cataloguing-in-Publication Data
A catalogue record for this book is available from the British Library

Library of Congress Cataloging-in-Publication Data
A catalog record for this book is available from the Library of Congress

ISBN: 978-0-08-100627-6

For information on all Chandos Publishing
visit our website at http://www.elsevier.com/

Working together
to grow libraries in
developing countries

www.elsevier.com • www.bookaid.org

Contents

Sources of all figures and tables: *Author's estimates based on data from China Statistics Yearbook, China Customs Statistics Yearbook, China Trade and External Economic Statistical Yearbook, China Commerce Yearbook, China labour Statistical Yearbook, China Population &Employment Statistics Yearbook, China Statistical Yearbook on Science and Technology, and China Energy Statistical Yearbook (Various issues).*

About the author

Wang Wei, PhD, is Professor of Economics at Tianjin University of Commerce in P.R. China. He has written one book, two textbooks, and more than 20 academic articles and chapters, and is interested in China's trade and development.

Acknowledgments

This book was supported by the MOE (the Ministry of Education in China) Project of Humanities and Social Science (Project No. 10YJC790259). The author acknowledges the China Statistics Yearbook, China Customs Statistics Yearbook, China Trade and External Economic Statistical Yearbook, China Commerce Yearbook, China labour Statistical Yearbook, China Population & Employment Statistics Yearbook, China Statistical Yearbook on Science and Technology, and China Energy Statistical Yearbook as invaluable sources of data.

Introduction: key elements of a transformation in China

1

1.1 Background

In recent years, two important interrelated developments have occurred that transformed the fundamental nature of Chinese economy. The first is the global community calling for fostering economic growth in a more inclusive manner, with China embracing inclusive growth to make the markets work for all. The second is the explosive growth of China's trade and China's rapid emergence as an export powerhouse due to having taken advantage of the processing trade regime based on vertical specialization and slicing up the value chain. The literature for each of these two separate topics is large and growing. However, very few books quantitatively assess these two trends together.

For China, development has always been the top priority throughout the approximately 30 years of reform and opening up. Up to 2007, China's gross domestic product (GDP) grew at an average rate of 11%, with trade surplus equaling 10% of the GDP. Since the global crisis, the trade surplus has fallen sharply into the range of 3−4% of the GDP.

Since its market-oriented economic reform in 1978, China's income inequality situation has seemingly deteriorated (Mah, 2013). For growth to be sustainable and effective in reducing poverty, it needs to be inclusive (Kraay, 2004; Berg and Ostry, 2011). How can the micro and macro dimensions of inequality and growth be integrated to reflect both the pace and distribution of economic growth? The links between inequality and growth are many and complex. Greater inclusiveness depends on the distribution of income and employment creation dimensions. The inclusive growth approach has a longer-term perspective, because the focus is on productive employment as a means of increasing the incomes of poor and excluded groups and raising their standard of living (Ianchovichina and Lundstrom, 2009). In the domestic context, inclusive growth means a country's economic and social development should guarantee a higher living standard for its people while not imposing serious damages on the environment. Realizing inclusive growth, resolving the social issues emerging from economic development, and laying a solid social foundation for trade promotion, foreign direct investment facilitation, and long-term economic development are all major issues. China's macroeconomic regulation in pursuing development in a scientific way should focus on transforming economic growth patterns and adjusting economic structures. To bring about these structural changes, China must turn to a growth model driven by technological progress and higher production efficiency.

In the past 30 years, China's exports have grown at an annualized rate of 19%, which is more than twice the rate of the growth of world exports (Ma et al., 2009).

As a result, China's share of world trade has surpassed that of Japan, the United States, and Germany to become the world's largest exporter. China's foreign trade is, to a large extent, vertically specialized. China's exports contain a substantial amount of inputs imported mostly from the East Asian supply chain, as illustrated by Koopman et al. (2008). Conventional trade models do not consider vertically specialized trade. One way to quantify the importance of the vertical trade is to look at the share of processing exports in China's total exports. The China Customs General Administration's trade database exclusively records China's foreign trade transactions of goods. Processing exports are significant to China's foreign trade, accounting for 55% of China's exports to the world in 2005 (Ferrantino et al., 2007). In 2008, 47% of China's exports were classified as processing exports (ie, they use imported intermediate inputs). Processing trade by foreign-invested enterprises (FIEs) is that conducted by three types of FIEs: wholly owned FIEs; foreign-invested joint ventures; and Sino-foreign cooperative firms. Processing trade includes two main types of transactions: processing and assembling and processing with imported materials (Xu and Lu, 2009).The emergence of China has intensified international segmentation of production processes within Asia, but it has not created an autonomous engine for the region's trade because Asia still depends on outside markets for its final exports (Gaulier et al. 2007; Liao et al., 2012). In reality, imports of intermediate goods sometimes involve trade between a parent and its subsidiaries in the same transnational corporation. This kind of relationship usually exists in the intermediate goods trade between China and developed countries (Liao et al., 2012).

1.2   Six components of the problem of inclusive growth in China

What is inclusive growth? The concept of inclusive growth was first created and advocated by Asian Development Bank (ADB) economists in 2007. It means to spread the benefits of globalization and development and to realize "balanced social and economic progress through sustainable development." Some definitions of inclusive growth are interchangeable with definitions of pro-poor growth—defined as growth associated with poverty reduction (Grosse et al., 2008; Habito, 2009; Rauniyar and Kanbur, 2010; Ranieri et al., 2013). Ianchovichina and Gable (2012) describe inclusive growth as increasing the pace of growth and enlarging the size of the economy by increasing productive employment opportunities and providing a level playing field for investment. Inclusive growth is the most important source of continued and sustained economic growth (Anand et al., 2013a,b).

The proxy used in this book is an attempt to capture inclusive growth by accounting for six components of the problem of inclusive growth in China. To enlarge the size of the economy, generate productive employment, accelerate poverty reduction, strengthen indigenous innovation, lower environmental damage, upgrade utilization of foreign capital at the required scale, and avoid middle-income trap, China will have to achieve sustained and inclusive growth, which critically depends on "reform and opening up" policies. For this reason, questions of macroeconomic stability, employment generation, poverty and economic disparity, environmental sustainability, technological innovation, utilization of foreign capital, and inclusive growth should be more prominently reflected in the Thirteenth 5-Year Plan.

Greater inclusiveness depends on the distribution of income, rapid GDP growth, employment creation, stimulation of technological innovation, poverty alleviation with prevention of irreversible environmental damage, and FDI absorption dimensions, among other factors. Six components of the problem of inclusive growth in China presented in this book cover a range of different perspectives on GDP growth, employment, income, environment, innovation, and FDI. Each of these makes clear contributions to the inclusive growth process in China, and together they provide an overview of some of the most important challenges that policymakers are facing in the pursuit of sustaining economic growth (Anwar and Sun, 2012; Xu and Li, 2008; Long et al., 2015; Daumal and Ozyurt, 2011; Feenstra and Hanson, 1999; Feenstra and Hanson, 2001; Fung et al., 2004; Hijzen, 2007; HKTDC, 2007; Hopenhayn, 1992a,b; Krugman, 2000; Dallas, 2014; Tang, 2011; Taylor, 1993, 1994; Gao, 2005; Topel, 1997; Yang et al., 2014).

1.3 Analytical framework

China's prominence in vertical specialization and transition to inclusive growth have raised numerous questions and created new challenges. What has driven inclusive growth in China? Why does vertically specialized trade matter for inclusive growth in China? How does rapid growth and new composition of trade affect growth toward more inclusiveness in China? Do data support the argument? What policy implications can be readily derived from empirical results? Increasingly, it appears that the answers to these questions may be found by studying the impact of vertical specialization on inclusive growth in China.

China is a major player in vertical specialization. A great deal of processing trade takes place, and many of the raw and auxiliary materials, parts and components, accessories, and packaging materials are imported from abroad duty-free. The finished products are re-exported after they have been processed or assembled by enterprises. Production for processing exports uses imported intermediates more intensively than for normal exports and domestic use. Hence, the policies that focus on aggregate trade flow may be very misleading.

Little attention has been given to the potential difference in the contribution to inclusive growth between conventional trade and processing trade. The links between vertical specialization and inclusive growth are many and complex. This book provides evidence of the links between vertical specialization and inclusive growth in China, focusing on deconstructing the inclusive growth effects of China's vertically specialized trade into six components, specifically GDP growth, employment, wages, environment, innovation, and foreign direct investment, and providing a comprehensive measure of the inclusive growth effects of the vertically specialized trade in China. Based on the deconstruction, this book describes and illustrates

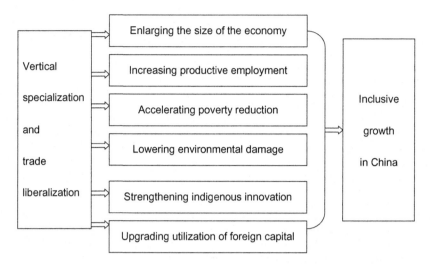

Figure 1.1 Analytical framework of driving inclusive growth through vertical specialization.

the different impacts of conventional trade and processing trade on inclusive growth and explores the policy implications toward more inclusive growth. Moreover, the impact of China's regime of processing trade policy on inclusive growth is significant in the context of vertical specialization. The analysis stresses the importance of integrating into vertical specialization to promote inclusive growth.

Our central tenet is that China's integration into vertical specialization enhances the positive impacts of trade liberalization on economic growth, employment, income, innovation capacity, and opening up and also weakens the negative impacts of trade liberalization on the environment. We incorporate these six dimensions of impact into our framework because they are some of the most salient outcomes of inclusive growth and the primary focus of interest in the inclusive growth and sustainable development literature. Moreover, our China Statistical Yearbook data allow us to examine these six dimensions. This study is not an attempt to exhaustively review the literature on trade liberalization impacts and replicate the findings. Rather, we provide a baseline framework that encompasses the multiple impacts of vertical specialization and apply a globalization-based view to reveal the underlying reason behind the inclusive growth in China. Fig. 1.1 presents our analytical framework. Table A1 provides a summary of the measures for all indicators in this study.

1.3.1 What are the overall messages of the book?

First, *Achieving Inclusive Growth in China through Vertical Specialization* provides a comprehensive overview of Chinese vertical specialization and effects on inclusive growth in China from the perspective of GDP growth, foreign capital utilization, employment, income, wage, environment and energy consumption, and indigenous innovation. It aims to test alternative explanations and provide empirical evidence in support of specific mechanisms that could enhance synergies between vertically specialized trade and inclusive growth by engaging in a wide range of globalization and trade liberalization and positioning to gain from mainstreaming inclusiveness considerations in trade-driven growth strategies.

Second, *Achieving Inclusive Growth in China through Vertical Specialization* uses a longer-term perspective because the focus is on productive employment as a means of increasing the incomes of poor and excluded groups and raising their standard of living. The book uses the spreading the benefits of economic globalization and development among all countries, regions, and people and the realization of balanced economic and social progress through sustainable development as ideas seeking to ensure equal access to opportunities and to balance economic and social development with environmental costs. This book investigates the impact of vertical specialization on the inclusive growth performance of China during the period of 1981−2012 using the vector error correction (VEC) model under the time series framework. The Johansen-Juselius procedure is applied to test the cointegration relationship between variables, followed by the VEC regression model. The empirical results trace a long-term equilibrium relationship in the variables.

Third, our book provides evidence of the links between vertically specialized trade or global value chains and inclusive growth outcomes, focusing on China. It examines the impact on labor demand and wages and disaggregates the effects whenever possible by skill level. The available empirical evidence strongly suggests that the types of activities undertaken by vertical specialization participants influence labor market outcomes in China.

Fourth, stronger-than-expected growth in China's foreign trade during the past decades has surprised the market and prompted many analysts to look for further hints of underlying economic strength. *Achieving Inclusive Growth in China through Vertical Specialization* aims to foster an understanding of how vertically specialized trade can help implement strategies for inclusive growth and sustainable development. The purpose of our book is to provide econometric evidence regarding the links between vertically specialized trade and inclusive growth by focusing on China in the era of globalized supply chains.

Fifth, the United States−China bilateral trade deficit is discussed because the bilateral trade deficit has been cited many times by US politicians and by the US Trade Representative as an important indicator of the existence of unfair trading practices. The aim of *Achieving Inclusive Growth in China through Vertical Specialization* is to identify the determinants of more inclusive growth in China and offer an assessment of their relative importance. This book proposes that China's external trade will succeed in becoming sustainable and responsible only if it can shift toward more inclusive growth. This requires, when accompanied by global trade liberalization, integrating into vertical specialization and shifting toward more inclusive growth to interact in a bi-directional, mutually beneficial way.

Sixth, the aim of *Achieving Inclusive Growth in China through Vertical Specialization* is to assess the different impacts of China's vertically specialized trade and ordinary trade for more inclusive growth. It uses data analysis and econometric methods applied to Chinese data from 1981 to 2012.

"The ultimate purpose of inclusive growth is to spread the benefits of economic globalization and economic development among all economies, regions and people and to realize balanced economic and social progress through sustainable development" (Hu, 2010). Integrating into vertical specialization is vital for achieving inclusive growth and sustainable development in China. However, inclusive growth in China has three pillars: economic, social, and environmental sustainability. After making the case for a change toward more inclusive growth patterns, these country-focused chapters cover six important dimensions of inclusive development in China: (1) GDP growth; (2) employment; (3) income; (4) innovation; (5) climate and environment; and (6) opening up.

In a world of deeply integrated economies, solutions to these problems of inclusive growth lie in integrating into global production fragmentation or vertical specialization. Success in inclusive growth will enable China to continue to grow well for another decade or more.

In summary, the topics in this book all have policy implications for the continued work against inclusive growth in China, understanding vertical specialization and trade liberalization, and dealing with economic imbalances in contemporary China. We hope that this book can serve as a starting point for further research in each of these areas.

Appendix

Table A1 Indicators and measures

Indicators	Indicators and measures
GDP growth	Indices of GDP
	Indices of gross national income
	Indices of primary industry GDP
	Indices of secondary industry GDP
	Indices of industry GDP
	Indices of construction GDP
	Indices of tertiary industry GDP
	Indices of whole and retail trades GDP
	Indices of per capita GDP
Employment	Number of total employed persons
	Number of employed persons at year-end in urban areas
	Number of employed persons at year-end in rural areas
	Number of economically active populations
	Number of employed persons at year-end by primary industry
	Number of employed persons at year-end by secondary industry
	Number of employed persons at year-end by tertiary industry
Income	Total wages of employed persons by registration status/GDP
	Index of average monetary wage of urban unit employment
	Per capita annual disposable income of urban households/per capita annual net income of rural households
	Engel's coefficient of rural households (%) minus Engel's coefficient of urban households (%)
Environment	Total energy consumption (10^4 tee)
	Petroleum consumption (10^4 tee)

(*Continued*)

Table A1 **(Continued)**

Indicators	Indicators and measures
Innovation	Natural gas consumption (10^4 tee)
	Hydro power, nuclear power, and other power consumption (10^4 tee)
	Ratio of appropriation for science and technology to total government budgetary expenditure
	Ratio of total intramural expenditure on R&D to GDP
Opening-up	Foreign direct investment, net inflows (BoP, current US$)
	Number of foreign enterprise (unit)
	The ratio of FDI to GDP
	The ratio of the total amount of foreign capital used to GDP
	The ratio of foreign partner registered capital to GDP
Vertical specialization	Indices of imports by processing trade
	Imports by processing trade
	Indices of exports by processing trade
	Exports by processing trade
Ordinary trade	Indices of imports by conventional trade
	Imports by conventional trade
	Indices of exports by conventional trade
	Exports by conventional trade
Other trading forms	Indices of imports by other trading forms
	Imports by other trading forms
	Indices of exports by other trading forms
	Exports by other trading forms

FDI, foreign direct investment; GDP, gross domestic product; R&D, research and development; BoP, Balance of payments.

The evolving pattern of China's free trade from a vertically specialized perspective during the transition to inclusive growth in China

2

2.1 Introduction

Since its reform and opening up period, China has made remarkable strides in expanding foreign trade and driving inclusive growth. Integrating into the global value chain has been a nearly global phenomenon in the past three decades. This is clearly reflected in the increasing disparities between different trade types, with the processing trade becoming faster than the conventional trade in China. The economics literature has attributed this mainly to vertical specialization, opening up, and factors endowment in China.

During the past decades, in response to inclusive sustainable economic development, China has given high priority to making structural adjustments and transforming the growth model, and has expanded the scope and depth of opening up. At the end of 2014, China's gross domestic products (GDP) reached 63.6 trillion Yuan. The strategy of developing the Silk Road Economic Belt and 21st Century Maritime Silk Road entered the implementation phase, the registered urban unemployment rate was 4.09%, research and development spending accounted for more than 2% of the GDP, energy intensity was cut, the growth rate of the per capita disposable income of rural residents outpaced that of those living in urban areas, the number of rural people living in poverty was reduced, and the urban−rural income gap continued to narrow.

A large portion of China's foreign trade is vertically specialized, because China imports intermediate inputs from other economies in the East Asian supply chain, assembles them into final goods, and exports them to overseas markets. Conventional trade models do not consider vertically specialized trade. Customs in China classify each import and export transaction into processing and nonprocessing categories. Processing exports are defined as exports that use imported intermediate inputs. During the 1980s, China installed a processing trade regime that grants duty exemptions on imported raw materials and other inputs as long as they are used solely for export purposes. Imported intermediate inputs for processing trade purposes are eligible for import tax rebates (Dean et al., 2009; Tong and Zheng, 2008; Lemoine and Ünal-Kezenci, 2004).

The academic literature and recent events in different parts of the world have highlighted the detrimental impact of less inclusive economic growth

Achieving Inclusive Growth in China Through Vertical Specialization.

(eg, Berg and Ostry, 2011; Rajan, 2010). In this context, this chapter investigates the factors behind the expansion of exports in China by using a deconstruction technique. It finds that, in many ways, the processing trade was largely utilized to support the growth of foreign trade surplus during the transition to inclusive growth in China. In this chapter, Section 2.2 is an overview of inclusive growth policies and practices in China. In the following sections, we report the method of analysis, interpret the empirical findings, and provide concluding comments.

2.2   An overview of inclusive growth in China: policies and practices

Inclusive growth is a multidimensional concept in policy discussions and the Report on China's Economic and Social Development Plan (2011−2015). From 2011 to 2015, China fulfilled the goals of the Twelfth 5-Year Plan and made progress in implementing the Thirteenth 5-Year Plan, including the Three Major Strategies: "One Belt and One Road" strategy (the Silk Road Economic Belt and 21st Century Maritime Silk Road); the coordinated development of the Beijing-Tianjin-Hebei region; and the development of the Yangtze River economic belt. "The ultimate purpose of inclusive growth is to spread the benefits of economic globalization and economic development among all economies, regions and people and to realize balanced economic and social progress through sustainable development" (Hu, 2010).

In China, pursing development in a scientific way embodies the thinking for promoting inclusive growth driven by scientific and technological progress and by coordinated urban−rural development. China implemented the strategy of innovation-driven development, established national innovation demonstration zones, and formulated the Knowledge Innovation Program (2011−2020), an "Internet Plus" action plan, and the "Made in China 2025" strategy. Scientific and technological innovation provides support for boosting GDP growth to avoid falling into the "middle-income trap." A proactive employment policy is crucial to inclusive growth practices. Advancing urbanization accelerated reform of the registration of rural migrant workers as permanent urban residents in an orderly way. China expanded job opportunities for the rural migrant labor force, strengthened vocational skills training for rural migrant workers, and public employment service facilities and harmonious labor relations continued to improve. In increasing individual income in step with inclusive growth, China regulated income distribution mainly through taxation and transfer payments and raised the share of work remuneration in GDP. To narrow the gap between urban and rural areas, China encouraged the rural migrant labor force to participate in integrating urban and rural development and the program of poverty alleviation, helped the poor by providing work relief and relocating those in poverty-stricken areas, gave pairing assistance to underdeveloped localities, and provided access to education to the children of rural migrant labor forces in cities (Full text of President Hu's speech).

Faced with increasing resource constraints and severe environmental pollution, China strived for green, circular, and low-carbon growth, imposed a ceiling on total energy consumption, and supported the development of energy-efficient industries, new energy sources, and renewable energy sources. Energy consumption and environmental damage have been covered by the system of standards for evaluating sustainable growth to promote ecological progress. In response to globalization and vertical specialization, China did the following: implemented the win−win strategy of opening up; formed coastal, inland, and border areas of opening up with the building of China Pilot Free Trade Zones in Shanghai, Guangdong, Tianjin, and Fujian; transformed and upgraded processing trade expanding the import of advanced technology, key equipment, and parts and components; and made use of the comparative advantage in utilizing foreign capital and technology (Report on the Work of the Government, 2011−2015).

2.3 Comparative advantage and patterns of China's foreign trade: 1981−2012

2.3.1 Net exports

The net export ratio is a simple measure that reflects the magnitude of the trade balance between China and the world for a given commodity. It is constructed as follows:

$$NX_{ij} = \left(\frac{X_{ij} - M_{ij}}{X_{ij} + M_{ij}}\right) \bullet 100$$

where X_{ij} represents country i's exports of product j to the world and M_{ij} represents country i's imports of product j from the world. The index ranges between -100, when a good is imported but not exported, and $+100$, when a good is exported but not imported. The net exports ratio can be used as a very rough approximation regarding which country has the comparative advantage in an industry.

Table 2.1 shows that China has had a processing trade surplus from 1989 to 2012. This surplus has increased substantially since 1989. China had a conventional trade surplus from 1990 to 2000 and from 2005 to 2008. This has been associated with an increase in China's competitive advantage of processing trade.

2.3.2 Michaely index

The Michaely index is not an accurate measure of advantage. However, it is a reasonable proxy regarding the industries a nation has specialized in over time. A nation is said to specialize, or has a comparative advantage, in a commodity for which the MI is greater than 100. Formula of Michaely index (MI) is cited from Michaely, M. (1962/67) and Laursen (2015).

$$MI = (X_{ij}/X_i - M_{ij}/M_i) \bullet 100$$

Where X_{ij} represents country i's exports of product j, X_i is country i's total exports, M_{ij} is country i's imports of product j, and M_i represents country i's total imports.

Table 2.1 Net exports ratio: China and the world

	NIC	NIP	NIO
1981–1985	−3.945	−10.074	−50.129
1981	1.0543	−14.156	−27.854
1982	8.1692	−67.781	−72.5
1983	3.5758	−7.78	−47.059
1984	−1.461	−3.588	−78.834
1985	−22.199	−12.622	−39.683
1986–1990	−2.101	4.2002	−70.721
1986	−16.769	−8.788	−62.963
1987	1.4911	−6.239	−68.198
1988	−3.807	−3.583	−71.098
1989	−6.048	7.0936	−68.196
1990	15.0178	15.0747	−74.792
1991–1995	17.7682	10.7881	−79.346
1991	12.6811	12.8785	−74.291
1992	13.0142	11.3547	−80.785
1993	6.3385	9.7742	−74.586
1994	26.8232	9.0005	−85.882
1995	24.403	11.6075	−78.209
1996–2000	16.0011	18.7704	−71.969
1996	22.9746	15.0477	−81.11
1997	33.2843	17.3113	−72.807
1998	25.9127	20.7191	−69.545
1999	8.2743	20.2234	−67.235
2000	2.4856	19.5882	−67.188
2001–2005	1.5809	20.0538	−60.823
2001	−0.699	22.145	−68.382
2002	2.6672	19.1069	−64.448
2003	−1.519	19.5048	−62.481
2004	−0.923	19.3347	−61.561
2005	5.9577	20.6313	−55.499
2006–2010	4.2005	26.772	−35.396
2006	11.0981	22.707	−52.725
2007	11.4348	25.2614	−43.688
2008	7.35	28.167	−32.523
2009	−0.438	29.1008	−27.435
2010	−3.266	27.8811	−28.382
2011	−4.707	28.0089	−29.125
2012	−1.716	28.3791	−22.735

Note: NIC is the net export ratio of conventional trade, NIP is the net export ratio of processing trade, and NIO is the net export ratio of trade by other trading forms.

The index ranges between −100 and +100. A value of 100 implies that the export performance of country i for product j matches its relative size as an exporter, therefore suggesting that country i has a comparative advantage in that good.

From 1999 to 2012, China's strongest competitive advantage has been in processing trade rather than conventional trade. The MI for processing trade has been increasing, rising above 0 since 1984 (except for 1987). MI for conventional trade has been declining, falling below 0 since 2000 (except for 2006) (Table 2.2).

Table 2.2 **Michaely index**

	MIC	MIP	MIO
1981–1985	1.6972	−0.86	−0.836
1981	2.0139	−1.692	−0.277
1982	1.7635	−1.193	−0.617
1983	2.9463	−1.877	−1.069
1984	1.5991	−0.276	−1.323
1985	−1.454	2.0083	−0.555
1986–1990	2.9734	5.0178	−7.987
1986	−0.94	2.5431	−1.58
1987	8.5733	−0.781	−7.793
1988	4.9544	2.2581	−7.212
1989	−0.167	8.6344	−8.468
1990	8.001	5.7766	−13.778
1991–1995	13.4486	7.5502	−20.997
1991	6.7025	5.8599	−12.562
1992	9.7072	7.5083	−17.216
1993	10.489	13.2495	−23.728
1994	20.1478	5.9401	−26.088
1995	15.134	5.3433	−20.477
1996–2000	5.9235	10.6212	−16.544
1996	13.2509	10.9758	−24.227
1997	15.2432	5.1775	−20.421
1998	9.2622	7.9427	−17.202
1999	0.138	12.4786	−12.615
2000	−2.254	14.1171	−11.863
2001–2005	−2.639	14.8115	−12.17
2001	−4.54	16.8202	−12.283
2002	−1.915	13.8603	−11.947
2003	−3.924	15.7211	−11.777
2004	−3.157	15.7747	−12.619
2005	−1.022	13.1379	−12.116
2006–2010	−5.103	14.6835	−9.601
2006	0.8723	12.0517	−12.925
2007	−0.641	12.0621	−11.526
2008	−4.181	13.7793	−9.597
2009	−9.041	16.8002	−7.76
2010	−9.423	17.0195	−7.597
2011	−9.488	17.0562	−7.569
2012	−8.004	15.6415	−7.637

Note: MIC is the Michaely index of conventional trade, MIP is the Michaely index of processing trade, and MIO is the Michaely index of trade by other trading forms.

2.4 Concluding remarks and policy implications

We found that processing trade has statistically significant effects on China's trade surplus and comparative advantage. Once foreign trade is broken down into distinctive parts, two results emerge. First, China has declined in relative importance as a provider of conventional trade. China's conventional trade was outperformed. Second, China has become more important as a trading partner of processing trade for the world. Net exports (NE) analysis attributes this to the competitiveness of processing trade. NE suggests that China was not competitive in conventional trade. This is confirmed by the Michaely index. The two trends were facilitated by changes in Chinese government policies toward trade openness and processing trade, particularly policy changes related to China's WTO entry in 2001, which is in line with the results of other work (Xu and Lu, 2009).

How would China's foreign policy affect China's inclusive growth? China's export structure has shown a rapid shift toward vertically specialized trade. Thus, the evidence from our study highlights the importance of dividing foreign trade into different categories in identifying their impact on the inclusiveness of China's economic growth.

Identifying the sources of China's comparative advantage has important implications. If the shifting of China's trade structure is driven by vertical specialization in which firms import intermediate inputs to assemble final goods, then we must ask if there is any effect on inclusive growth in China. Without understanding this issue, we cannot make conclusive statements on how vertical specialization inclusive growth in China or on how the inclusive growth can be driven by trade liberalization. This also implies that changes in trade patterns should be taken into consideration when we evaluate policies for inclusive growth and government strategies for sustainable development.

Vertical specialization and enlarging the size of the economy: comparing impacts of conventional trade and processing trade patterns on GDP growth in China

3

3.1 Introduction

After 30 years of reform and opening up, China's economy has grown at an annual rate of 9.8% and has become the world's second largest economy. In 2010, China obtained two-digit growth, reaching 10.4%; in 2013, China's gross domestic product (GDP) grew by 7.7%, which remains mid-to-high growth worldwide. Opening up is an engine of China's economic growth. In 2001, China joined the World Trade Organization and integrated the Chinese economy into the world economy. China's share of the world trade has sharply increased from less than 1% more than 30 years ago to 10.5% in 2014.

China's Customs Statistics distinguishes between imports and exports linked to conventional trade, processing trade, and other trading forms. The former is a type of trade pattern of ordinary international trade (standard textbook); the latter (processing trade) is a type of trade pattern of achievement of integration into vertical specialization. Processing trade involves importing parts and components as intermediate goods in the manufacture of final products for exports. On the basis of vertical specialization, different trade patterns operate in a different way to induce economic growth activities. Thus, the question that may arise is in regard to what impact the three different types of trade patterns have on the gross national income (GNI), GDP, secondary industry GDP (SIGDP), tertiary industry GDP (TIGDP), and per capita GDP (PCGDP). Which type of trade pattern is more effective for the government to induce economic growth in China? In this chapter, the focus is on three different types of trade pattern, namely, conventional trade, processing trade, and other trading forms.

This chapter is organized as follows: the problem is described in Section 3.2. The different effects on economic growth are described under three different types of trade patterns in Section 3.3. Finally, we draw some conclusions and implications for further research in Section 3.4.

Achieving Inclusive Growth in China Through Vertical Specialization.

3.2 The nature of the relationship between trade openness and economic growth

How does trade openness affect economic growth? Greater trade liberalization produces antigrowth and pro-growth effects. The neoclassical economists argue that export growth is the main driver of economic growth (Helpman and Krugman, 1985; Hye et al., 2013). Bhagwati (1988) proposed that the growth led to the export hypothesis that economic growth stimulates both the supply and demand sides of the economy. The Hopenhayn—Melitz model selection effects increase the expected cost of introducing a new variety, and this tends to lead to slow growth. The pro-growth effect stems from the impact that freer trade has on the marginal cost of innovating (Baldwin and Robert-Nicoud, 2008). Grossman and Helpman (1991) developed an endogenous growth model whereby trade between a developed and less developed country can, under certain conditions, improve the long-term rate of growth in the less developed country. Taylor assembled the Ricardian trade model of Dornbusch et al. (1977) and Grossman and Helpman's (1991) quality ladder endogenous growth model in 1993 (de Souza and Batista, 2011). They reveal that greater trade openness brings about higher economic growth rates. Moreover, trade openness promotes the efficient allocation of resources, factor accumulation, technology diffusion, and knowledge spillovers. According to Kuroda (2006), Asia has been a showcase of economic performance where an outward trade policy takes a central role (Trejos and Barboza, 2015). Other explanations regarding the Singer-Prebisch thesis, however, suggest that trade openness might have a negative impact on growth (Tekin, 2012a,b). Spilimbergo (2000) presents a model in which trade between an advanced country and a less developed country can reduce long-term growth rates in the developed country. But is this the case for China? Is there a case of individual heterogeneity? Therefore, to answer these questions, this chapter surveys empirically the effects of trade on economic growth in China.

3.3 Empirical evidence of the impact of vertically specialized trade policy on the economic growth in China

3.3.1 Methodology and data

The variable groups are used in a different diagnostic test to perform time series analyses. It first tests for the order of integration in the data by using the augmented Dickey Fuller (ADF) unit root test; if the unit root is present, then stationarity is achieved by the first difference of the data. Having established the order of integration, it next tests for cointegration by applying the Johansen cointegration method, and a vector error correction model (VECM) has been used to assess both the long-term and short-term relationships between the variables. The results were further verified through impulse response functions (IRFs) and variance decomposition.

This chapter attempts to trace the long-term equilibrium relationship among indices of imports by conventional trade, indices of imports by processing trade, indices of exports by conventional trade, indices of exports by processing trade, indices of exports by conventional trade, indices of GNI, indices of GDP, indices of SIGDP, indices of TIGDP, and indices of PCGDP of China during the period 1981−2012 using the time series framework. Data in this chapter are calculated at constant prices. Preceding year = 100. All these variables are used and transformed into the natural logarithm form. All data have been obtained from the database of China Statistical Yearbook and China Trade and External Economic Statistical Yearbook published by the National Bureau of Statistics of China; the sample covers annual observations from 1981 to 2012. This study used the following variables groups in Table A1 to find the relationship:

LN PM = natural logarithm of indices of imports by processing trade (PM),
LN CM = natural logarithm of indices of imports by conventional trade (CM),
LNOM = natural logarithm of indices of imports by other trading forms (OM),
LN PX = natural logarithm of indices of exports by processing trade (PX),
LN CX = natural logarithm of indices of exports by conventional trade (CX),
LNOX = natural logarithm of indices of exports by other trading forms (OX),
LNGNI = natural logarithm of indices of gross national income (GNI),
LNGDP = natural logarithm of indices of gross domestic product (GDP),
LNSIGDP = natural logarithm of indices of secondary industry GDP (SIGDP),
LNTIGDP = natural logarithm of indices of tertiary industry GDP (TIGDP),
LNPCGDP = natural logarithm of indices of per capita GDP.

3.3.2   Unit root test for stationarity

To test if all the time series used for the study are stable and to explore the existence cointegration equations, the augmented Dickey Fuller (ADF) test for unit roots was conducted to determine the order of integration of all variables. The results of the ADF unit roots tests (see Table B1) show that all the variable series were integrated series of order I (1); therefore, there may exist some cointegration between the employed variables. Thus, we use Johansen's technique to conduct the cointegration test.

3.3.3   Results of Johansen's cointegration tests

Cointegration means economic variables share the same stochastic trend so that they are combined together in the long-term. Even if they deviate from each other in the short-term, they tend to come back to the trend in the long-term. A necessary condition for the cointegration test is that all the variables should be integrated at the same order or should contain a deterministic trend (Engle and Granger, 1991). The unit root test results show that all the time series of indices of imports by conventional trade, indices of imports by processing trade, indices of exports by conventional trade, indices of exports by processing trade, indices of exports by conventional trade, indices of GNI, indices of GDP, indices of SIGDP, indices of TIGDP, and indices of PCGDP are founded to be integrated with I (1) during 1981–2012. Therefore, these time series in the period are valid in the cointegration test. Once the variables are cointegrated, the short-term changes can be explained through the VECM (Engle and Granger, 1987). Following the cointegration test, the VECM was used to analyze the causality within the 10 variable groups, and this is described in the following section.

The results of trace statistic and the results of maximum Eigen statistics are shown in Tables C1–C10. Trace statistics and maximum Eigen statistics values help to find the rank(s) that shows the number of vector(s) containing long-term relations. It is evident that the null hypothesis of no rank is rejected. Therefore, the results of both trace and Max-Eigen statistics confirm that cointegration vectors exist in the model. It means long-term relationships prevail among the variables. In summary, the Johansen cointegration test results show the variable groups in Table A1 are cointegrated in the three periods and have a long-term equilibrium relationship from 1981 to 2012.

To distinguish the importance of vertical specialization trade for economic growth, we compare the effects of indices of imports and exports by conventional trade and indices of imports and exports by processing trade on indices of GNI, indices of GDP, indices of SIGDP, indices of TIGDP, and indices of PCGDP, respectively.

Following Johansen's technique, the normalized long-term cointegration relationships and the comparison coefficients are shown in Tables C1–C10. The normalized long-term cointegration relationships are very revealing. The observed signs are as anticipated. Moreover, the long-term relationships are also as expected, given the intrinsic interdependence between the variables. From Tables C1–C10, we can obtain the following equations for the long-term:

1. GNI, imports and exports by conventional trade, imports and exports by processing trade, and imports and exports by other trading forms:

$$LNGNI = \underset{(0.16022)}{-0.198926} \, LNCM + \underset{(0.25221)}{2.288227} \, LNPM - \underset{(0.15353)}{1.096156} \, LNOM \qquad (3.1)$$

$$LNGNI = \underset{(2.69392)}{1.531848} \, LNCX + \underset{(2.76033)}{8.990969} \, LNPX - \underset{(1.56298)}{9.35174} \, LNOX \qquad (3.2)$$

From the results of Eqs. (3.1) and (3.2), it can be seen that the 1% increase in imports by conventional trade (LNCM) will have a negative impact of 0.198926% on gross national income (LNGNI), the 1% increase in imports by processing trade (LNPM) will have a positive impact of 2.288227% on gross notional income (LNGNI), the 1% increase in LNOM will have a negative impact of 1.096156% on the LNGNI, the 1% increase in exports by conventional trade (LNCX) will have a positive impact of 1.531848%, the 1% increase in exports by processing trade (LNPX) will have a positive impact of 8.990969% on gross national income (LNGNI), and the 1% increase in LNGNI will have a negative impact of 9.35174% on the LNGNI.

Eqs. (3.1) and (3.2) show that the increase in imports and exports by processing trade could increase GNI in the long-term. This provides the support for evidence of the foreign trade and vertically specialized trade channels.

2. GDP, imports and exports by conventional trade, imports and exports by processing trade, and imports and exports by other trading forms:

$$\text{LNGDP} = -\underset{(0.26220)}{0.575569}\,\text{LNCM} + \underset{(0.41440)}{3.319504}\,\text{LNPM} - \underset{(0.25358)}{1.746966}\,\text{LNOM} \qquad (3.3)$$

$$\text{LNGDP} = \underset{(1.64760)}{1.194768}\,\text{LNCX} + \underset{(1.68183)}{5.897643}\,\text{LNPX} - \underset{(0.94676)}{5.987458}\,\text{LNOX} \qquad (3.4)$$

From Eqs. (3.3) and (3.4), we observe that the 1% increase in imports by conventional trade (LNCM) will have a negative impact of 0.575569% on gross domestic product (LNGDP), the 1% increase in imports by processing trade (LNPM) will have a positive impact of 3.319504% on gross domestic product (LNGDP), the 1% increase in LNOM will have a negative impact of 1.746966% on the LNGDP, the 1% increase in exports by conventional trade (LNCX) will have a positive impact of 1.194768% on gross domestic product (LNGDP), the 1% increase in exports by processing trade (LNPX) will have a positive impact of 5.897643% on gross domestic product (LNGDP), and the 1% increase in LNOX will have a negative impact of 5.987458% on LNGDP.

Eqs. (3.3) and (3.4) demonstrate that the increase in imports and exports by processing trade can cause the increase in the GDP in the long-term; this confirms the existence of the vertical specialization channel.

3. SIGDP, imports and exports by conventional trade, imports and exports by processing trade, and imports and exports by other trading forms:

$$\text{LNSIGDP} = \underset{(0.41083)}{0.904918}\,\text{LNCM} + \underset{(0.64396)}{4.376530}\,\text{LNPM} - \underset{(0.40162)}{2.461771}\,\text{LNOM} \qquad (3.5)$$

$$\text{LNSIGDP} = \underset{(0.20955)}{0.687955}\,\text{LNCX} + \underset{(0.24888)}{1.39818}\,\text{LNPX} - \underset{(0.16618)}{1.076688}\,\text{LNOX} \qquad (3.6)$$

Eqs. (3.5) and (3.6) show that the 1% increase in imports by conventional trade will have a positive impact of 0.904918% on the secondary industry gross domestic products (LNSIGDP), the 1% increase in imports by processing trade will have a positive impact of 4.376530% on the secondary industry gross domestic products (LNSIGDP), the 1% increase in LNOM will have a negative impact of 2.461771% on the secondary industry gross domestic products (LNSIGDP), the 1% increase in exports by conventional trade will have a positive impact of 0.687955% on the second industry gross domestic products (LNSIGDP), the 1% increase in exports by processing trade will have a positive impact of 1.39818% on the second industry gross domestic products (LNSIGDP), and the 1% increase in LNOX will have a negative impact of 1.076688% on the LNSIGDP.

Eqs. (3.5) and (3.6) demonstrate that the increase in imports and exports by processing trade can cause an increase in the second industry GDPs in the long-term, and this confirms the existence of the vertical specialization channel.

4. TIGDP, imports and exports by conventional trade, imports and exports by processing trade, and imports and exports by other trading forms:

$$\text{LNTIGDP} = \underset{(0.10594)}{0.184272}\,\text{LNCM} + \underset{(0.17125)}{1.456961}\,\text{LNPM} - \underset{(0.10537)}{0.648673}\,\text{LNOM} \qquad (3.7)$$

$$\text{LNTIGDP} = \underset{(0.25522)}{0.563409 \text{ LNCX}} + \underset{(0.30105)}{1.377640 \text{ LNPX}} - \underset{(0.23615)}{0.935717 \text{ LNOX}} \qquad (3.8)$$

From Eqs. (3.7) and (3.8), we observe that the 1% increase in LNCM will have a positive impact of 0.184272% on LNTIGDP, the 1% increase in imports by processing trade will have a positive impact of 1.45696% on LNTIGDP, the 1% increase in LNOM will have a negative impact of 0.648673%, the 1% increase in exports by conventional trade will have a positive impact of 0.563409% on the TIGDP, the 1% increase in exports by processing trade will have a positive impact of 1.377640% on the TIGDP, and the 1% increase in LNOX will have a negative impact of 0.935717% on LNTIGDP.

Eqs. (3.7) and (3.8) suggest that imports and exports by processing trade are the sources of raising the TIGDP in China.

5. PCGDP, imports and exports by conventional trade, imports and exports by processing trade, and imports and exports by other trading forms:

$$\text{LNPCGDP} = \underset{(0.32355)}{-0.817631 \text{ LNCM}} + \underset{(0.51140)}{4.00969 \text{ LNPM}} - \underset{(0.31354)}{2.193281 \text{ LNOM}} \qquad (3.9)$$

$$\text{LNPCGDP} = \underset{(1.00249)}{1.085070 \text{ LNCX}} + \underset{(1.02081)}{3.629133 \text{ LNPX}} - \underset{(0.57962)}{3.657099 \text{ LNOX}} \qquad (3.10)$$

Furthermore, from Eqs. (3.9) and (3.10), we observe that the 1% increase in imports by conventional trade (LNCM) will have a negative impact of 0.817631% on the per capita GDP (LNPCGDP), the 1% increase in imports by processing trade (LNPM) will have a positive impact of 4.00969% on LNPCGDP, the 1% increase in imports by other trading forms (LNOM) will have a negative impact of 2.193281% on LNPCGDP, the 1% increase in exports by conventional trade will have a positive impact of 1.085070% on LNPCGDP, the 1% increase in exports by processing trade (LNPX) will have a positive impact of 3.629133% on the LNPCGDP, and the 1% increase in LNOX will have negative impact of 3.657099% on the LNPCGDP.

These equations show that the vertical specialization variables (imports and exports by processing trade) have important effects on the economic growth that connect the vertically specialized trade policy variables with the size of the economy variables (GNI, GDP, SIGDP, TIGDP, and PCGDP). These long-term equations support the existence of the vertical specialization channel in the trade policy transmission process in China.

Proposition 1. The contribution and importance of imports and exports by conventional trade to the increasing GNI are lower than that by processing trade.

Proposition 2. The contribution and importance of imports and exports by conventional trade to the increasing GDP are lower than that by processing trade.

Proposition 3. The contribution and importance of imports and exports by conventional trade to the SIGDP are lower than that by processing trade.

Proposition 4. The contribution and importance of imports by conventional trade to the increasing TIGDP are lower than that by processing trade.

Proposition 5. The contribution and importance of imports by conventional trade to the increasing PCGDP are lower than that by processing trade.

3.3.4   The vector error correction model

Given the cointegration results, we should construct the VECMs to analyze the short-term dynamic behavior of the model. The results of the VECM are shown in Tables D1–D10. The presence of cointegration requires at least one of the coefficients of the error correction terms to be statistically significant. The coefficients of variables indicate the short-term impact.

From the results in Tables D1–D10, for D (LNOM) and D (LNOX), the coefficient of error correction term is negative, signaling that the system is stable and converges to the equilibrium track after some disturbance in the system. High absolute values of the error correction terms indicate that if a deviation from long-term equilibrium happens as a result of a shock, then the adjustment speed toward long-term equilibrium will be high and there will be full adjustment of deviation. For D (LNPM) and D (LNPX) in Tables D1–D10, the error correction terms are positive, signaling that the disequilibrium is not corrected.

3.3.5   Granger causality tests

The structures of the causal relationships between variables were analyzed through the Granger causality approach. Tables E1–E10 show the Granger causality results and block exogeneity tests.

The results of Tables E1–E10 reveal the dynamic behavior of all variables, which is a requisite for endogeneity and, hence, validate the VECM methodology. Granger causality allows causal relationships to be identified in all equations. In brief, for all significance levels, the Granger causality detected and its direction is: $D(LNPM) \rightarrow D(LNGNI)$; $D(LNPM) \rightarrow D(LNGDP)$; $D(LNPM) \rightarrow D(LNTIGDP)$; $D(LNPM) \rightarrow D(LNPCGDP)$. Globally, the block exogeneity outcome corroborates the endogeneity of the variables, strengthening the appropriateness of using the VEC modeling. When a particular variable helps to predict future values of another variable, causal relationships are present.

3.3.6   Impulse response function

Finally, to scrutinize the behavior of each variable once confronted with an increase in a single specific variable and the duration of its effect, the IRFs are exhibited. The IRF curves simulated by analytic method are reported in Figures F1–F10. These indicate how a 1-time positive shock of 1 standard deviation (SD) (± 2 SE innovations) in the conventional trade and processing trade endures regarding the economic growth of China. We consider the response of five variables to 1-SD in the innovation of conventional trade and processing trade.

Figs. F1, F3, F5, and F9 illustrate that the responses of the LNGNI, LNGDP, LNSIGDP, and LNPCGDP to a 1-SD shock on LNCM are negative and powerful, with a persistent effect; however, the responses of the LNGNI, LNGDP, LNSIGDP, and LNPCGDP to a 1-SD shock on LNPM are positive and increase abruptly. Fig. F7 shows that the impulse responses of LNTIGDP to a 1-SD shock on LNCM and on LNPM are positive. However, the influence of LNCM is lower than that of LNPM.

Figs. F2, F4, F6, and F10 illustrate that the responses of the LNGNI, LNGDP, LNSIGDP, and LNPCGDP to a 1-SD shock on LNCX are positive and powerful, with a persistent effect; however, the influence of LNCX is lower than that of LNPX.

The IRFs provided the support of causality status between these time variables in the multivariate VECM system.

3.3.7   Variance decomposition

The forecast error variance decomposition follows. It aims to capture the intensity of the response of a variable in the face of shocks suffered on the other variables. Tables G1−G10 reveal the percentages of the forecast error variance in all variables generated by a shock on each of the other variables.

In Tables G1−G10, the first columns are the periods that are set to a maximum of 30. The data in the SE (standard error) column are the forecasting variances of various periods, which are caused by the change of the present or future value.

In Table G1, LNGNI, LNCM, LNPM, and LNOM are the contributions of the innovation to forecasting variance, respectively, which sum to 100. It can be seen from Table G1 that, at the end of the forecast period, LNPM explains approximately 6.863527% of the forecast error variance. This is approximately 6 percentage points higher than in the LNCM case.

In Tables G2, G4, G6, and G10, LNGNI, LNCX, LNPX, and LNOX are the contributions of the innovations to forecasting variance, respectively, which sum to 100. It can be seen that at the end of the forecast period, LNPX explains a higher percentage of the forecast error variance than that in the LNCX case.

When focused on Tables G3, G5, G7, and G9, it can be seen that the impact of a shock to LNCM on LNGDP, LNSIGDP, LNTIGDP, and LNPCGDP is relatively low when compared with the impact of a shock to LNPM.

This fact suggests that, in China, processing trade plays a more important role than conventional trade, which is true (see Proposition 1−5).

3.4   Concluding remarks and policy implications

To stimulate economic growth, the government needs to formulate appropriate policy. This chapter compares two types of trade in a vertical specialization and global production network in which Chinese enterprises conduct processing trade. By means of vertical specialization theory, we investigate and compare the economic growth effects of trade in China under the two trade patterns, that is, conventional trade and processing trade. Finally, we compare the economic growth effects of two trade patterns to explore the better trade-promoting policy. The results show that conventional trade patterns are all lower than those of processing trade. Therefore, the government should use a vertically specialized trade strategy to encourage economic growth toward more inclusive growth in China.

By disaggregating the total imports and exports into imports and exports by conventional trade and imports and exports by processing trade, we estimate the different effects of two types of imports on GNI, GDP, SIGDP, TIGDP, and PCGDP of

China, and we seek more evidence for the higher impact of vertical specialization than conventional trade on economic growth and enlarging the size of the economy in China during the transition.

This study provides evidence of economic growth from trade through conventional trade and processing trade. It shows that the results are stronger for transitional economies, implying that imports and exports by processing trade can act as an important and positive boost to economic growth. This study shows that China's conventional trade and processing trade cause an increase in China's GNI, GDP, SIGDP, TIGDP, and PCGDP. This fact could suggest that the increase in GNI, GDP, SIGDP, TIGDP, and PCGDP of China requires the increasing importance of vertical specialization of export production rather than ordinary trade. In the mean time, while processing trade was becoming an increasingly importance source for economic growth in China during the transition, the relative importance of the conventional trade as a source of China's economic growth was declining. This could signal that some of the resources freed in the economy are being allocated for integrating into global vertical specialization, in part because of the changing engines of economic growth during the transition to inclusive growth in China.

Further, two types of measures could be recommended to trade policymakers. They should encourage greater imports of parts and intermediates to enhance the effects of vertical specialization on economic growth. However, the trade policymakers should promote policies that lower the entry barriers facing foreign enterprises and improve access to the market. These measures are essential to increased openness, helping toward inclusive growth, and relating to the role played by imported intermediates available in the emerging markets.

Appendix A Variables grouping

Table A1 **Variables grouping**

Group number	Variables	Sample range
1	LNGNI, LNCM, LNPM, and LNOM	1981−2012
2	LNGNI, LNPX, LNCX, and LNOX	1981−2012
3	LNGDP, LNCM, LNPM, and LNOM	1981−2012
4	LNGDP, LNPX, LNCX, and LNOX	1981−2012
5	LNSIGDP, LNCM, LNPM, and LNOM	1981−2012
6	LNSIGDP, LNPX, LNCX, and LNOX	1981−2012
7	LNTIGDP, LNCM, LNPM, and LNOM	1981−2012
8	LNTIGDP, LNPX, LNCX, and LNOX	1981−2012
9	LNPCGDP, LNCM, LNPM, and LNOM	1981−2012
10	LNPCGDP, LNPX, LNCX, and LNOX	1981−2012

Note: PM is indices of imports by processing trade, CM is indices of imports by conventional trade, OM is indices of imports by other trading forms, PX is indices of exports by processing trade, CX is indices of exports by conventional trade, OX is indices of exports by other trading forms, GNI stands for indices of gross national income, GDP stands for indices of gross domestic product, SIGDP stands for indices of secondary industry GDP, TIGDP stands for indices of tertiary industry GDP, PCGDP stands for indices of per capita GDP. Data in this table are calculated at constant prices. Preceding year = 100.

Appendix B   The results of unit root tests

Table B1 **Augmented Dickey Fuller test on unit roots for all variables**

S\NO.	Variables	Test type (C,T,P)	ADF test statistic	Order of integration
1	LNCM	(0,0,0)	0.192686	I(1)
2	D(LNCM)	(0,0,0)	− 6.190714*	I(0)
3	LNPM	(0,0,0)	− 0.233714	I(1)
4	D(LNPM)	(0,0,0)	− 5.684092*	I(0)
5	LNOM	(0,0,0)	− 0.097811	I(1)
6	D(LNOM)	(0,0,0)	− 7.175608*	I(0)
7	LNCX	(0,0,0)	0.586035	I(1)
8	D(LNCX)	(0,0,0)	− 8.757645*	I(0)
9	LNPX	(0,0,0)	− 0.047070	I(1)
10	D(LNPX)	(0,0,0)	− 9.234865*	I(0)
11	LNOX	(0,0,0)	− 0.029691	I(1)
12	D(LNOX)	(0,0,0)	− 9.772892*	I(0)
13	LNGNI	(0,0,0)	0.238696	I(1)
14	D(LNGNI)	(0,0,0)	− 5.031681*	I(0)
15	LNGDP	(0,0,0)	0.282775	I(1)
16	D(LNGDP)	(0,0,0)	− 4.814375*	I(0)
17	LNSIGDP	(0,0,0)	− 0.342928	I(0)
18	D(LNSIGDP)	(0,0,0)	− 5.229153*	I(1)
19	LNTIGDP	(0,0,0)	− 0.310213	I(0)
20	D(LNTIGDP)	(0,0,0)	− 4.691221*	I(1)
21	LNPCGDP	(0,0,0)	− 2.664853	I(0)
22	D(PCGDP)	(0,0,0)	− 4.858135*	I(0)

Note: C, T, and P in test type stand for constant, trend, and lag orders, respectively. At three remarkable levels, when the ADF value is greater than the critical value, the corresponding series has unit root. D stands for the first differential of the variables.
*denote the rejection of the null hypothesis of unit root at the 1% significance levels.

Appendix C   Results of cointegration tests

Table C1 **Cointegration test result (series: LNGNI, LNCM, LNPM, and LNOM)**

Included observations: 30 after adjustments Trend assumption: No deterministic trend Lags interval (in first differences): 1−1				
Unrestricted cointegration rank test (trace)				
Hypothesized number of CE(s)	**Eigenvalue**	**Trace statistic**	**0.05 Critical value**	**Probability**[a]
None[b]	0.664439	62.79141	40.17493	0.0001
At most 1[b]	0.548995	30.03282	24.27596	0.0084
At most 2	0.177292	6.144511	12.32090	0.4186
At most 3	0.009617	0.289896	4.129906	0.6514
Trace test indicates 2 cointegrating equations at the 0.05 level				
Unrestricted cointegration rank test (Maximum Eigenvalue)				
Hypothesized number of CE(s)	**Eigenvalue**	**Max-Eigen statistic**	**0.05 Critical value**	**Probability**[a]
None[b]	0.664439	32.75858	24.15921	0.0027
At most 1[b]	0.548995	23.88831	17.79730	0.0054
At most 2	0.177292	5.854615	11.22480	0.3665
At most 3	0.009617	0.289896	4.129906	0.6514
Max-eigenvalue test indicates 2 cointegrating equations at the 0.05 level				

1 Cointegrating equation		**Log likelihood**	**122.7990**
Normalized cointegrating coefficients (standard error in parentheses)			
LNGNI	LNCM	LNPM	LNOM
1.000000	0.198926 (0.16022)	− 2.288227 (0.25221)	1.096156 (0.15353)

[a]MacKinnon−Haug−Michelis (1999) *P* values.
[b]Rejection of the hypothesis at the 0.05 level.

Table C2 Cointegration test result (series: LNGNI, LNCX, LNPX, and LNOX)

Sample (adjusted): 1984—2012
Included observations: 29 after adjustments
Trend assumption: No deterministic trend
Lags interval (in first differences): 1—2

Unrestricted cointegration rank test (trace)

Hypothesized number of CE(s)	Eigenvalue	Trace statistic	0.05 Critical value	Probability[a]
None[b]	0.655044	43.69139	40.17493	0.0213
At most 1	0.297955	12.82560	24.27596	0.6364
At most 2	0.084017	2.566635	12.32090	0.8982
At most 3	0.000747	0.021677	4.129906	0.9042

Trace test indicates 1 cointegrating equation at the 0.05 level

Unrestricted cointegration rank test (Maximum Eigenvalue)

Hypothesized number of CE(s)	Eigenvalue	Max-Eigen statistic	0.05 Critical value	Probability[a]
None[b]	0.655044	30.86579	24.15921	0.0053
At most 1	0.297955	10.25896	17.79730	0.4583
At most 2	0.084017	2.544958	11.22480	0.8548
At most 3	0.000747	0.021677	4.129906	0.9042

Max-eigenvalue test indicates 1 cointegrating equation at the 0.05 level

1 Cointegrating equation		Log likelihood	120.8503

Normalized cointegrating coefficients (standard error in parentheses)

LNGNI	LNCX	LNPX	LNOX
1.000000	− 1.531848	− 8.990969	9.351740
	(2.69392)	(2.76033)	(1.56298)

[a]MacKinnon—Haug—Michelis (1999) P values.
[b]Rejection of the hypothesis at the 0.05 level.

Table C3 Cointegration test result (series: LNGDP, LNCM, LNPM, and LNOM)

Sample (adjusted): 1983−2012
Included observations: 30 after adjustments
Trend assumption: No deterministic trend
Lags interval (in first differences): 1−1

Unrestricted cointegration rank test (trace)

Hypothesized number of CE(s)	Eigenvalue	Trace statistic	0.05 Critical value	Probability[a]
None[b]	0.650906	61.37988	40.17493	0.0001
At most 1[b]	0.546617	29.80747	24.27596	0.0091
At most 2	0.175091	6.076895	12.32090	0.4267
At most 3	0.010030	0.302413	4.129906	0.6439

Trace test indicates 2 cointegrating equations at the 0.05 level

Unrestricted cointegration rank test (Maximum Eigenvalue)

Hypothesized number of CE(s)	Eigenvalue	Max-Eigen statistic	0.05 Critical value	Probability[a]
None[b]	0.650906	31.57242	24.15921	0.0041
At most 1[b]	0.546617	23.73057	17.79730	0.0057
At most 2	0.175091	5.774482	11.22480	0.3760
At most 3	0.010030	0.302413	4.129906	0.6439

Max-eigenvalue test indicates 2 cointegrating equations at the 0.05 level

1 Cointegrating equation		**Log likelihood**	**121.4358**

Normalized cointegrating coefficients (standard error in parentheses)

LNGDP	LNCM	LNPM	LNOM
1.000000	0.575569	− 3.319504	1.746966
	(0.26220)	(0.41440)	(0.25358)

[a]MacKinnon−Haug−Michelis (1999) P values.
[b]Rejection of the hypothesis at the 0.05 level.

Table C4 Cointegration test result (series: LNGDP, LNCX, LNPX, and LNOX)

Sample (adjusted): 1984–2012
Included observations: 29 after adjustments
Trend assumption: No deterministic trend
Lags interval (in first differences): 1–2

Unrestricted cointegration rank test (trace)

Hypothesized number of CE(s)	Eigenvalue	Trace statistic	0.05 Critical value	Probability[a]
None[b]	0.679602	45.22115	40.17493	0.0143
At most 1	0.285136	12.21357	24.27596	0.6878
At most 2	0.081156	2.479363	12.32090	0.9074
At most 3	0.000855	0.024819	4.129906	0.8975

Trace test indicates 1 cointegrating equation at the 0.05 level

Unrestricted cointegration rank test (Maximum Eigenvalue)

Hypothesized number of CE(s)	Eigenvalue	Max-Eigen statistic	0.05 Critical value	Probability[a]
None[b]	0.679602	33.00758	24.15921	0.0025
At most 1	0.285136	9.734208	17.79730	0.5136
At most 2	0.081156	2.454544	11.22480	0.8672
At most 3	0.000855	0.024819	4.129906	0.8975

Max-eigenvalue test indicates 1 cointegrating equation at the 0.05 level

1 Cointegrating equation	Log likelihood	121.7930

Normalized cointegrating coefficients (standard error in parentheses)

LNGDP	LNCX	LNPX	LNOX
1.000000	− 1.194768	− 5.897643	5.987458
	(1.64760)	(1.68183)	(0.94676)

[a]MacKinnon–Haug–Michelis (1999) P values.
[b]Rejection of the hypothesis at the 0.05 level.

Table C5 Cointegration test result (series: LNSIGDP, LNCM, LNPM, and LNOM)

Sample (adjusted): 1983–2012
Included observations: 30 after adjustments
Trend assumption: No deterministic trend
Lags interval (in first differences): 1–1

Unrestricted cointegration rank test (trace)

Hypothesized number of CE(s)	Eigenvalue	Trace statistic	0.05 Critical value	Probability[a]
None[b]	0.604631	53.48821	40.17493	0.0014
At most 1[b]	0.473105	25.65012	24.27596	0.0334
At most 2	0.190656	6.427476	12.32090	0.3858
At most 3	0.002714	0.081546	4.129906	0.8146

Trace test indicates 2 cointegrating equations at the 0.05 level

Unrestricted cointegration rank test (Maximum Eigenvalue)

Hypothesized number of CE(s)	Eigenvalue	Max-Eigen statistic	0.05 Critical value	Probability[a]
None[b]	0.604631	27.83810	24.15921	0.0152
At most 1[b]	0.473105	19.22264	17.79730	0.0303
At most 2	0.190656	6.345930	11.22480	0.3120
At most 3	0.002714	0.081546	4.129906	0.8146

Max-eigenvalue test indicates 2 cointegrating equations at the 0.05 level

1 Cointegrating equation	**Log likelihood**	**104.5541**

Normalized cointegrating coefficients (standard error in parentheses)

LNSIGDP	LNCM	LNPM	LNOM
1.000000	0.904918	− 4.376530	2.461771
	(0.41083)	(0.64396)	(0.40162)

[a]MacKinnon–Haug–Michelis (1999) P values.
[b]Rejection of the hypothesis at the 0.05 level.

Table C6 Cointegration test result (series: LNSIGDP, LNCX, LNPX, and LNOX)

Sample (adjusted): 1985−2012
Included observations: 28 after adjustments
Trend assumption: No deterministic trend
Lags interval (in first differences): 1−3

Unrestricted cointegration rank test (trace)

Hypothesized number of CE(s)	Eigenvalue	Trace statistic	0.05 Critical value	Probability[a]
None[b]	0.741622	60.51493	40.17493	0.0002
At most 1	0.452826	22.62161	24.27596	0.0797
At most 2	0.156303	5.737958	12.32090	0.4687
At most 3	0.034362	0.979042	4.129906	0.3739

Trace test indicates 1 cointegrating equation at the 0.05 level

Unrestricted cointegration rank test (Maximum Eigenvalue)

Hypothesized number of CE(s)	Eigenvalue	Max-Eigen statistic	0.05 Critical value	Probability[a]
None[b]	0.741622	37.89331	24.15921	0.0004
At most 1	0.452826	16.88365	17.79730	0.0682
At most 2	0.156303	4.758916	11.22480	0.5119
At most 3	0.034362	0.979042	4.129906	0.3739

Max-eigenvalue test indicates 1 cointegrating equation at the 0.05 level

1 Cointegrating equation		Log likelihood	126.8285

Normalized cointegrating coefficients (standard error in parentheses)

LNSIGDP	LNCX	LNPX	LNOX
1.000000	− 0.687955	− 1.398180	1.076688
	(0.20955)	(0.24888)	(0.16618)

[a]MacKinnon−Haug−Michelis (1999) P values.
[b]Rejection of the hypothesis at the 0.05 level.

Table C7 Cointegration test result (series: LNTIGDP, LNCM, LNPM, and LNOM)

Sample (adjusted): 1983—2012
Included observations: 30 after adjustments
Trend assumption: No deterministic trend
Lags interval (in first differences): 1—1

Unrestricted cointegration rank test (trace)

Hypothesized number of CE(s)	Eigenvalue	Trace statistic	0.05 Critical value	Probability[a]
None[b]	0.624405	59.73756	40.17493	0.0002
At most 1[b]	0.553079	30.36022	24.27596	0.0076
At most 2	0.169111	6.198998	12.32090	0.4122
At most 3	0.021147	0.641225	4.129906	0.4838

Trace test indicates 2 cointegrating equations at the 0.05 level

Unrestricted cointegration rank test (Maximum Eigenvalue)

Hypothesized number of CE(s)	Eigenvalue	Max-Eigen statistic	0.05 Critical value	Probability[a]
None[b]	0.624405	29.37735	24.15921	0.0090
At most 1[b]	0.553079	24.16122	17.79730	0.0048
At most 2	0.169111	5.557773	11.22480	0.4027
At most 3	0.021147	0.641225	4.129906	0.4838

Max-eigenvalue test indicates 2 cointegrating equations at the 0.05 level

1 Cointegrating equation		**Log likelihood**	**114.1711**

Normalized cointegrating coefficients (standard error in parentheses)

LNTIGDP	LNCM	LNPM	LNOM
1.000000	− 0.184272	− 1.456961	0.648673
	(0.10594)	(0.17125)	(0.10537)

[a]MacKinnon—Haug—Michelis (1999) P values.
[b]Rejection of the hypothesis at the 0.05 level.

Table C8 Cointegration test result (series: LNTIGDP, LNCX, LNPX, and LNOX)

Sample (adjusted): 1985–2012
Included observations: 28 after adjustments
Trend assumption: No deterministic trend
Lags interval (in first differences): 1–3

Unrestricted cointegration rank test (trace)

Hypothesized number of CE(s)	Eigenvalue	Trace statistic	0.05 Critical value	Probability[a]
None[b]	0.592004	54.55203	40.17493	0.0010
At most 1[b]	0.523063	29.45006	24.27596	0.0102
At most 2	0.261332	8.719667	12.32090	0.1861
At most 3	0.008474	0.238295	4.129906	0.6839

Trace test indicates 2 cointegrating equations at the 0.05 level

Unrestricted cointegration rank test (Maximum Eigenvalue)

Hypothesized number of CE(s)	Eigenvalue	Max-Eigen statistic	0.05 Critical value	Probability[a]
None[b]	0.592004	25.10197	24.15921	0.0372
At most 1[b]	0.523063	20.73039	17.79730	0.0176
At most 2	0.261332	8.481372	11.22480	0.1460
At most 3	0.008474	0.238295	4.129906	0.6839

Max-eigenvalue test indicates 2 cointegrating equations at the 0.05 level

1 Cointegrating equation		Log likelihood	140.4000

Normalized cointegrating coefficients (standard error in parentheses)

LNTIGDP	LNCX	LNPX	LNOX
1.000000	− 0.563409	− 1.377640	0.935717
	(0.25522)	(0.30105)	(0.23615)

[a]MacKinnon–Haug–Michelis (1999) P values.
[b]Rejection of the hypothesis at the 0.05 level.

Table C9 Cointegration test result (series: LNPCGDP, LNCM, LNPM, and LNOM)

Sample (adjusted): 1983−2012
Included observations: 30 after adjustments
Trend assumption: No deterministic trend
Lags interval (in first differences): 1−1

Unrestricted cointegration rank test (trace)

Hypothesized number of CE(s)	Eigenvalue	Trace statistic	0.05 Critical value	Probability[a]
None[b]	0.659621	62.79305	40.17493	0.0001
At most 1[b]	0.561143	30.46219	24.27596	0.0073
At most 2	0.168775	5.754719	12.32090	0.4666
At most 3	0.006945	0.209081	4.129906	0.7039

Trace test indicates 2 cointegrating equations at the 0.05 level

Unrestricted cointegration rank test (Maximum Eigenvalue)

Hypothesized number of CE(s)	Eigenvalue	Max-Eigen statistic	0.05 Critical value	Probability[a]
None[b]	0.659621	32.33086	24.15921	0.0031
At most 1[b]	0.561143	24.70748	17.79730	0.0039
At most 2	0.168775	5.545638	11.22480	0.4043
At most 3	0.006945	0.209081	4.129906	0.7039

Max-eigenvalue test indicates 2 cointegrating equations at the 0.05 level

1 Cointegrating equation		Log likelihood	121.9169

Normalized cointegrating coefficients (standard error in parentheses)

LNPCGDP	LNCM	LNPM	LNOM
1.000000	0.817631	− 4.009690	2.193281
	(0.32355)	(0.51140)	(0.31354)

[a]MacKinnon−Haug−Michelis (1999) *P* values.
[b]Rejection of the hypothesis at the 0.05 level.

Table C10 Cointegration test result (series: LNPCGDP, LNCX, LNPX, and LNOX)

Sample (adjusted): 1984−2012
Included observations: 29 after adjustments
Trend assumption: No deterministic trend
Lags interval (in first differences): 1−2

Unrestricted cointegration rank test (trace)

Hypothesized number of CE(s)	Eigenvalue	Trace statistic	0.05 Critical value	Probability[a]
None[b]	0.676599	44.64586	40.17493	0.0166
At most 1	0.278771	11.90889	24.27596	0.7129
At most 2	0.080137	2.431730	12.32090	0.9122
At most 3	0.000322	0.009341	4.129906	0.9370

Trace test indicates 1 cointegrating equations at the 0.05 level

Unrestricted cointegration rank test (Maximum Eigenvalue)

Hypothesized number of CE(s)	Eigenvalue	Max-Eigen statistic	0.05 Critical value	Probability[a]
None[b]	0.676599	32.73696	24.15921	0.0027
At most 1	0.278771	9.477164	17.79730	0.5416
At most 2	0.080137	2.422388	11.22480	0.8715
At most 3	0.000322	0.009341	4.129906	0.9370

Max-eigenvalue test indicates 1 cointegrating equation at the 0.05 level

1 Cointegrating equation		Log likelihood	122.5799

Normalized cointegrating coefficients (standard error in parentheses)

LNPCGDP	LNCX	LNPX	LNOX
1.000000	− 1.085070 (1.00249)	− 3.629133 (1.02081)	3.657099 (0.57962)

[a]MacKinnon−Haug−Michelis (1999) P values.
[b]Rejection of the hypothesis at the 0.05 level.

Appendix D   Results of vector error correction model

Table D1 Vector error correction estimates (series: LNGNI, LNCM, LNPM, and LNOM)

Sample (adjusted): 1983–2012 Included observations: 30 after adjustments Standard errors in parentheses ( ) and t-statistics in brackets [ ]				
Cointegrating equation	**CointEq1**			
LNGNI(−1)	1.000000			
LNCM(−1)	0.198926			
	(0.16022)			
	[1.24157]			
LNPM(−1)	−2.288227			
	(0.25221)			
	[−9.07255]			
LNOM(−1)	1.096156			
	(0.15353)			
	[7.13988]			
Error correction	**D(LNGNI)**	**D(LNCM)**	**D(LNPM)**	**D(LNOM)**
CointEq1	− 0.069239	0.032378	0.166096	−0.802456
	(0.01780)	(0.20189)	(0.12797)	(0.28823)
	[−3.88898]	[0.16038]	[1.29791]	[−2.78408]

Table D2 Vector error correction estimates (series: LNGNI, LNCX, LNPX, and LNOX)

Sample (adjusted): 1984–2012 Included observations: 29 after adjustments Standard errors in parentheses ( ) and t-statistics in brackets [ ]				
Cointegrating equation	**CointEq1**			
LNGNI(−1)	1.000000			
LNCX(−1)	−1.531848			
	(2.69392)			
	[−0.56863]			
LNPX(−1)	−8.990969			
	(2.76033)			
	[−3.25721]			
LNOX(−1)	9.351740			
	(1.56298)			
	[5.98329]			
Error correction	**D(LNGNI)**	**D(LNCX)**	**D(LNPX)**	**D(LNOX)**
CointEq1	−0.004252	− 0.001952	0.015396	−0.117719
	(0.00223)	(0.01394)	(0.01079)	(0.03706)
	[−1.90444]	[−0.13996]	[1.42731]	[−3.17634]

Table D3 Vector error correction estimates (series: LNGDP, LNCM, LNPM, and LNOM)

Sample (adjusted): 1983–2012
Included observations: 30 after adjustments
Standard errors in parentheses ( ) and t-statistics in brackets [ ]

Cointegrating equation	CointEq1			
LNGDP(−1)	1.000000			
LNCM(−1)	0.575569			
	(0.26220)			
	[2.19518]			
LNPM(−1)	−3.319504			
	(0.41440)			
	[−8.01031]			
LNOM(−1)	1.746966			
	(0.25358)			
	[6.88912]			
Error correction	**D(LNGDP)**	**D(LNCM)**	**D(LNPM)**	**D(LNOM)**
CointEq1	− 0.042443	− 0.045606	0.087071	− 0.488299
	(0.01052)	(0.12576)	(0.08056)	(0.18020)
	[−4.03484]	[−0.36265]	[1.08086]	[−2.70974]

Table D4 Vector error correction estimates (series: LNGDP, LNCX, LNPX, and LNOX)

Sample (adjusted): 1984–2012
Included observations: 29 after adjustments
Standard errors in parentheses ( ) and t-statistics in brackets [ ]

Cointegrating equation	CointEq1			
LNGDP(−1)	1.000000			
LNCX(−1)	−1.194768			
	(1.64760)			
	[−0.72515]			
LNPX(−1)	−5.897643			
	(1.68183)			
	[−3.50667]			
LNOX(−1)	5.987458			
	(0.94676)			
	[6.32416]			
Error correction	**D(LNGDP)**	**D(LNCX)**	**D(LNPX)**	**D(LNOX)**
CointEq1	−0.006667	−0.002355	0.025538	−0.182335
	(0.00342)	(0.02142)	(0.01655)	(0.05642)
	[−1.95018]	[−0.10997]	[1.54264]	[−3.23182]

Table D5 Vector error correction estimates (series: LNSIGDP, LNCM, LNPM, and LNOM)

Sample (adjusted): 1983–2012
Included observations: 30 after adjustments
Standard errors in parentheses ( ) and t-statistics in brackets [ ]

Cointegrating equation		CointEq1		
LNSIGDP(−1)		1.000000		
LNCM(−1)		0.904918		
		(0.41083)		
		[2.20265]		
LNPM(−1)		− 4.376530		
		(0.64396)		
		[−6.79625]		
LNOM(−1)		2.461771		
		(0.40162)		
		[6.12954]		
Error correction	**D(LNSIGDP)**	**D(LNCM)**	**D(LNPM)**	**D(LNOM)**
CointEq1	− 0.036234	− 0.086242	0.050938	− 0.348014
	(0.01226)	(0.08860)	(0.05532)	(0.12306)
	[−2.95544]	[−0.97334]	[0.92084]	[−2.82800]

Table D6 Vector error correction estimates (series: LNSIGDP, LNCX, LNPX, and LNOX)

Sample (adjusted): 1985–2012
Included observations: 28 after adjustments
Standard errors in parentheses ( ) and t-statistics in brackets [ ]

Cointegrating equation		CointEq1		
LNSIGDP(−1)		1.000000		
LNCX(−1)		−0.687955		
		(0.20955)		
		[−3.28305]		
LNPX(−1)		−1.398180		
		(0.24888)		
		[−5.61798]		
LNOX(−1)		1.076688		
		(0.16618)		
		[6.47887]		
Error correction	**D(LNSIGDP)**	**D(LNCX)**	**D(LNPX)**	**D(LNOX)**
CointEq1	−0.125805	−0.015619	0.266141	−1.196736
	(0.03111)	(0.18727)	(0.12545)	(0.49756)
	[−4.04444]	[−0.08340]	[2.12156]	[−2.40520]

Table D7 **Vector error correction estimates (series: LNTIGDP, LNCM, LNPM, and LNOM)**

Sample (adjusted): 1983−2012
Included observations: 30 after adjustments
Standard errors in parentheses ( ) and t-statistics in brackets [ ]

Cointegrating equation	CointEq1			
LNTIGDP(−1)	1.000000			
LNCM(−1)	−0.184272			
	(0.10594)			
	[−1.73947]			
LNPM(−1)	−1.456961			
	(0.17125)			
	[−8.50776]			
LNOM(−1)	0.648673			
	(0.10537)			
	[6.15603]			
Error correction	**D(LNTIGDP)**	**D(LNCM)**	**D(LNPM)**	**D(LNOM)**
CointEq1	−0.093950	0.482429	0.314443	−1.237307
	(0.03316)	(0.33950)	(0.20420)	(0.46712)
	[−2.83354]	[1.42100]	[1.53990]	[−2.64878]

Table D8 **Vector error correction estimates (series: LNTIGDP, LNCX, LNPX, and LNOX)**

Sample (adjusted): 1985−2012
Included observations: 28 after adjustments
Standard errors in parentheses ( ) and t-statistics in brackets [ ]

Cointegrating equation	CointEq1			
LNTIGDP(−1)	1.000000			
LNCX(−1)	− 0.563409			
	(0.25522)			
	[−2.20756]			
LNPX(−1)	−1.377640			
	(0.30105)			
	[−4.57608]			
LNOX(−1)	0.935717			
	(0.23615)			
	[3.96240]			
Error correction	**D(LNTIGDP)**	**D(LNCX)**	**D(LNPX)**	**D(LNOX)**
CointEq1	− 0.070353	0.141036	0.396575	− 0.381528
	(0.03121)	(0.21868)	(0.15002)	(0.54843)
	[−2.25398]	[0.64493]	[2.64341]	[−0.69567]

Table D9 Vector error correction estimates (series: LNPCGDP, LNCM, LNPM, and LNOM)

Sample (adjusted): 1983–2012
Included observations: 30 after adjustments
Standard errors in parentheses ( ) and t-statistics in brackets [ ]

Cointegrating equation	CointEq1
LNPCGDP(−1)	1.000000
LNCM(−1)	0.817631
	(0.32355)
	[2.52708]
LNPM(−1)	−4.009690
	(0.51140)
	[−7.84054]
LNOM(−1)	2.193281
	(0.31354)
	[6.99517]

Error correction	D(LNPCGDP)	D(LNCM)	D(LNPM)	D(LNOM)
CointEq1	−0.033060	−0.053765	0.062697	−0.385568
	(0.00841)	(0.09869)	(0.06412)	(0.14287)
	[−3.92933]	[−0.54481]	[0.97785]	[−2.69871]

Table D10 Vector error correction estimates (series: LNPCGDP, LNCX, LNPX, and LNOX)

Sample (adjusted): 1984–2012
Included observations: 29 after adjustments
Standard errors in parentheses ( ) and t-statistics in brackets [ ]

Cointegrating equation	CointEq1
LNPCGDP(−1)	1.000000
LNCX(−1)	−1.085070
	(1.00249)
	[−1.08238]
LNPX(−1)	−3.629133
	(1.02081)
	[−3.55516]
LNOX(−1)	3.657099
	(0.57962)
	[6.30944]

Error correction	D(LNPCGDP)	D(LNCX)	D(LNPX)	D(LNOX)
CointEq1	−0.010821	− 0.002037	0.043165	−0.295386
	(0.00553)	(0.03552)	(0.02721)	(0.09381)
	[−1.95634]	[−0.05736]	[1.58623]	[−3.14873]

Appendix E   VEC Granger causality/block exogeneity Wald tests

Table E1 **VEC Granger causality/block exogeneity Wald tests (series: LNGNI, LNCM, LNPM, and LNOM)**

Sample: 1981–2012
Included observations: 30

Dependent variable: D(LNGNI)

Excluded	Chi-sq	df	Probability
D(LNCM)	3.704046	1	0.0543
D(LNPM)	9.837869	1	0.0017
D(LNOM)	18.92997	1	0.0000
All	26.65476	3	0.0000

Dependent variable: D(LNCM)

Excluded	Chi-sq	df	Probability
D(LNGNI)	10.31168	1	0.0013

Dependent variable: D(LNPM)

Excluded	Chi-sq	df	Probability
D(LNGNI)	0.009111	1	0.9240

Dependent variable: D(LNOM)

Excluded	Chi-sq	df	Probability
D(LNGNI)	0.000109	1	0.9917

Table E2 VEC Granger causality/block exogeneity Wald tests (series: LNGNI, LNCX, LNPX, and LNOX)

Sample: 1981–2012 Included observations: 29			
Dependent variable: D(LNGNI)			
Excluded	**Chi-sq**	**df**	**Probability**
D(LNCX)	2.133158	2	0.3442
D(LNPX)	1.008378	2	0.6040
D(LNOX)	2.668048	2	0.2634
All	5.023027	6	0.5409
Dependent variable: D(LNCX)			
Excluded	**Chi-sq**	**df**	**Probability**
D(LNGNI)	1.854846	2	0.3956
Dependent variable: D(LNPX)			
Excluded	**Chi-sq**	**df**	**Probability**
D(LNGNI)	0.543815	2	0.7619
Dependent variable: D(LNOX)			
Excluded	**Chi-sq**	**df**	**Probability**
D(LNGNI)	6.111380	2	0.0471

Table E3 VEC Granger causality/block exogeneity Wald tests (series: LNGDP, LNCM, LNPM, and LNOM)

Sample: 1981–2012
Included observations: 30

Dependent variable: D(LNGDP)

Excluded	Chi-sq	df	Probability
D(LNCM)	2.524397	1	0.1121
D(LNPM)	7.492824	1	0.0062
D(LNOM)	22.36579	1	0.0000
All	28.37371	3	0.0000

Dependent variable: D(LNCM)

Excluded	Chi-sq	df	Probability
D(LNGDP)	9.800136	1	0.0017

Dependent variable: D(LNPM)

Excluded	Chi-sq	df	Probability
D(LNGDP)	0.096956	1	0.7555

Dependent variable: D(LNOM)

Excluded	Chi-sq	df	Probability
D(LNGDP)	0.039104	1	0.8432

Table E4 VEC Granger causality/block exogeneity Wald tests (series: LNGDP, LNCX, LNPX, and LNOX)

Sample: 1981−2012
Included observations: 29

Dependent variable: D(LNGDP)

Excluded	Chi-sq	df	Probability
D(LNCX)	1.661272	2	0.4358
D(LNPX)	0.845771	2	0.6552
D(LNOX)	2.851922	2	0.2403
All	3.791210	6	0.7049

Dependent variable: D(LNCX)

Excluded	Chi-sq	df	Probability
D(LNGDP)	2.200120	2	0.3329

Dependent variable: D(LNPX)

Excluded	Chi-sq	df	Probability
D(LNGDP)	0.778664	2	0.6775

Dependent variable: D(LNOX)

Excluded	Chi-sq	df	Probability
D(LNGDP)	7.115056	2	0.0285

Table E5 VEC Granger causality/block exogeneity Wald tests (series: LNSIGDP, LNCM, LNPM, and LNOM)

Sample: 1981–2012
Included observations: 30

Dependent variable: D(LNSIGDP)

Excluded	Chi-sq	df	Probability
D(LNCM)	5.251155	1	0.0219
D(LNPM)	1.568629	1	0.2104
D(LNOM)	11.66626	1	0.0006
All	20.39259	3	0.0001

Dependent variable: D(LNCM)

Excluded	Chi-sq	df	Probability
D(LNSIGDP)	8.014305	1	0.0046

Dependent variable: D(LNPM)

Excluded	Chi-sq	df	Probability
D(LNSIGDP)	0.791254	1	0.3737

Dependent variable: D(LNOM)

Excluded	Chi-sq	df	Probability
D(LNSIGDP)	0.396748	1	0.5288

Table E6 VEC Granger causality/block exogeneity Wald tests (series: LNSIGDP, LNCX, LNPX, and LNOX)

Sample: 1981−2012
Included observations: 28

Dependent variable: D(LNSIGDP)

Excluded	Chi-sq	df	Probability
D(LNCX)	7.796208	3	0.0504
D(LNPX)	1.549248	3	0.6710
D(LNOX)	14.47137	3	0.0023
All	21.95196	9	0.0090

Dependent variable: D(LNCX)

Excluded	Chi-sq	df	Probability
D(LNSIGDP)	3.243206	3	0.3556

Dependent variable: D(LNPX)

Excluded	Chi-sq	df	Probability
D(LNSIGDP)	4.856561	3	0.1826

Dependent variable: D(LNOX)

Excluded	Chi-sq	df	Probability
D(LNSIGDP)	7.656864	3	0.0537

Table E7 **VEC Granger causality/block exogeneity Wald tests (series: LNTIGDP, LNCM, LNPM, and LNOM)**

Sample: 1981–2012
Included observations: 30

Dependent variable: D(LNTIGDP)

Excluded	Chi-sq	df	Probability
D(LNCM)	7.939025	1	0.0048
D(LNPM)	3.232368	1	0.0722
D(LNOM)	13.39381	1	0.0003
All	18.81269	3	0.0003

Dependent variable: D(LNCM)

Excluded	Chi-sq	df	Probability
D(LNTIGDP)	5.597627	1	0.0180

Dependent variable: D(LNPM)

Excluded	Chi-sq	df	Probability
D(LNTIGDP)	0.031980	1	0.8581

Dependent variable: D(LNOM)

Excluded	Chi-sq	df	Probability
D(LNTIGDP)	0.672964	1	0.4120

Table E8 VEC Granger causality/block exogeneity Wald tests (series: LNTIGDP, LNCX, LNPX, and LNOX)

Sample: 1981−2012
Included observations: 28

Dependent variable: D(LNTIGDP)

Excluded	Chi-sq	df	Probability
D(LNCX)	2.668979	3	0.4455
D(LNPX)	1.353094	3	0.7166
D(LNOX)	6.903685	3	0.0750
All	12.48627	9	0.1873

Dependent variable: D(LNCX)

Excluded	Chi-sq	df	Probability
D(LNTIGDP)	5.522622	3	0.1373

Dependent variable: D(LNPX)

Excluded	Chi-sq	df	Probability
D(LNTIGDP)	6.158488	3	0.1041

Dependent variable: D(LNOX)

Excluded	Chi-sq	df	Probability
D(LNTIGDP)	16.40336	3	0.0009

Table E9 VEC Granger causality/block exogeneity Wald tests (LNPCGDP, LNCM, LNPM, and LNOM)

Sample: 1981−2012
Included observations: 30

Dependent variable: D(LNPCGDP)

Excluded	Chi-sq	df	Probability
D(LNCM)	2.432526	1	0.1188
D(LNPM)	6.776124	1	0.0092
D(LNOM)	20.10149	1	0.0000
All	26.59423	3	0.0000

Dependent variable: D(LNCM)

Excluded	Chi-sq	df	Probability
D(LNPCGDP)	10.10085	1	0.0015

Dependent variable: D(LNPM)

Excluded	Chi-sq	df	Probability
D(LNPCGDP)	0.086874	1	0.7682

Dependent variable: D(LNOM)

Excluded	Chi-sq	df	Probability
D(LNPCGDP)	0.040458	1	0.8406

Table E10 **VEC Granger causality/block exogeneity Wald tests (series: LNPCGDP, LNCX, LNPX, and LNOX)**

Sample: 1981–2012 Included observations: 29			
Dependent variable: D(LNPCGDP)			
Excluded	**Chi-sq**	**df**	**Probability**
D(LNCX)	1.641308	2	0.4401
D(LNPX)	0.794047	2	0.6723
D(LNOX)	2.913280	2	0.2330
All	4.039764	6	0.6713
Dependent variable: D(LNCX)			
Excluded	**Chi-sq**	**df**	**Probability**
D(LNPCGDP)	2.199690	2	0.3329
Dependent variable: D(LNPX)			
Excluded	**Chi-sq**	**df**	**Probability**
D(LNPCGDP)	0.940504	2	0.6248
Dependent variable: D(LNOX)			
Excluded	**Chi-sq**	**df**	**Probability**
D(LNPCGDP)	7.015831	2	0.0300

Appendix F Impulse responses function

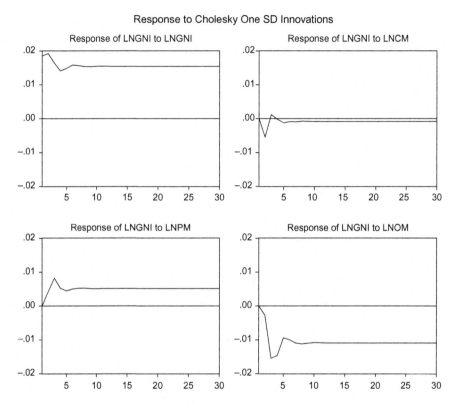

Figure F1 Impulse response functions (between LNGNI, LNCM, LNPM, and LNOM).

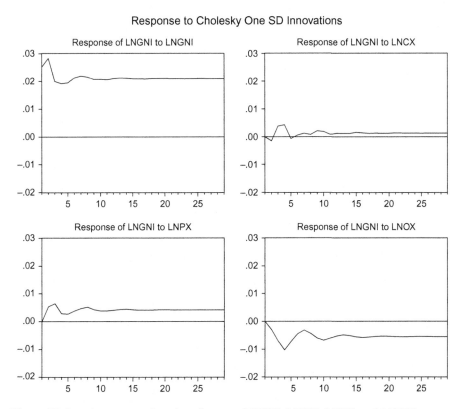

Figure F2 Impulse response functions (between LNGNI, LNCX, LNPX, and LNOX).

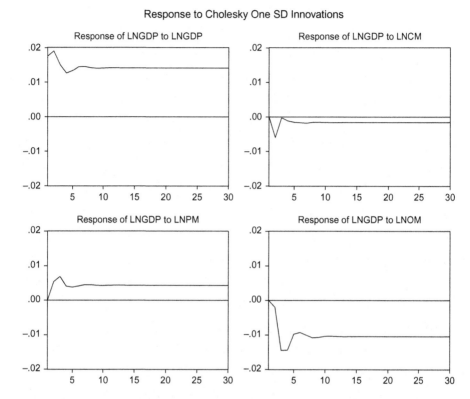

Figure F3 Impulse response functions (between LNGDP, LNCM, LNPM, and LNOM).

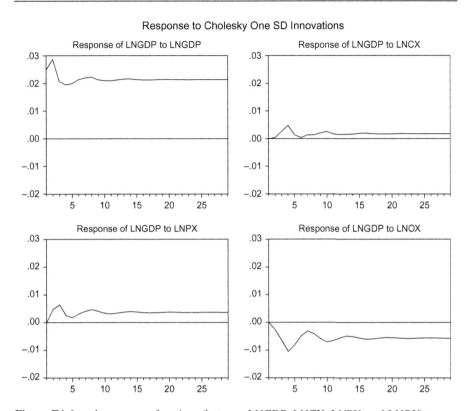

Figure F4 Impulse response functions (between LNGDP, LNCX, LNPX, and LNOX).

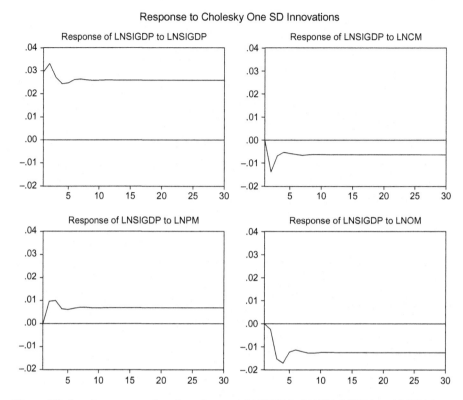

Response to Cholesky One SD Innovations

Figure F5 Impulse response functions (between LNSIGDP, LNCM, LNPM, and LNOM).

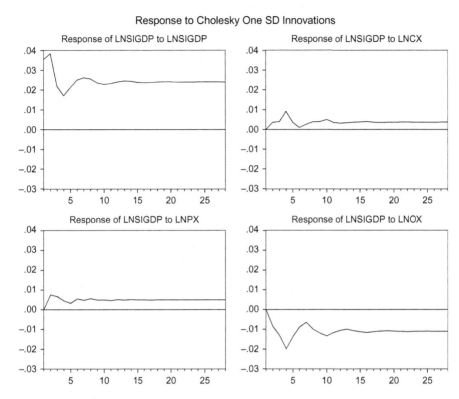

Figure F6 Impulse response functions (between LNSIGDP, LNCX, LNPX, and LNOX).

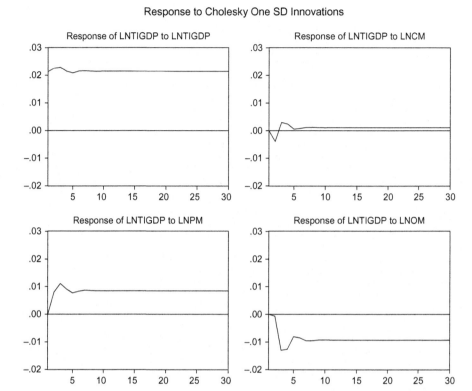

Figure F7 Impulse response functions (between LNTIGDP, LNCM, LNPM, and LNOM).

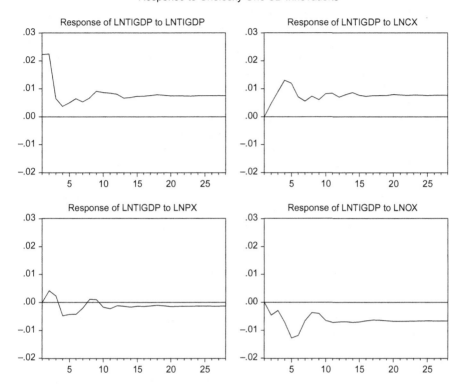

Figure F8 Impulse response functions (between LNTIGDP, LNCX, LNPX, and LNOX).

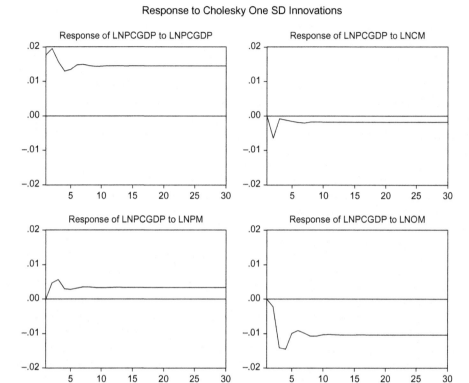

Figure F9 Impulse response functions (between LNPCGDP, LNCM, LNPM, and LNOM).

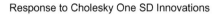

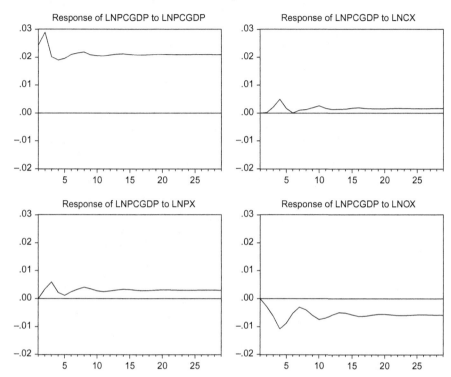

Figure F10 Impulse response functions (between LNPCGDP, LNCX, LNPX, and LNOX).

Appendix G   Results of variance decomposition

Table G1 **Decomposition of LNGNI (Cholesky ordering: LNGNI, LNCM, LNPM, and LNOM)**

Period	SE	LNGNI	LNCM	LNPM	LNOM
1	0.018558	100.0000	0.000000	0.000000	0.000000
2	0.027748	92.79919	3.872965	2.346303	0.981547
3	0.036708	73.03711	2.316214	6.390714	18.25596
4	0.042303	66.15813	1.747029	6.363289	25.73156
5	0.046069	66.26875	1.543817	6.320667	25.86677
6	0.050002	66.31857	1.341958	6.387094	25.95238
7	0.053805	65.77091	1.188542	6.483590	26.55696
8	0.057337	65.16585	1.064233	6.567706	27.20221
9	0.060607	64.78868	0.970408	6.605798	27.63511
10	0.063690	64.57453	0.897401	6.635583	27.89249
11	0.066653	64.37675	0.835489	6.666310	28.12145
12	0.069496	64.18672	0.783096	6.692736	28.33745
13	0.072222	64.02565	0.738552	6.714527	28.52127
14	0.074847	63.89243	0.700279	6.732667	28.67463
15	0.077384	63.77795	0.666989	6.748592	28.80647
16	0.079840	63.67589	0.637676	6.762821	28.92361
17	0.082224	63.58479	0.611701	6.775403	29.02811
18	0.084540	63.50382	0.588545	6.786573	29.12106
19	0.086794	63.43139	0.567766	6.796589	29.20426
20	0.088991	63.36600	0.549014	6.805639	29.27935
21	0.091135	63.30661	0.532004	6.813855	29.34753
22	0.093230	63.25250	0.516505	6.821337	29.40966
23	0.095279	63.20301	0.502326	6.828181	29.46648
24	0.097284	63.15756	0.489304	6.834466	29.51867
25	0.099249	63.11568	0.477303	6.840259	29.56676
26	0.101176	63.07695	0.466208	6.845615	29.61123
27	0.103067	63.04104	0.455919	6.850582	29.65246
28	0.104924	63.00765	0.446352	6.855200	29.69080
29	0.106749	62.97652	0.437434	6.859505	29.72654
30	0.108543	62.94744	0.429101	6.863527	29.75993

Table G2 Decomposition of LNGNI (Cholesky ordering: LNGNI, LNCX, LNPX, and LNOX)

Period	SE	LNGNI	LNCX	LNPX	LNOX
1	0.025221	100.0000	0.000000	0.000000	0.000000
2	0.038424	97.32222	0.145337	1.934665	0.597782
3	0.044491	92.70230	0.853894	3.529547	2.914260
4	0.049787	88.85944	1.422988	3.142679	6.574890
5	0.054019	88.47041	1.223413	2.922562	7.383612
6	0.058340	89.09364	1.058404	2.928812	6.919148
7	0.062581	89.67097	0.958652	3.106316	6.264066
8	0.066522	89.81994	0.862699	3.353256	5.964108
9	0.070084	89.63270	0.869262	3.388544	6.109490
10	0.073517	89.39564	0.854968	3.344225	6.405168
11	0.076676	89.37479	0.797351	3.322355	6.505501
12	0.079779	89.46642	0.761061	3.326390	6.446128
13	0.082806	89.58883	0.726259	3.357591	6.327323
14	0.085726	89.64264	0.696032	3.399858	6.261465
15	0.088531	89.63210	0.684213	3.412198	6.271484
16	0.091249	89.60955	0.667844	3.412341	6.310266
17	0.093863	89.61303	0.647645	3.412876	6.326451
18	0.096423	89.63706	0.632162	3.416487	6.314287
19	0.098925	89.66951	0.616153	3.426538	6.287801
20	0.101365	89.68890	0.602690	3.438082	6.270326
21	0.103746	89.69509	0.593077	3.444119	6.267716
22	0.106071	89.69767	0.582827	3.447814	6.271685
23	0.108342	89.70367	0.572844	3.450722	6.272765
24	0.110569	89.71381	0.563974	3.453961	6.268253
25	0.112754	89.72575	0.555176	3.458603	6.260466
26	0.114898	89.73484	0.547476	3.463298	6.254389
27	0.117003	89.74091	0.540767	3.466844	6.251474
28	0.119069	89.74576	0.534193	3.469798	6.250248
29	0.121099	89.75086	0.528042	3.472324	6.248770

Table G3 **Decomposition of LNGDP (Cholesky ordering: LNGDP, LNCM, LNPM, and LNOM)**

Period	SE	LNGDP	LNCM	LNPM	LNOM
1	0.017580	100.0000	0.000000	0.000000	0.000000
2	0.027193	90.80166	4.798716	3.870348	0.529273
3	0.034990	73.41664	2.903998	6.183730	17.49563
4	0.040104	65.76009	2.294115	5.722716	26.22308
5	0.043555	65.09462	2.074506	5.597975	27.23290
6	0.047034	65.30984	1.906921	5.562516	27.22072
7	0.050473	65.01007	1.782313	5.615059	27.59255
8	0.053731	64.33026	1.656099	5.650228	28.36341
9	0.056734	63.82196	1.561448	5.644816	28.97177
10	0.059547	63.55112	1.490525	5.641033	29.31732
11	0.062250	63.35213	1.431921	5.643547	29.57241
12	0.064853	63.15483	1.381625	5.648386	29.81516
13	0.067357	62.96789	1.337746	5.651608	30.04275
14	0.069766	62.81003	1.300042	5.653057	30.23687
15	0.072093	62.67919	1.267423	5.654366	30.39902
16	0.074348	62.56480	1.238716	5.655876	30.54061
17	0.076538	62.46146	1.213178	5.657327	30.66804
18	0.078666	62.36831	1.190330	5.658547	30.78281
19	0.080739	62.28492	1.169812	5.659580	30.88569
20	0.082759	62.20995	1.151288	5.660521	30.97824
21	0.084731	62.14189	1.134469	5.661397	31.06224
22	0.086658	62.07970	1.119125	5.662200	31.13897
23	0.088544	62.02272	1.105072	5.662930	31.20928
24	0.090390	61.97036	1.092157	5.663598	31.27388
25	0.092199	61.92210	1.080246	5.664215	31.33344
26	0.093973	61.87744	1.069227	5.664787	31.38855
27	0.095715	61.83600	1.059001	5.665317	31.43968
28	0.097425	61.79744	1.049488	5.665811	31.48726
29	0.099106	61.76147	1.040614	5.666271	31.53164
30	0.100759	61.72785	1.032318	5.666701	31.57313

Table G4 Decomposition of LNGDP (Cholesky ordering: LNGDP, LNCX, LNPX, and LNOX)

Period	SE	LNGDP	LNCX	LNPX	LNOX
1	0.024964	100.0000	0.000000	0.000000	0.000000
2	0.038442	97.96565	0.009158	1.537973	0.487223
3	0.044701	94.02084	0.348705	3.151407	2.479048
4	0.050173	89.78724	1.174407	2.732409	6.305944
5	0.054666	89.01413	1.055862	2.406252	7.523752
6	0.058976	89.59182	0.911294	2.348116	7.148773
7	0.063181	90.23014	0.837061	2.459265	6.473532
8	0.067310	90.48950	0.780365	2.648148	6.081992
9	0.071003	90.35572	0.786785	2.699413	6.158080
10	0.074509	90.02673	0.831882	2.647789	6.493595
11	0.077752	89.93431	0.809054	2.591684	6.664956
12	0.080885	90.02098	0.779440	2.573180	6.626396
13	0.083955	90.16381	0.757078	2.585199	6.493912
14	0.086957	90.24739	0.738317	2.615143	6.399150
15	0.089830	90.24532	0.734678	2.626447	6.393557
16	0.092606	90.20268	0.735764	2.618753	6.442802
17	0.095275	90.18913	0.727865	2.607123	6.475879
18	0.097876	90.21012	0.718767	2.601293	6.469823
19	0.100423	90.24823	0.709800	2.602916	6.439054
20	0.102916	90.27612	0.702144	2.608905	6.412835
21	0.105347	90.28424	0.698283	2.611689	6.405792
22	0.107720	90.28185	0.695390	2.610459	6.412296
23	0.110034	90.28311	0.691278	2.607777	6.417836
24	0.112302	90.29175	0.686968	2.606014	6.415263
25	0.114528	90.30506	0.682526	2.606126	6.406286
26	0.116714	90.31643	0.678598	2.607375	6.397592
27	0.118860	90.32297	0.675686	2.608064	6.393278
28	0.120967	90.32646	0.673109	2.607845	6.392589
29	0.123035	90.33008	0.670464	2.607156	6.392298

Table G5 **Decomposition of LNSIGDP (Cholesky ordering: LNSIGDP, LNCM, LNPM, and LNOM)**

Period	SE	LNSIGDP	LNCM	LNPM	LNOM
1	0.029618	100.0000	0.000000	0.000000	0.000000
2	0.047664	87.22303	8.402560	4.096113	0.278295
3	0.058266	80.18011	7.009325	5.675921	7.134645
4	0.065987	76.16208	6.115831	5.368435	12.35366
5	0.072028	75.72702	5.784115	5.212987	13.27588
6	0.078012	75.81790	5.580428	5.161442	13.44023
7	0.083791	75.62548	5.469093	5.180267	13.72516
8	0.089156	75.29778	5.345810	5.192768	14.16365
9	0.094150	75.04784	5.238451	5.181619	14.53209
10	0.098873	74.90002	5.157514	5.171082	14.77138
11	0.103399	74.78921	5.093422	5.165852	14.95152
12	0.107745	74.68501	5.039695	5.163228	15.11206
13	0.111919	74.58967	4.992651	5.160610	15.25707
14	0.115940	74.50831	4.951687	5.157646	15.38236
15	0.119826	74.43949	4.916198	5.155008	15.48930
16	0.123590	74.37928	4.885110	5.152852	15.58276
17	0.127244	74.32538	4.857529	5.151007	15.66609
18	0.130795	74.27700	4.832853	5.149334	15.74081
19	0.134252	74.23361	4.810675	5.147803	15.80791
20	0.137623	74.19451	4.790654	5.146420	15.86841
21	0.140913	74.15903	4.772488	5.145172	15.92331
22	0.144128	74.12666	4.755923	5.144036	15.97338
23	0.147272	74.09701	4.740756	5.142995	16.01924
24	0.150351	74.06976	4.726818	5.142038	16.06138
25	0.153368	74.04465	4.713967	5.141155	16.10023
26	0.156327	74.02142	4.702080	5.140338	16.13616
27	0.159231	73.99986	4.691051	5.139581	16.16950
28	0.162083	73.97981	4.680792	5.138876	16.20052
29	0.164886	73.96112	4.671225	5.138219	16.22944
30	0.167641	73.94364	4.662282	5.137605	16.25648

Table G6 **Decomposition of LNSIGDP (Cholesky ordering: LNSIGDP, LNCX, LNPX, and LNOX)**

Period	SE	LNSIGDP	LNCX	LNPX	LNOX
1	0.035536	100.0000	0.000000	0.000000	0.000000
2	0.053656	95.07456	0.461118	1.928440	2.535884
3	0.059903	89.60258	0.809989	2.758723	6.828708
4	0.066180	80.07193	2.590047	2.707056	14.63097
5	0.071020	78.48721	2.507740	2.557658	16.44739
6	0.076038	79.35199	2.205281	2.741946	15.70079
7	0.080888	80.66635	2.054182	2.764424	14.51505
8	0.085714	80.81230	2.036761	2.882269	14.26867
9	0.089924	80.32480	2.044042	2.907200	14.72395
10	0.093986	79.41892	2.154790	2.926893	15.49939
11	0.097698	79.18528	2.124324	2.928979	15.76142
12	0.101351	79.23890	2.071918	2.965613	15.72357
13	0.104926	79.41967	2.039091	2.977953	15.56329
14	0.108454	79.42593	2.022837	3.006503	15.54473
15	0.111799	79.32603	2.018863	3.019017	15.63609
16	0.115051	79.15693	2.028230	3.031316	15.78352
17	0.118177	79.08816	2.016859	3.039261	15.85572
18	0.121242	79.06849	2.003893	3.051925	15.87569
19	0.124240	79.07969	1.992759	3.060355	15.86720
20	0.127183	79.06191	1.985014	3.071377	15.88170
21	0.130045	79.02561	1.980663	3.078745	15.91498
22	0.132846	78.97715	1.978446	3.086018	15.95838
23	0.135581	78.94735	1.972904	3.092027	15.98772
24	0.138266	78.92759	1.967527	3.098554	16.00633
25	0.140902	78.91580	1.962293	3.104083	16.01782
26	0.143493	78.89937	1.958000	3.109885	16.03274
27	0.146035	78.88009	1.954625	3.114701	16.05058
28	0.148534	78.85896	1.951733	3.119357	16.06995

Table G7 Decomposition of LNTIGDP (Cholesky ordering: LNTIGDP, LNCM, LNPM, and LNOM)

Period	SE	LNTIGDP	LNCM	LNPM	LNOM
1	0.021375	100.0000	0.000000	0.000000	0.000000
2	0.032321	92.49456	1.443016	6.025128	0.037291
3	0.043222	79.75571	1.285654	9.926490	9.032142
4	0.050748	75.71414	1.159017	10.41049	12.71635
5	0.055973	76.07594	0.962493	10.43424	12.52733
6	0.061144	76.16432	0.826227	10.57777	12.43168
7	0.066139	75.80168	0.738831	10.75780	12.70169
8	0.070714	75.52849	0.675233	10.87054	12.92575
9	0.074959	75.39843	0.623085	10.94039	13.03810
10	0.078980	75.30788	0.580394	10.99950	13.11223
11	0.082822	75.21581	0.546072	11.05209	13.18602
12	0.086493	75.13391	0.517694	11.09568	13.25271
13	0.090011	75.06843	0.493528	11.13160	13.30644
14	0.093396	75.01378	0.472739	11.16237	13.35111
15	0.096663	74.96565	0.454737	11.18927	13.39034
16	0.099824	74.92308	0.438997	11.21286	13.42506
17	0.102887	74.88564	0.425101	11.23363	13.45563
18	0.105862	74.85247	0.412739	11.25208	13.48271
19	0.108756	74.82276	0.401676	11.26860	13.50696
20	0.111574	74.79599	0.391717	11.28348	13.52881
21	0.114323	74.77176	0.382706	11.29695	13.54859
22	0.117008	74.74974	0.374511	11.30919	13.56656
23	0.119632	74.72963	0.367027	11.32037	13.58298
24	0.122200	74.71118	0.360166	11.33062	13.59803
25	0.124715	74.69422	0.353853	11.34005	13.61188
26	0.127180	74.67855	0.348025	11.34876	13.62467
27	0.129599	74.66404	0.342627	11.35682	13.63651
28	0.131973	74.65057	0.337615	11.36431	13.64750
29	0.134305	74.63803	0.332947	11.37128	13.65774
30	0.136597	74.62632	0.328591	11.37779	13.66730

Table G8 Decomposition of LNTIGDP (Cholesky ordering: LNTIGDP, LNCX, LNPX, and LNOX)

Period	SE	LNTIGDP	LNCX	LNPX	LNOX
1	0.022338	100.0000	0.000000	0.000000	0.000000
2	0.032641	94.35233	2.062938	1.633255	1.951475
3	0.034664	87.24272	8.443460	1.881759	2.432057
4	0.038211	72.75892	18.61490	3.118177	5.508003
5	0.042559	60.02347	22.94170	3.523111	13.51172
6	0.045425	54.72864	22.58652	3.955066	18.72977
7	0.046581	53.35137	22.90669	3.949298	19.79264
8	0.047786	52.66356	24.13488	3.806694	19.39487
9	0.049204	53.12477	24.29423	3.631616	18.94938
10	0.051084	52.16910	25.13931	3.485279	19.20631
11	0.052995	51.02036	25.87293	3.422286	19.68442
12	0.054516	50.38495	26.10429	3.282847	20.22791
13	0.055935	49.28701	26.79891	3.180459	20.73362
14	0.057490	48.09529	27.63154	3.097169	21.17600
15	0.058892	47.37936	28.03084	3.003514	21.58629
16	0.060179	46.87256	28.31989	2.933592	21.87396
17	0.061460	46.46365	28.65322	2.855267	22.02786
18	0.062759	46.14557	28.93226	2.763581	22.15859
19	0.064036	45.77255	29.20562	2.691717	22.33011
20	0.065327	45.29040	29.54252	2.640085	22.52700
21	0.066578	44.87403	29.80972	2.586784	22.72947
22	0.067780	44.50999	30.02752	2.536319	22.92617
23	0.068962	44.14856	30.26914	2.491056	23.09124
24	0.070126	43.84238	30.48525	2.444052	23.22832
25	0.071260	43.58125	30.66532	2.399142	23.35429
26	0.072386	43.31970	30.84896	2.359926	23.47141
27	0.073502	43.07346	31.02209	2.322018	23.58243
28	0.074598	42.84394	31.17730	2.285711	23.69305

Table G9 **Decomposition of LNPCGDP (Cholesky ordering: LNPCGDP, LNCM, LNPM, and LNOM)**

Period	SE	LNPCGDP	LNCM	LNPM	LNOM
1	0.017740	100.0000	0.000000	0.000000	0.000000
2	0.027659	91.13765	5.389847	2.836372	0.636135
3	0.035282	75.90166	3.365187	4.283437	16.44972
4	0.040435	68.06402	2.650217	3.793457	25.49231
5	0.043876	67.21293	2.380083	3.625292	26.78170
6	0.047333	67.54079	2.202478	3.554603	26.70213
7	0.050778	67.39461	2.075825	3.566824	26.96274
8	0.054057	66.76255	1.937528	3.568255	27.73167
9	0.057072	66.24252	1.829958	3.540687	28.38684
10	0.059889	65.97675	1.749818	3.518336	28.75510
11	0.062593	65.80587	1.685511	3.505043	29.00358
12	0.065203	65.63381	1.630462	3.496756	29.23897
13	0.067715	65.45974	1.581807	3.488795	29.46966
14	0.070132	65.30966	1.539742	3.480534	29.67007
15	0.072464	65.18768	1.503447	3.473277	29.83560
16	0.074726	65.08301	1.471631	3.467260	29.97810
17	0.076922	64.98813	1.443320	3.462081	30.10647
18	0.079057	64.90173	1.417938	3.457382	30.22295
19	0.081136	64.82420	1.395124	3.453075	30.32760
20	0.083162	64.75472	1.374535	3.449183	30.42156
21	0.085141	64.69179	1.355847	3.445675	30.50669
22	0.087074	64.63424	1.338794	3.442485	30.58448
23	0.088966	64.58142	1.323171	3.439557	30.65585
24	0.090818	64.53289	1.308809	3.436861	30.72144
25	0.092633	64.48816	1.295564	3.434374	30.78190
26	0.094413	64.44678	1.283309	3.432074	30.83784
27	0.096160	64.40837	1.271937	3.429941	30.88975
28	0.097876	64.37263	1.261354	3.427955	30.93806
29	0.099563	64.33928	1.251483	3.426103	30.98313
30	0.101221	64.30811	1.242253	3.424371	31.02526

Table G10 **Decomposition of LNPCGDP (Cholesky ordering: LNPCGDP, LNCX, LNPX, and LNOX)**

Period	SE	LNPCGDP	LNCX	LNPX	LNOX
1	0.024387	100.0000	0.000000	0.000000	0.000000
2	0.038091	98.64545	0.002565	0.797685	0.554302
3	0.044004	94.90918	0.238802	2.405027	2.446991
4	0.049421	89.92733	1.196845	2.099931	6.775893
5	0.053899	88.73450	1.105338	1.807552	8.352608
6	0.058124	89.32773	0.950504	1.727639	7.994128
7	0.062158	90.11941	0.857784	1.795485	7.227316
8	0.066153	90.50370	0.792674	1.959942	6.743686
9	0.069735	90.40530	0.787712	2.013282	6.793705
10	0.073183	89.98695	0.841262	1.970110	7.201675
11	0.076364	89.82446	0.819941	1.913008	7.442594
12	0.079416	89.91238	0.783566	1.888465	7.415591
13	0.082393	90.09887	0.754809	1.892421	7.253895
14	0.085313	90.22535	0.731114	1.918113	7.125425
15	0.088113	90.23942	0.723979	1.929675	7.106923
16	0.090827	90.18233	0.725394	1.922467	7.169804
17	0.093435	90.15300	0.716903	1.908972	7.221128
18	0.095970	90.17399	0.705304	1.900359	7.220346
19	0.098450	90.22572	0.693596	1.899270	7.181410
20	0.100880	90.26896	0.683459	1.903851	7.143728
21	0.103252	90.28477	0.677907	1.906297	7.131021
22	0.105569	90.28122	0.674328	1.904598	7.139859
23	0.107829	90.27952	0.669439	1.900776	7.150269
24	0.110041	90.28893	0.663912	1.897618	7.149544
25	0.112212	90.30725	0.658091	1.896479	7.138181
26	0.114346	90.32468	0.652843	1.896950	7.125531
27	0.116440	90.33515	0.648919	1.897186	7.118747
28	0.118497	90.33982	0.645647	1.896469	7.118063
29	0.120517	90.34370	0.642340	1.895085	7.118877

Vertical specialization and increasing productive employment: comparing impacts of conventional trade and processing trade patterns on labor market in China

4.1 Introduction

The analysis of inclusive growth looks for ways to increase the pace of growth by utilizing more fully parts of the labor force trapped in low-productivity activities or completely excluded from the growth process. The presence of intermediate goods suggests the relevance of the theory of vertical specialization, in which foreign direct investment plays a major role. The labor market effects of vertical specialization have become increasingly important from a policy point of view because they are closely linked to the concepts of inclusive growth in China, with a substantial vertical specialization presence. Vertical specialization intensively involve firms located in China, and it is important to understand whether firms entering international production networks can create important employment opportunities in China (Ma et al., 2015).

On the basis of vertical specialization, different trade pattern operate in a different way to create employment activities. In this chapter, the focus is on two different types of trade patterns, namely, conventional trade and processing trade. China's Customs Statistics distinguishes between imports and exports linked to conventional trade and processing trade. The former is a type of trade pattern of ordinary international trade in standard textbook; the latter is a type of trade pattern of achievement of integrating into vertical specialization. Processing trade involves importing parts and components as intermediate goods in the manufacture of final products for exports. Thus, questions may arise regarding the impact of the two different types of trade patterns on the total number of employed persons, number of employed persons at year-end in urban areas, number of employed persons at year-end in rural areas, economically active population (EAP), number of employed persons at year-end by primary industry, number of employed persons at year-end by secondary industry, and number of employed persons at year-end by tertiary industry. Which type of subsidies is more effective for the government to induce employment?

Achieving Inclusive Growth in China Through Vertical Specialization.

The purpose of this chapter is to examine the relationship between vertical specialization and national economies: their labor market effects. Specifically, it focuses on the impact of imports and exports by processing trade on China labor markets. This chapter is organized as follows: the problem is described in Section 4.2. The different effects on labor market are presented under two different types of subsidies in Section 4.3. Finally, we draw some conclusions and implications for further research in Section 4.4.

4.2 Trade and labor markets

If trade is driven by Ricardian comparative advantage, then trade liberalization will result in a reduction in unemployment. However, trade driven by Heckscher–Ohlin is expected to reduce unemployment only if the country in question is labor-abundant (Dutt et al., 2009). Although both importing and exporting activities may create an internal restructuring process and bring about efficiency gains (Halpern et al., 2005; Wagner, 2007, 2012), the impact on employment is more uncertain (Lo Turco and Maggion, 2013). Whether trade affects the level of equilibrium unemployment is "primarily an empirical issue." Yet, "there is very little empirical work on the aggregate employment effects of trade policies" (Davidson and Matusz, 2004; Felbermayr et al., 2011). For example, imported inputs (parts and components) may directly substitute for domestic labor with a consequent reduction in employment. However, imported inputs enhance the possibilities for improving competitiveness and leading to an expansion of the scale of output and, thus, of employment.

The labor market effects of vertical specialization have become increasingly important from a policy point of view because they are closely linked to the concepts of economic upgrading within inclusive growth. Economic upgrading sometimes translates into improvements for workers (Barrientos et al., 2010; Milberg and Winkler, 2011). The growth of intermediate imports and the insourcing of higher skill intensive production stages might drive an increase in skill intensity in the developing country manufacturing sector (Feenstra and Hanson, 1997). Fajnzylber and Fernandes (2004) contrast China and Brazil. In the former, importing or exporting intermediates is associated with stronger demand for skilled labor. In Brazil, however, the opposite is true. The reasons for this difference are the simple assembly or the extent of processing trade (ie, export of final goods based on assembly of imported intermediates) undertaken in China relative to Brazil (Shepherd, 2013). Dai et al. (2011) found that exporters in China are generally larger than other firms, although the effect is muted somewhat for firms engaged in processing trade. Feenstra and Hong (2007) showed that using China's employment/export ratios from earlier years to forecast the country's employment growth from 1997 to 2005 would result in serious overestimates, because the employment/export ratios changed significantly due to changes in wages, technological progress, and changes in export composition.

In sum, overall declines in unemployment with trade opening can be shown, but this outcome will be influenced by the labor market conditions.

4.3 Empirical evidence of the impact of vertically specialized trade policy on the labor market in China

4.3.1 Methodology and data

Further, the variable groups are tested in a different diagnostic test to perform time series analysis. First, the order of integration in the data is tested by using the augmented Dickey Fuller (ADF) unit root test; if the unit root is present, then stationarity is achieved by the first differencing of the data. Having established the order of integration, it next tests for cointegration by applying the Johansen cointegration method, and a vector error correction model (VECM) has been used to assess both the long-term as well as short-term relationship between the variables. Finally, a VECM is used. The results were further verified through impulse response functions (IRFs) and variance decomposition.

The chapter attempts to trace the long-term equilibrium relationship between exports by processing trade, exports by conventional trade, imports by processing trade, imports by conventional trade, total employed persons, number of employed persons at year-end in urban rural areas, number of employed persons at year-end in rural areas, EAP, number of employed persons at year-end by primary industry, number of employed persons at year-end by secondary industry, and number of employed persons at year-end by tertiary industry of China during the period of 1981−2012 using the time series framework. All these variables are used and transformed into natural logarithm form. All data have been obtained from the database of China Statistical Yearbook and China Trade and External Economic Statistical Yearbook published by National Bureau of Statistics of China; the sample covers 32 annual observations.

This study used the variable groups in Table B1 to find the relationship.

LN PX = natural logarithm of exports by processing trade (PX),
LN CX = natural logarithm of exports by conventional trade (CX),
LN PM = natural logarithm of imports by processing trade (PM),
LN CM = natural logarithm of imports by conventional trade (CM),
LNTE = natural logarithm of total employed persons (TE),
LNUE = natural logarithm of number of employed persons at year-end in urban areas (UE),
LNRE = natural logarithm of number of employed persons at year-end in rural areas (RE),
LNEAP = natural logarithm of economically active population (EAP),
LNPIP = natural logarithm of number of employed persons at year-end by primary industry (PIP),
LNSIP = natural logarithm of number of employed persons at year-end by secondary industry (SIP),
LNTIP = natural logarithm of number of employed persons at year-end by tertiary industry (TIP).

4.3.2   Unit root test for stationarity

The ADF test for unit roots was conducted for all the time series used for the study. Table B1 shows the result of unit root tests using the ADF unit root test at the first difference level. The null hypothesis of nonstationarity is performed at the 1% and the 5% significance levels. In Table B1, the result of the ADF test illustrates that all the data series are nonstationary at level. However, the result of the ADF test on the first difference strongly supports that all data series are stationary after the first difference at the 1% or 5% significance levels. The ADF results show that all the variable series were integrated series of order I (1).

4.3.3   Results of Johansen's cointegration tests

Cointegration means economic variables share the same stochastic trend so that they are combined together in the long-term. Even if they deviate from each other in the short-term, they tend to come back to the trend in the long-term. A necessary condition for the cointegration test is that all the variables should be integrated at the same order or contain a deterministic trend (Engle and Granger, 1991). The unit root test results show that all the time series of exports by processing trade, exports by conventional trade, imports by processing trade, imports by conventional trade, total employed persons, number of employed persons at year-end in urban rural areas, number of employed persons at year-end in rural areas, EAP, number of employed persons at year-end by primary industry, number of employed persons at year-end by secondary industry, and number of employed persons at year-end by tertiary industry are integrated at first difference but are not integrated at level form during the period from 1981 to 2012. Therefore, these time series in the period are valid in the cointegration test. Once the variables are cointegrated, the short-term changes can be explained through the VECM (Engle and Granger, 1987). Following the cointegration test, the VECM was used to analyze the causality within the seven variable groups, and this is described in the following section.

Through test iterations, we found that when the largest lag order equals three, the AIC reaches the minimum. SC reaches the minimum when the lag order equals one. So, the LR test is chosen as a tradeoff. The original hypothesis test is the largest lag order equal to one. Schwarz information criterion (SIC), final prediction error (FPE), and Hannan-Quinn information criterion (HQ) confirm lag length one (1). After ascertaining lag length, we apply the Johansen cointegration test, and the results of this test are given in Tables C1−C14. The results are based on the Johansen cointegration test, reporting the hypothesized number of cointegration equations in the first left column, the eigenvalue, the likelihood ratio statistics, and the 5% critical value.

The results of trace statistics and the results of maximum Eigen statistics are shown in Tables C1−C14. Trace statistics and maximum Eigen statistics values help to find the rank(s) that shows the number of vector(s) containing long-term relations. It is evident that the null hypothesis of no rank is rejected at the 1% significant level.

Moreover, the results reveal that null hypothesis of no rank was also rejected at the 1% level of significance. Therefore, the results of both trace and max-Eigen statistics confirm that one cointegration vector exists in the model. It means the long-term relationship prevails among the variables. In summary, the Johansen cointegration test results show the 14 variable groups in Table A1 are cointegrated and have a long-term equilibrium relationship during 1981−2012.

To distinguish the effect between imports and exports by conventional trade and imports by processing trade, we compared the effects of total employed persons (TE), number of employed persons at year-end in urban areas (UE), number of employed persons at year-end in rural areas (RE), economically active population (EAP), number of employed persons at year-end by primary industry (PIP), number of employed persons at year-end by secondary industry (SIP), and number of employed persons at year-end by tertiary industry (TIP). Following Johansen's technique, the normalized long-term cointegration relationships and the comparison coefficients are shown in Tables C1−C14. The normalized long-term cointegration relationships are very revealing. The observed signs are as anticipated. Moreover, the long-term relationships are also as expected, given the intrinsic interdependence between the variables. The results can be expressed as follows:

1. Total employed persons, imports and exports by conventional trade, and imports and exports by processing trade:

$$\text{LNTE} = -\underset{(1.23366)}{0.292264}\ \text{LNCM} + \underset{(1.17312)}{2.597418}\ \text{LNPM} \tag{4.1}$$

$$\text{LNTE} = -\underset{(1.56982)}{1.107964}\ \text{LNCX} + \underset{(1.50868)}{3.356340}\ \text{LNPX} \tag{4.2}$$

We can see the results from Eqs. (4.1) and (4.2) that the 1% increase in imports by conventional trade (LNCM) will have a negative impact of 0.292264% on total employed persons (LNTE), the 1% increase in imports by processing trade (LNPM) will have a positive impact of 2.597418% on total employed persons (LNTE), the 1% increase in exports by conventional trade (LNCX) will have a negative impact of 1.107964% on total employed persons (LNTE), and the 1% increase in exports by processing trade (LNPX) will have a positive impact of 3.35634% on total employed persons (LNTE).

Eqs. (4.1) and (4.2) shows that the increase in imports and exports by processing trade could increase total employed persons in the long-term. This provides the supports for evidence of the foreign trade and vertically specialized trade channels.

2. Number of employed persons at year-end in urban areas, imports and exports by conventional trade, and imports and exports by processing trade:

$$\text{LNUE} = -\underset{(0.58782)}{0.205225}\ \text{LNCM} + \underset{(0.54710)}{1.856411}\ \text{LNPM} \tag{4.3}$$

$$\text{LNUE} = -\underset{(1.83073)}{0.151620}\ \text{LNCX} + \underset{(1.78011)}{3.331855}\ \text{LNPX} \tag{4.4}$$

We can see from the previous equations that in the longer-term, the 1% increase in imports by conventional trade (LNCM) will have an adverse effect of 0.205225% on the number of employed persons at year-end in urban areas (LNUE), the 1% increase in imports by processing trade (LNPM) will have a positive impact of 1.856411% on the number of employed persons at year-end in urban areas (LNUE), the 1% increase in exports by conventional trade (LNCX) will have an negative effect of 0.15162% on the number of employed persons at year-end in urban areas (LNUE), and the 1% increase in exports by processing trade (LNPX) will have a positive impact of 3.331855% on the number of employed persons at year-end in urban areas (LNUE).

Eqs. (4.3) and (4.4) demonstrate that the increase in imports and exports by processing trade can cause the increase in the number of employed persons at year-end in urban areas in the long-term. This confirms the existence of the vertical specialization channel.

3. Number of employed persons at year-end in rural areas, imports and exports by conventional trade, and imports and exports by processing trade:

$$\text{LNRE} = -\underset{(2.71415)}{0.599911} \text{LNCM} + \underset{(2.64948)}{4.031328} \text{LNPM} \tag{4.5}$$

$$\text{LNRE} = -\underset{(1.46246)}{0.611893} \text{LNCX} + \underset{(1.39894)}{2.816825} \text{LNPX} \tag{4.6}$$

Eq. (4.5) reveals that in the longer-term, the 1% increase in imports by conventional trade (LNCM) will have an adverse effect of 0.599911% on the number of employed persons at year-end in rural areas (LNRE) and the 1% increase in imports by processing trade (LNPM) will have a positive impact of 4.031328% on the number of employed persons at year-end in rural areas (LNRE). Eq. (4.6) reveals that the 1% increase in exports by conventional trade (LNCX) will have an adverse effect of 0.611893% on the number of employed persons at year-end in rural areas (LNRE) and the 1% increase in exports by processing trade (LNPX) will have a positive impact of 2.816825% on the number of employed persons at year-end in rural areas (LNRE).

Eqs. (4.5) and (4.6) shows that the increase in imports and exports by processing trade could increase the number of employed persons at year-end in rural areas in the long-term. This confirms the existence of the vertical specialization channel.

4. Economically active population, imports and exports by conventional trade, and imports and exports by processing trade:

$$\text{LNEAP} = -\underset{(1.18131)}{0.249089} \text{LNCM} + \underset{(1.12110)}{2.544901} \text{LNPM} \tag{4.7}$$

$$\text{LNEAP} = -\underset{(1.51673)}{0.957982} \text{LNCX} + \underset{(1.45974)}{3.257376} \text{LNPX} \tag{4.8}$$

Eq. (4.6) reveals that the 1% increase in imports by conventional trade (LNCM) will have an adverse effect of 0.249089% on economically active population (LNEAP) and the 1% increase in imports by processing trade (LNPM) will have a positive impact of 2.544901% on economically active population (LNEAP). Eq. (4.7) reveals that the 1% increase in exports by conventional trade (LNCX) will have an adverse effect of 0.957982% on economically active population (LNEAP) and the 1% increase in exports by processing trade (LNPX) will have a positive impact of 3.257376% on economically active population (LNEAP).

Eqs. (4.7) and (4.8) show that the increase in imports and exports by processing trade could increase the economically active population in the long-term. This provides support for evidence of the vertically specialized trade channels.

5. Number of employed persons at year-end by primary industry, imports and exports by conventional trade, and imports and exports by processing trade:

$$\text{LNPIP} = -\underset{(1.02761)}{0.173471}\,\text{LNCM} + \underset{(1.00064)}{2.321904}\,\text{LNPM} \tag{4.9}$$

$$\text{LNPIP} = -\underset{(0.38631)}{1.909295}\,\text{LNCX} + \underset{(0.37471)}{3.053029}\,\text{LNPX} \tag{4.10}$$

We can see from the previous equations that in the longer-term, the 1% increase in imports by conventional trade (LNCM) will have an adverse effect of 0.173471% on the number of employed persons at year-end by primary industry (LNPIP) and the 1% increase in imports by processing trade (LNPM) will have a positive impact of 2.321904% on the number of employed persons at year-end by primary industry (LNPIP). The 1% increase in exports by conventional trade (LNCX) will have a negative effect of 1.909295% on the number of employed persons at year-end by primary industry (LNPIP) and the 1% increase in exports by processing trade (LNPX) will have a positive impact of 3.053029% on the number of employed persons at year-end by primary industry (LNPIP).

Eqs. (4.9) and (4.10) demonstrate that the increase in imports and exports by processing trade can cause the increase in the number of employed persons at year-end by primary industry in the long-term. This confirms the existence of the vertical specialization channel.

6. Number of employed persons at year-end by secondary industry, imports and exports by conventional trade, and imports and exports by processing trade:

$$\text{LNSIP} = -\underset{(0.48139)}{0.113645}\,\text{LNCM} + \underset{(0.45346)}{1.492470}\,\text{LNPM} \tag{4.11}$$

$$\text{LNSIP} = -\underset{(1.47696)}{2.386625}\,\text{LNCX} + \underset{(1.39236)}{4.028120}\,\text{LNPX} \tag{4.12}$$

Eq. (4.11) reveals that the 1% increase in imports by conventional trade (LNCM) will have an adverse effect of 0.113645% on the number of employed persons at year-end by secondary industry (LNSIP). The 1% increase in imports by processing trade (LNPM) will have a positive impact of 1.492470 % on the number of employed persons at year-end by secondary industry (LNSIP). Eq. (4.12) reveals that the 1% increase in exports by conventional trade (LNCX) will have an adverse effect of 2.386625% on the number of employed persons at year-end by secondary industry (LNSIP). The 1% increase in exports by processing trade (LNPX) will have a positive impact of 4.02812% on the number of employed persons at year-end by secondary industry (LNSIP).

Eqs. (4.11) and (4.12) show that the increase in imports and exports by processing trade could increase the number of employed persons at year-end by secondary industry in the long-term. This provides the supports for evidence of the vertically specialized trade channels.

7. Number of employed persons at year-end by tertiary industry, imports and exports by conventional trade, and imports and exports by processing trade:

$$\text{LNTIP} = -\underset{(0.49849)}{1.781351}\,\text{LNCM} + \underset{(0.48304)}{3.139817}\,\text{LNPM} \tag{4.13}$$

$$\text{LNTIP} = -\underset{(0.45904)}{0.536178}\,\text{LNCX} + \underset{(0.43013)}{1.755503}\,\text{LNPX} \tag{4.14}$$

We can see from the previous equations that in the longer-term, the 1% increase in imports by conventional trade (LNCM) will have an adverse effect of 1.781351% on the number of employed persons at year-end by tertiary industry (LNTIP) and the 1% increase in imports by processing trade (LNPM) will have a positive impact of 3.139817% on the number of employed persons at year-end by tertiary industry (LNTIP). The 1% increase in exports by conventional trade (LNCX) will have a negative effect of 0.536178% on the number of employed persons at year-end by tertiary industry (LNTIP) and the 1% increase in exports by processing trade (LNPX) will have a positive impact of 1.755503% on the number of employed persons at year-end by tertiary industry (LNTIP).

Eqs. (4.13) and (4.14) demonstrate that the increase in imports and exports by processing trade can cause the increase in the number of employed persons at year-end by tertiary industry in the long-term. This confirms the existence of the vertical specialization channel.

In fact, these equations reveal the contribution of the vertical specialization variables (imports and exports by processing trade) to employment, which connects the vertically specialized trade policy variables with the labor market variables (TE, UE, RE, EAP, PIP, SIP, and TIP). These long-term equations support the existence of the vertical specialization channel in the trade policy transmission process in China.

Proposition 1. The contribution and importance of conventional trade for increasing total employed persons are lower than processing trade.

Proposition 2. The contribution and importance of conventional trade for increasing the number of employed persons at year-end in urban areas are lower than processing trade.

Proposition 3. The contribution and importance of conventional trade for increasing the number of employed persons at year-end in rural areas are lower than processing trade.

Proposition 4. The contribution and importance of conventional trade for increasing the economically active population are lower than processing trade.

Proposition 5. The contribution and importance of conventional trade for increasing the number of employed persons at year-end by primary industry are lower than processing trade.

Proposition 6. The contribution and importance of conventional trade for increasing the number of employed persons at year-end by secondary industry are lower than processing trade.

Proposition 7. The contribution and importance of conventional trade for increasing the number of employed persons at year-end by tertiary industry are lower than processing trade.

4.3.4 The vector error correction model

Given the cointegration results, we should construct the VECMs to analyze the short-term dynamic behavior of the model. The results of the VCEM are shown on Tables D1−D14, where EC is the error correction term (the cointegration term) since the deviation from long-run equilibrium is corrected gradually through a series of partial short-run adjustments (Johansen, 1995; Juselius, 2006).

The presence of cointegration requires at least one of the coefficients of the error correction terms to be statistically significant. The coefficients of variables indicate the short-term impact. A significant coefficient implies that past equilibrium errors play a role in determining the current outcomes. The negative sign indicates that the adjustment is in the right direction to restore the long-term relationship. The magnitude of the error correction model (-1) coefficient indicates that the speed of adjustment.

The negative sign of the estimated error correction coefficients suggest from low to moderate speed of convergence to equilibrium. For D (LNPX), the error correction terms are negative in Tables D2, D4, D6, Tables 8 and 12, signaling that the system is stable and converges to the equilibrium track after some disturbance in the system.

4.3.5 Granger causality tests

The structures of the causal relationships between variables were analyzed through the Granger causality approach. The Granger causality test is a statistical hypothesis test for determining whether one time series is useful for forecasting another. If probability value is less than any α level, then the hypothesis would be rejected at that level.

In Table E1, when nine lags are applied, the hypothesis that LNCM does not involve Granger causality of LNTE can be rejected at the 1% level of significance, and the hypothesis that LNPM does not involve Granger causality of LNTE can be rejected at the 5% level of significance. Thus, we found unidirectional causality running from LNCM to LNTE, and we found unidirectional causality running from LNPM to LNTE. In Table E2, when nine lags were applied, we found unidirectional causality running from LNCX to LNTE at the 1% level of significance and unidirectional causality running from LNPX to LNTE at the 5% level of significance. In Table E3, when nine lags were applied, we found unidirectional causality running from LNCM to LNUE at the 1% level of significance and unidirectional causality running from LNPM to LNUE at the 5% level of significance. When five lags, six lags, and eight lags were applied, we found unidirectional causality running from LNUE to LNCM at the 10% level of significance. In Table E4, when six lags were applied, we found unidirectional causality running from LNPX to LNUE at the 10% level of significance. When nine lags were applied, we found unidirectional causality running from LNCX to LNUE at the 1% level of significance and unidirectional causality running from LNPX to LNUE at the 5% level of significance. The results in Table E5 indicate the existence of a unidirectional causality running from LNCM to LNRE when one lag and two lags were applied at the 1% and the 5% levels of significance. Unidirectional causality running from LNPM to LNRE when one lag and two lags were applied at the 1% and 5% levels of significance was revealed. The results in Table E6 indicate the existence of unidirectional causality running from LNCX to LNRE when one, two, and three lags were applied at the 1%, 5%, and 10% levels of significance. Unidirectional causality running from LNPX to LNRE when one, two, and three lags were applied at the 1%, 5%, and 10% levels of significance was also revealed.

The results in Table E7 indicate the existence of unidirectional causality running from LNCM to LNEAP when six and nine lags were applied at the 10% level of significance. Unidirectional causality running from LNPM to LNEAP when nine lags were applied at the 5% level of significance was also revealed. The results in Table E8 indicate the existence of unidirectional causality running from LNCX to LNEAP when nine lags were applied at the 5% level of significance. Unidirectional causality running from LNPX to LNEAP when nine lags were applied at the 1% level of significance was revealed. The results in Table E9 indicate the existence of a unidirectional causality running from LNCM to LNPIP when one lag and four lags were applied at the 1% and 10% levels of significance. Unidirectional causality running from LNPM to LNPIP when one lag and four lags were applied at the 1% and 10% level of significance was revealed. The results in Table E10 indicate the existence of a unidirectional causality running from LNCX to LNPIP when one lag and two lags were applied at the 1% and 10% levels of significance. Unidirectional causality running from LNPX to LNPIP when one lag was applied at the 1% level of significance was revealed. In Table E11, when one lag, two lags, three lags, and four lags were applied, we found unidirectional causality running from LNCM to LNSIP at the 5% and 10% levels of significance, respectively. When one lag and three lags were applied, we found unidirectional causality running from LNPM to LNSIP at the 10% level of significance. In Table E12, when one lag, two lags, and three lags were applied, we found unidirectional causality running from LNCX to LNSIP at the 5% and 10% levels of significance, respectively. Unidirectional causality running from LNPX to LNSIP when three lags, six lags, seven lags, and eight lags were applied at the 10% and 5% levels of significance was revealed. The results in Table E13 indicate the existence of a bidirectional causality running from LNCM to LNTIP when nine lags were applied at the 10% level of significance. The results in Table E14 indicate the existence of a unidirectional causality running from LNPX to LNTIP when one lag was applied at the 10% level of significance.

4.3.6 Impulse response function

Finally, to scrutinize the behavior of each variable once confronted with an increase in a single specific variable, as well as the duration of its effect, the IRFs are exhibited. The IRF curves simulated by analytic method are reported in Figs. F1−F10. How a one-time positive shock of 1 standard deviation (SD) (±2 SE (standard error) innovations) to the conventional trade and processing trade endures on the economic growth of China is shown. We consider the response of seven variables to 1 SD innovation of conventional trade and processing trade.

In Figs. F1, F3, F5, F7, F11, and F13, following an imports by conventional trade shock (an innovation in LNCM), the employment variables (LNTE, LNUE, LNRE, LNEAP, LNSIP, and LNTIP) increase fast (positive change rate). Following an imports by processing trade shock (an innovation in LNPM), the employment variables (LNTE, LNUE, LNRE, LNEAP, LNSIP, and LNTIP) increase immediately (positive change rate). Therefore, we should conclude that the effects of the trade policy shocks are transmitted through the mutual effects of the conventional trade channel and processing trade channel based on the results in this case.

Figs. F2, F4, F6, F8, and F12 illustrate that the response of the LNTE, LNUE, LNRE, LNEAP, and LNSIP to a 1 SD shock on LNCX and LNPX are positive and powerful, with a persistent effect. However, the influence of LNCX is lower than that of LNPX.

This suggests the existence of the vertical specialization channel and conventional trade channel in China's trade policy transmission process. Furthermore, we can conclude that the effects of trade policy shock on increasing productive employment through vertical specialization and conventional trade channels are different. The results support the argument that the trade policy does have an impact on the increasing productive employment in the long-term.

4.3.7 Variance decomposition

The forecast error variance decomposition follows. It aims to capture the intensity of the response of a variable in the face of shocks suffered on the other variables. Tables G1−G10 reveal the percentages of the forecast error variance in all variables generated by a shock on each of the other variables.

In Tables G1−10, the first columns are the periods that are set to a maximum of 15. The data in the SE column are the forecasting variances of various periods, which are caused by the change of the present or future value.

In Tables G1, G3, G5, G7, G9, G11, and G13, the employment variables (LNTE, LNUE, LNRE, LNEAP, LNPIP, LNSIP, and LNTIP), LNCM, and LNPM are the contributions of the innovations to forecasting variance, respectively, which sum to 100. It can be seen that the impact of a shock to LNPM on the employment variables (LNTE, LNUE, LNRE, LNEAP, LNPIP, LNSIP, and LNTIP) is relatively low when compared with the impact of a shock to LNCM on the employment variables (LNTE, LNUE, LNRE, LNEAP, LNPIP, LNSIP, and LNTIP). For example, in Table G1, at the end of the forecast period, LNCM explains approximately 22% of the forecast error variance. This is approximately 13% higher than in the LNPM case.

In Tables G2, G4, G6, G8, and G12, the employment variables (LNTE, LNUE, LNRE, LNEAP, and LNSIP) are largely influenced by the exports by processing trade (LNPX). For example, in Table G2, at the end of the forecast period, LNPX explains approximately 77% of the forecast error variance. This is approximately 62% higher than in the LNCX case.

4.4 Concluding remarks and policy implications

By disaggregating the total imports and exports into imports and exports by conventional trade and imports and exports by processing trade, we estimate the different effects of two types of imports on the total employed persons (TE), number of employed persons at year-end in urban areas (UE), number of employed persons at year-end in rural areas (RE), economically active population (EAP), number of employed persons at year-end by primary industry (PIP), number of employed persons at year-end by secondary industry (SIP), and number of employed persons at year-end by tertiary industry (TIP), and we seek more evidence for the higher impact of vertical specialization on increasing employment based on ordinary trade.

To encourage enterprises to increase employment, the government needs to formulate appropriate policy. This chapter compares two types of trade in a vertical specialization and global production network, in which Chinese enterprises conduct processing trade. By means of the vertical specialization theory, we investigate and compare the employment effects of trade in China under the two trade patterns, that is, conventional trade and processing trade. Finally, we compare the employment effects of two trade patterns to explore the better trade-promoting policy. The results show that under conventional trade patterns, the total employed persons, number of employed persons at year-end in urban areas, number of employed persons at year-end in rural areas, economically active population, number of employed persons at year-end by primary industry, number of employed persons at year-end by secondary industry, and number of employed persons at year-end by tertiary industry are all lower than those of processing trade. Therefore, the government should use a vertically specialized trade strategy to encourage employment in urban and rural areas for more inclusive growth in China.

This study shows that China's total employed persons, especially number of employed persons in rural areas, is caused by imports and exports by conventional trade in the short-term and long-term. Imports and exports by processing trade cause an increase in China's employment. In other words, while imports and exports by processing trade were becoming an increasingly importance source for total employed persons, especially the number of employed persons in rural areas in China, the relative importance of the rest of imports and exports by conventional trade as a source of employment in China was declining, in part because many foreign firms were shifting their export-oriented manufacturing facilities to China based on vertical specialization. This could signal that some of the resources freed-up in the economy are being allocated for the imports and exports by processing trade, and these are stimulating the increase of employment during the transition to inclusive growth in China. In view of this, two types of measures could be recommended to labor market policymakers. They should encourage greater incorporation into vertical specialization to enhance its effect on the labor market. However, the policymakers should promote policies that increase processed imported intermediates without hampering imports of final goods. Thus, measures to promote imports of parts and components are welcome and crucial to accommodate the foreign investment made in developing countries.

The prominence of imports and exports by processing trade in the endogenous adjustment process of the economically active population including number of employed persons by primary industry, secondary industry, and tertiary industry is another major finding of this study. Imports and exports by processing trade are central to putting the labor market on course to meet the targets of inclusive growth. Thus, it is recommended that policymakers should begin making efforts to stimulate greater integration into global vertical specialization by improving practices of production fragmentation. These measures are essential to accommodate labor demand for employed persons by primary industry, secondary industry, and tertiary industry in the inclusive growth as a whole.

Appendix A   Variables grouping

Table A1 **Variables grouping**

Group number	Variables	Sample range
1	LNTE, LNPM, LNCM	1981−2012
2	LNTE, LNPX, LNCX	1981−2012
3	LNUE, LNPM, LNCM	1981−2012
4	LNUE, LNPX, LNCX	1981−2012
5	LNRE, LNPM, LNCM	1981−2012
6	LNRE, LNPX, LNCX	1981−2012
7	LNEAP, LNPM, LNCM	1981−2012
8	LNEAP, LNPX, LNCX	1981−2012
9	LNPIP, LNPM, LNCM	1981−2012
10	LNPIP, LNPX, LNCX	1981−2012
11	LNSIP, LNPM, LNCM	1981−2012
12	LNSIP, LNPX, LNCX	1981−2012
13	LNTIP, LNPM, LNCM	1981−2012
14	LNTIP, LNPX, LNCX	1981−2012

Note: PM is imports by processing trade, CM is imports by conventional trade, PX is exports by processing trade, CX is exports by conventional trade, TE stands for total employed persons (10,000 persons), UE stands for number of employed persons at year-end in urban rural areas, RE stands for number of employed persons at year-end in rural areas, EAP stands for economically active population (10,000 persons), PIP stands for number of employed persons at year-end by primary industry, SIP stands for number of employed persons at year-end by secondary industry, TIP stands for number of employed persons at year-end by tertiary industry.

Appendix B   The results of unit root tests

Table B1 Augmented Dickey Fuller test on unit roots for all variables

S\No.	Variables	Test type (C,T,P)	ADF test statistic	Order of integration
1	LNPM	(C,T,0)	−1.261698	I(1)
2	D(LNPM)	(C,T,0)	−4.351388*	I(0)
3	LNCM	(C,T,0)	−1.265244	I(1)
4	D(LNCM)	(C,T,0)	−4.968410*	I(0)
5	LNPX	(C,T,0)	−1.034865	I(1)
6	D(LNPX)	(C,T,0)	−4.158776**	I(0)
7	LNCX	(C,T,0)	−1.780058	I(1)
8	D(LNCX)	(C,T,0)	−6.235275*	I(0)
9	LNTE	(C,T,0)	−1.170025	I(1)
10	D(LNTE)	(C,T,0)	−5.877516*	I(0)
11	LNUE	(C,T,0)	−3.246828***	I(1)
12	D(LNUE)	(C,T,0)	−6.575841*	I(0)
13	LNRE	(C,T,0)	−0.555368	I(1)
14	D(LNRE)	(C,T,0)	−5.626039*	I(0)
15	LNEAP	(C,T,0)	−1.147836	I(1)
16	D(LNEAP)	(C,T,0)	−5.831589*	I(0)
17	LNPIP	(C,T,0)	−0.251425	I(1)
18	D(LNPIP)	(C,T,0)	−3.880519**	I(0)
19	LNSIP	(C,T,0)	−2.111070	I(1)
20	D(LNSIP)	(C,T,0)	−4.470785*	I(0)
21	LNTIP	(C,T,0)	−0.787652	I(1)
22	D(LNTIP)	(C,T,0)	−6.310533*	I(0)

Note: C, T, and P in test type stand for constant, trend, and lag orders, respectively. At three remarkable levels, when ADF value is greater than critical value, corresponding series has unit root. D stands for the first differential of the variables.
***, **, and *denote the rejection of the null hypothesis of unit root at the 10%, 5%, and 1% significance levels, respectively.

Appendix C   Results of cointegration tests

Table C1 Cointegration test result (series: LNTE, LNCM, and LNPM)

Sample (adjusted): 1985–2012
Included observations: 28 after adjustments
Trend assumption: No deterministic trend
Lags interval (in first differences): 2–3

Unrestricted cointegration rank test (trace)

Hypothesized number of CE(s)	Eigenvalue	Trace statistic	0.05 Critical value	Probability[a]
None[b]	0.534472	32.78792	24.27596	0.0034
At most 1	0.329085	11.37963	12.32090	0.0715
At most 2	0.007276	0.204463	4.129906	0.7071

Trace test indicates 1 cointegrating equation at the 0.05 level

Unrestricted cointegration rank test (maximum eigenvalue)

Hypothesized number of CE(s)	Eigenvalue	Max-eigen statistic	0.05 Critical value	Probability[a]
None[b]	0.534472	21.40830	17.79730	0.0137
At most 1	0.329085	11.17516	11.22480	0.0510
At most 2	0.007276	0.204463	4.129906	0.7071

Max-eigenvalue test indicates 1 cointegrating equation at the 0.05 level

1 Cointegrating equation		Log likelihood	109.0063

Normalized cointegrating coefficients (standard error in parentheses)

LNTE	LNCM	LNPM
1.000000	0.292264	−2.597418
	(1.23366)	(1.17312)

[a]MacKinnon−Haug−Michelis (1999) *P* values.
[b]Rejection of the hypothesis at the 0.05 level.

Table C2 Cointegration test result (series: LNTE, LNCX, and LNPX)

Sample (adjusted): 1984–2012
Included observations: 29 after adjustments
Trend assumption: No deterministic trend
Lags interval (in first differences): 1–2

Unrestricted cointegration rank test (trace)

Hypothesized number of CE(s)	Eigenvalue	Trace statistic	0.05 Critical value	Probability[a]
None[b]	0.418993	24.51613	24.27596	0.0466
At most 1	0.259037	8.769346	12.32090	0.1830
At most 2	0.002583	0.075011	4.129906	0.8222

Trace test indicates 1 cointegrating equation at the 0.05 level

Unrestricted cointegration rank test (maximum eigenvalue)

Hypothesized number of CE(s)	Eigenvalue	Max-eigen statistic	0.05 Critical value	Probability[a]
None	0.418993	15.74679	17.79730	0.0991
At most 1	0.259037	8.694335	11.22480	0.1348
At most 2	0.002583	0.075011	4.129906	0.8222

Max-eigenvalue test indicates no cointegration at the 0.05 level

1 Cointegrating equation		Log likelihood	125.0845

Normalized cointegrating coefficients (standard error in parentheses)

LNTE	LNCX	LNPX
1.000000	1.107964	−3.356340
	(1.56982)	(1.50868)

[a]MacKinnon–Haug–Michelis (1999) P values.
[b]Rejection of the hypothesis at the 0.05 level.

Table C3 Cointegration test result (series: LNUE, LNCM, and LNPM)

Sample (adjusted): 1985–2012
Included observations: 28 after adjustments
Trend assumption: No deterministic trend
Lags interval (in first differences): 2–3

Unrestricted cointegration rank test (trace)

Hypothesized number of CE(s)	Eigenvalue	Trace statistic	0.05 Critical value	Probability[a]
None[b]	0.547296	30.42303	24.27596	0.0074
At most 1	0.254562	8.232575	12.32090	0.2192
At most 2	0.000237	0.006624	4.129906	0.9467

Trace test indicates 1 cointegrating equation at the 0.05 level

Unrestricted cointegration rank test (maximum eigenvalue)

Hypothesized number of CE(s)	Eigenvalue	Max-eigen statistic	0.05 Critical value	Probability[a]
None[b]	0.547296	22.19046	17.79730	0.0102
At most 1	0.254562	8.225951	11.22480	0.1605
At most 2	0.000237	0.006624	4.129906	0.9467

Max-eigenvalue test indicates 1 cointegrating equation at the 0.05 level

1 Cointegrating equation		**Log likelihood**	**107.9932**

Normalized cointegrating coefficients (standard error in parentheses)

LNUE	LNCM	LNPM
1.000000	0.205225	−1.856411
	(0.58782)	(0.54710)

[a]MacKinnon–Haug–Michelis (1999) P values.
[b]Rejection of the hypothesis at the 0.05 level.

Table C4 Cointegration test result (series: LNUE, LNCX, and LNPX)

Sample (adjusted): 1984−2012
Included observations: 29 after adjustments
Trend assumption: No deterministic trend
Lags interval (in first differences): 1−2

Unrestricted cointegration rank test (trace)

Hypothesized number of CE(s)	Eigenvalue	Trace statistic	0.05 Critical value	Probability[a]
None[b]	0.484849	29.23644	24.27596	0.0109
At most 1	0.288596	10.00088	12.32090	0.1187
At most 2	0.004333	0.125942	4.129906	0.7699

Trace test indicates 1 cointegrating equation at the 0.05 level

Unrestricted cointegration rank test (maximum eigenvalue)

Hypothesized number of CE(s)	Eigenvalue	Max-eigen statistic	0.05 Critical value	Probability[a]
None[b]	0.484849	19.23556	17.79730	0.0302
At most 1	0.288596	9.874935	11.22480	0.0856
At most 2	0.004333	0.125942	4.129906	0.7699

Max-eigenvalue test indicates 1 cointegrating equation at the 0.05 level

1 Cointegrating equation	Log likelihood	122.4055

Normalized cointegrating coefficients (standard error in parentheses)

LNUE	LNCX	LNPX
1.000000	0.151620 (1.83073)	−3.331855 (1.78011)

[a]MacKinnon−Haug−Michelis (1999) P values.
[b]Rejection of the hypothesis at the 0.05 level.

Table C5 Cointegration test result (series: LNRE, LNCM, and LNPM)

Sample (adjusted): 1985−2012
Included observations: 28 after adjustments
Trend assumption: No deterministic trend
Lags interval (in first differences): 2−3

Unrestricted cointegration rank test (trace)

Hypothesized number of CE(s)	Eigenvalue	Trace statistic	0.05 Critical value	Probability[a]
None[b]	0.475209	30.15381	24.27596	0.0081
At most 1	0.348843	12.10068	12.32090	0.0544
At most 2	0.003158	0.088568	4.129906	0.8068

Trace test indicates 1 cointegrating equation at the 0.05 level

Unrestricted cointegration rank test (maximum eigenvalue)

Hypothesized number of CE(s)	Eigenvalue	Max-eigen statistic	0.05 Critical value	Probability[a]
None[b]	0.475209	18.05313	17.79730	0.0457
At most 1[b]	0.348843	12.01211	11.22480	0.0363
At most 2	0.003158	0.088568	4.129906	0.8068

Max-eigenvalue test indicates 2 cointegrating equations at the 0.05 level

1 Cointegrating equation		**Log likelihood**	**109.3446**

Normalized cointegrating coefficients (standard error in parentheses)

LNRE	LNCM	LNPM
1.000000	0.599911	−4.031328
	(2.71415)	(2.64948)

[a]MacKinnon−Haug−Michelis (1999) *P* values.
[b]Rejection of the hypothesis at the 0.05 level.

Table C6 Cointegration test result (series: LNRE, LNCX, and LNPX)

Sample (adjusted): 1984–2012
Included observations: 29 after adjustments
Trend assumption: No deterministic trend
Lags interval (in first differences): 1–2

Unrestricted cointegration rank test (trace)

Hypothesized number of CE(s)	Eigenvalue	Trace statistic	0.05 Critical value	Probability[a]
None[b]	0.409723	25.36086	24.27596	0.0364
At most 1	0.268759	10.07312	12.32090	0.1157
At most 2	0.033754	0.995758	4.129906	0.3693

Trace test indicates 1 cointegrating equation at the 0.05 level

Unrestricted cointegration rank test (maximum eigenvalue)

Hypothesized number of CE(s)	Eigenvalue	Max-eigen statistic	0.05 Critical value	Probability[a]
None	0.409723	15.28774	17.79730	0.1147
At most 1	0.268759	9.077366	11.22480	0.1165
At most 2	0.033754	0.995758	4.129906	0.3693

Max-eigenvalue test indicates no cointegration at the 0.05 level

1 Cointegrating equation		Log likelihood	124.3908
Normalized cointegrating coefficients (standard error in parentheses)			

LNRE	LNCX	LNPX
1.000000	0.611893	−2.816825
	(1.46246)	(1.39894)

[a]MacKinnon–Haug–Michelis (1999) P values.
[b]Rejection of the hypothesis at the 0.05 level.

Table C7 Cointegration test result (series: LNEAP, LNCM, and LNPM)

Sample (adjusted): 1985−2012
Included observations: 28 after adjustments
Trend assumption: No deterministic trend
Lags interval (in first differences): 2−3

Unrestricted cointegration rank test (trace)

Hypothesized number of CE(s)	Eigenvalue	Trace statistic	0.05 Critical value	Probability[a]
None[b]	0.546445	33.18769	24.27596	0.0029
At most 1	0.320025	11.04978	12.32090	0.0809
At most 2	0.008896	0.250215	4.129906	0.6761

Trace test indicates 1 cointegrating equation at the 0.05 level

Unrestricted cointegration rank test (maximum eigenvalue)

Hypothesized number of CE(s)	Eigenvalue	Max-eigen statistic	0.05 Critical value	Probability[a]
None[b]	0.546445	22.13791	17.79730	0.0104
At most 1	0.320025	10.79956	11.22480	0.0593
At most 2	0.008896	0.250215	4.129906	0.6761

Max-eigenvalue test indicates 1 cointegrating equation at the 0.05 level

1 Cointegrating equation		Log likelihood	109.1766

Normalized cointegrating coefficients (standard error in parentheses)

LNEAP	LNCM	LNPM
1.000000	0.249089	−2.544901
	(1.18131)	(1.12110)

[a]MacKinnon−Haug−Michelis (1999) *P* values.
[b]Rejection of the hypothesis at the 0.05 level.

Table C8 Cointegration test result (series: LNEAP, LNCX, and LNPX)

Sample (adjusted): 1984–2012
Included observations: 29 after adjustments
Trend assumption: No deterministic trend
Lags interval (in first differences): 1–2

Unrestricted cointegration rank test (trace)

Hypothesized number of CE(s)	Eigenvalue	Trace statistic	0.05 Critical value	Probability[a]
None[b]	0.441966	25.80765	24.27596	0.0318
At most 1	0.260237	8.890922	12.32090	0.1755
At most 2	0.005144	0.149567	4.129906	0.7494

Trace test indicates 1 cointegrating equation at the 0.05 level

Unrestricted cointegration rank test (maximum eigenvalue)

Hypothesized number of CE(s)	Eigenvalue	Max-eigen statistic	0.05 Critical value	Probability[a]
None	0.441966	16.91672	17.79730	0.0674
At most 1	0.260237	8.741355	11.22480	0.1324
At most 2	0.005144	0.149567	4.129906	0.7494

Max-eigenvalue test indicates no cointegration at the 0.05 level

1 Cointegrating equation		Log likelihood	125.3340

Normalized cointegrating coefficients (standard error in parentheses)

LNEAP	LNCX	LNPX
1.000000	0.957982	−3.257376
	(1.51673)	(1.45974)

[a]MacKinnon–Haug–Michelis (1999) P values.
[b]Rejection of the hypothesis at the 0.05 level.

Table C9 Cointegration test result (series: LNPIP, LNCM, and LNPM)

Sample (adjusted): 1985−2012
Included observations: 28 after adjustments
Trend assumption: No deterministic trend
Lags interval (in first differences): 2−3

Unrestricted cointegration rank test (trace)

Hypothesized number of CE(s)	Eigenvalue	Trace statistic	0.05 Critical value	Probability[a]
None[b]	0.543293	36.78672	24.27596	0.0008
At most 1[b]	0.402202	14.84275	12.32090	0.0185
At most 2	0.015475	0.436699	4.129906	0.5722

Trace test indicates 2 cointegrating equations at the 0.05 level

Unrestricted cointegration rank test (maximum eigenvalue)

Hypothesized number of CE(s)	Eigenvalue	Max-eigen statistic	0.05 Critical value	Probability[a]
None[b]	0.543293	21.94397	17.79730	0.0112
At most 1[b]	0.402202	14.40605	11.22480	0.0134
At most 2	0.015475	0.436699	4.129906	0.5722

Max-eigenvalue test indicates 2 cointegrating equations at the 0.05 level

1 Cointegrating equation		Log likelihood	100.6546

Normalized cointegrating coefficients (standard error in parentheses)

LNPIP	LNCM	LNPM
1.000000	0.173471	−2.321904
	(1.02761)	(1.00064)

[a]MacKinnon−Haug−Michelis (1999) P values.
[b]Rejection of the hypothesis at the 0.05 level.

Table C10 Cointegration test result (series: LNPIP, LNCX, and LNPX)

Sample (adjusted): 1986–2012
Included observations: 27 after adjustments
Trend assumption: No deterministic trend
Lags interval (in first differences): 3–4

Unrestricted cointegration rank test (trace)

Hypothesized number of CE(s)	Eigenvalue	Trace statistic	0.05 Critical value	Probability[a]
None[b]	0.836875	61.32766	24.27596	0.0000
At most 1[b]	0.335892	12.37026	12.32090	0.0490
At most 2	0.047673	1.318864	4.129906	0.2932

Trace test indicates 2 cointegrating equations at the 0.05 level

Unrestricted cointegration rank test (maximum eigenvalue)

Hypothesized number of CE(s)	Eigenvalue	Max-eigen statistic	0.05 Critical value	Probability[a]
None[b]	0.836875	48.95740	17.79730	0.0000
At most 1	0.335892	11.05140	11.22480	0.0536
At most 2	0.047673	1.318864	4.129906	0.2932

Max-eigenvalue test indicates 1 cointegrating equation at the 0.05 level

1 Cointegrating equation	Log likelihood	119.3809

Normalized cointegrating coefficients (standard error in parentheses)

LNPIP	LNCX	LNPX
1.000000	1.909295 (0.38631)	−3.053029 (0.37471)

[a]MacKinnon–Haug–Michelis (1999) P values.
[b]Rejection of the hypothesis at the 0.05 level.

Table C11 Cointegration test result (series: LNSIP, LNCM, and LNPM)

Sample (adjusted): 1985−2012
Included observations: 28 after adjustments
Trend assumption: No deterministic trend
Lags interval (in first differences): 2−3

Unrestricted cointegration rank test (trace)

Hypothesized number of CE(s)	Eigenvalue	Trace statistic	0.05 critical value	Probability[a]
None[b]	0.597165	48.46340	24.27596	0.0000
At most 1[b]	0.460587	23.00500	12.32090	0.0006
At most 2[b]	0.184810	5.721355	4.129906	0.0199

Trace test indicates 3 cointegrating equations at the 0.05 level

Unrestricted cointegration rank test (maximum eigenvalue)

Hypothesized number of CE(s)	Eigenvalue	Max-eigen statistic	0.05 Critical value	Probability[a]
None[b]	0.597165	25.45840	17.79730	0.0029
At most 1[b]	0.460587	17.28365	11.22480	0.0039
At most 2[b]	0.184810	5.721355	4.129906	0.0199

Max-eigenvalue test indicates 3 cointegrating equations at the 0.05 level

1 Cointegrating equation		Log likelihood	99.58070

Normalized cointegrating coefficients (standard error in parentheses)

LNSIP	LNCM	LNPM
1.000000	0.113645	−1.492470
	(0.48139)	(0.45346)

[a]MacKinnon−Haug−Michelis (1999) P values.
[b]Rejection of the hypothesis at the 0.05 level.

Table C12 Cointegration test result (series: LNSIP, LNCX, and LNPX)

Included observations: 30 after adjustments Trend assumption: No deterministic trend Lags interval (in first differences): 1−1				
Unrestricted cointegration rank test (trace)				
Hypothesized number of CE(s)	**Eigenvalue**	**Trace statistic**	**0.05 Critical value**	**Probability**[a]
None[b] At most 1[b] At most 2[b]	0.392913 0.305961 0.138899	30.41562 15.44311 4.486316	24.27596 12.32090 4.129906	0.0075 0.0145 0.0406
Trace test indicates 3 cointegrating equations at the 0.05 level				
Unrestricted cointegration rank test (maximum eigenvalue)				
Hypothesized number of CE(s)	**Eigenvalue**	**Max-eigen statistic**	**0.05 Critical value**	**Probability**[a]
None At most 1 At most 2[b]	0.392913 0.305961 0.138899	14.97251 10.95680 4.486316	17.79730 11.22480 4.129906	0.1266 0.0557 0.0406
Max-eigenvalue test indicates no cointegration at the 0.05 level				
1 Cointegrating equation		**Log likelihood**		**111.1587**
Normalized cointegrating coefficients (standard error in parentheses)				
LNSIP 1.000000	LNCX 2.386625 (1.47696)	LNPX −4.028120 (1.39236)		

[a]MacKinnon−Haug−Michelis (1999) P values.
[b]Rejection of the hypothesis at the 0.05 level.

Table C13 Cointegration test result (series: LNTIP, LNCM, and LNPM)

Sample (adjusted): 1986–2012
Included observations: 27 after adjustments
Trend assumption: No deterministic trend
Lags interval (in first differences): 3–4

Unrestricted cointegration rank test (trace)

Hypothesized number of CE(s)	Eigenvalue	Trace statistic	0.05 Critical value	Probability[a]
None[b]	0.668313	44.18814	24.27596	0.0001
At most 1[b]	0.391939	14.39190	12.32090	0.0222
At most 2	0.034928	0.959921	4.129906	0.3792

Trace test indicates 2 cointegrating equations at the 0.05 level

Unrestricted cointegration rank test (maximum eigenvalue)

Hypothesized number of CE(s)	Eigenvalue	Max-eigen statistic	0.05 Critical value	Probability[a]
None[b]	0.668313	29.79624	17.79730	0.0005
At most 1[b]	0.391939	13.43198	11.22480	0.0202
At most 2	0.034928	0.959921	4.129906	0.3792

Max-eigenvalue test indicates 2 cointegrating equations at the 0.05 level

1 Cointegrating equation		**Log likelihood**	**105.7981**

Normalized cointegrating coefficients (standard error in parentheses)

LNTIP	LNCM	LNPM
1.000000	1.781351	−3.139817
	(0.49849)	(0.48304)

[a]MacKinnon–Haug–Michelis (1999) P values.
[b]Rejection of the hypothesis at the 0.05 level.

Table C14 Cointegration test result (series: LNTIP, LNCX, and LNPX)

Sample (adjusted): 1984−2012
Included observations: 29 after adjustments
Trend assumption: No deterministic trend
Lags interval (in first differences): 1−2

Unrestricted cointegration rank test (trace)

Hypothesized number of CE(s)	Eigenvalue	Trace statistic	0.05 Critical value	Probability[a]
None[b]	0.458483	31.35434	24.27596	0.0055
At most 1[b]	0.373215	13.56628	12.32090	0.0308
At most 2	0.000652	0.018901	4.129906	0.9105

Trace test indicates 2 cointegrating equations at the 0.05 level

Unrestricted cointegration rank test (maximum eigenvalue)

Hypothesized number of CE(s)	Eigenvalue	Max-eigen statistic	0.05 Critical value	Probability[a]
None	0.458483	17.78806	17.79730	0.0502
At most 1[b]	0.373215	13.54738	11.22480	0.0192
At most 2	0.000652	0.018901	4.129906	0.9105

Max-eigenvalue test indicates no cointegration at the 0.05 level

1 Cointegrating equation		Log likelihood	113.0284

Normalized cointegrating coefficients (standard error in parentheses)

LNTIP	LNCX	LNPX
1.000000	0.536178	−1.755503
	(0.45904)	(0.43013)

[a]MacKinnon−Haug−Michelis (1999) *P* values.
[b]Rejection of the hypothesis at the 0.05 level.

Appendix D   Results of vector error correction model

Table D1 Vector error correction estimates (series: LNTE, LNCM, and LNPM)

Sample (adjusted): 1985–2012 Included observations: 28 after adjustments Standard errors in parentheses ( ) and t-statistics in brackets [ ]			
Cointegrating equation	**CointEq1**		
LNTE(−1) LNCM(−1) LNPM(−1)	1.000000 0.292264 (1.23366) [0.23691] −2.597418 (1.17312) [−2.21411]		
Error correction	**D(LNTE)**	**D(LNCM)**	**D(LNPM)**
CointEq1 R-squared Adj. R-squared	0.001212 (0.00136) [0.89310] 0.383231 0.207011	−0.027078 (0.00994) [−2.72476] 0.244012 0.028015	0.010719 (0.00629) [1.70310] 0.386365 0.211040

Table D2 Vector error correction estimates (series: LNTE, LNCX, and LNPX)

Included observations: 29 after adjustments Standard errors in parentheses ( ) and t-statistics in brackets [ ]			
Cointegrating equation	**CointEq1**		
LNTE(−1) LNCX(−1) LNPX(−1)	1.000000 1.107964 (1.56982) [0.70579] −3.356340 (1.50868) [−2.22469]		
Error correction	**D(LNTE)**	**D(LNCX)**	**D(LNPX)**
CointEq1 R-squared Adj. R-squared	−0.001321 (0.00124) [−1.06444] 0.506091 0.371388	−0.024470 (0.00834) [−2.93469] 0.067410 −0.186933	−0.004962 (0.00726) [−0.68317] 0.277574 0.080549

Table D3 Vector error correction estimates (series: LNUE, LNCM, and LNPM)

Sample (adjusted): 1985–2012 Included observations: 28 after adjustments Standard errors in parentheses ( ) and t-statistics in brackets [ ]			
Cointegrating equation	**CointEq1**		
LNUE(−1) LNCM(−1) LNPM(−1)	1.000000 0.205225 (0.58782) [0.34913] −1.856411 (0.54710) [−3.39317]		
Error correction	**D(LNUE)**	**D(LNCM)**	**D(LNPM)**
CointEq1 R-squared Adj. R-squared	−0.002437 (0.00301) [−0.81063] 0.144606 −0.099793	−0.011943 (0.01889) [−0.63237] 0.328474 0.136609	0.043674 (0.01143) [3.82153] 0.502443 0.360284

Table D4 Vector error correction estimates (series: LNUE, LNCX, and LNPX)

Sample (adjusted): 1984–2012 Included observations: 29 after adjustments Standard errors in parentheses ( ) and t-statistics in brackets [ ]			
Cointegrating equation	**CointEq1**		
LNUE(−1) LNCX(−1) LNPX(−1)	1.000000 0.151620 (1.83073) [0.08282] −3.331855 (1.78011) [−1.87171]		
Error correction	**D(LNUE)**	**D(LNCX)**	**D(LNPX)**
CointEq1 R-squared Adj. R-squared	−0.003870 (0.00100) [−3.86221] 0.331844 0.149620	−0.013560 (0.00597) [−2.27265] 0.152463 −0.078683	−0.003776 (0.00523) [−0.72200] 0.335517 0.154294

Table D5 Vector error correction estimates (series: LNRE, LNCM, and LNPM)

Sample (adjusted): 1985–2012 Included observations: 28 after adjustments Standard errors in parentheses ( ) and t-statistics in brackets [ ]			
Cointegrating equation	**CointEq1**		
LNRE(−1) LNCM(−1) LNPM(−1)	1.000000 0.599911 (2.71415) [0.22103] −4.031328 (2.64948) [−1.52155]		
Error correction	**D(LNRE)**	**D(LNCM)**	**D(LNPM)**
CointEq1 R-squared Adj. R-squared	0.001751 (0.00068) [2.56867] 0.546819 0.417339	−0.016803 (0.00480) [−3.49764] 0.296217 0.095136	−4.30E-05 (0.00326) [−0.01319] 0.343269 0.155632

Table D6 Vector error correction estimates (series: LNRE, LNCX, and LNPX)

Sample (adjusted): 1984–2012 Included observations: 29 after adjustments Standard errors in parentheses ( ) and t-statistics in brackets [ ]			
Cointegrating equation	**CointEq1**		
LNRE(−1) LNCX(−1) LNPX(−1)	1.000000 0.611893 (1.46246) [0.41840] −2.816825 (1.39894) [−2.01354]		
Error correction	**D(LNRE)**	**D(LNCX)**	**D(LNPX)**
CointEq1 R-squared Adj. R-squared	0.001906 (0.00143) [1.33021] 0.607704 0.500714	−0.025613 (0.00903) [−2.83502] 0.093180 −0.154135	−0.005270 (0.00791) [−0.66619] 0.290335 0.096790

Table D7 Vector error correction estimates (series: LNEAP, LNCM, and LNPM)

Sample (adjusted): 1985−2012 Included observations: 28 after adjustments Standard errors in parentheses ( ) and t-statistics in brackets [ ]			
Cointegrating equation	**CointEq1**		
LNEAP(−1) LNCM(−1) LNPM(−1)	1.000000 0.249089 (1.18131) [0.21086] −2.544901 (1.12110) [−2.27000]		
Error correction	**D(LNEAP)**	**D(LNCM)**	**D(LNPM)**
CointEq1 R-squared Adj. R-squared	0.001044 (0.00138) [0.75399] 0.392526 0.218961	−0.026813 (0.01015) [−2.64116] 0.236166 0.017927	0.011676 (0.00639) [1.82786] 0.388031 0.213183

Table D8 Vector error correction estimates (series: LNEAP, LNCX, and LNPX)

Sample (adjusted): 1984−2012 Included observations: 29 after adjustments Standard errors in parentheses ( ) and t-statistics in brackets [ ]			
Cointegrating equation	**CointEq1**		
LNEAP(−1) LNCX(−1) LNPX(−1)	1.000000 0.957982 (1.51673) [0.63161] −3.257376 (1.45974) [−2.23147]		
Error correction	**D(LNEAP)**	**D(LNCX)**	**D(LNPX)**
CointEq1 R-squared Adj. R-squared	−0.001848 (0.00122) [−1.51747] 0.522635 0.392444	−0.024595 (0.00816) [−3.01303] 0.084832 −0.164759	−0.005541 (0.00715) [−0.77461] 0.282688 0.087058

Table D9 Vector error correction estimates (series: LNPIP, LNCM, and LNPM)

Vector Error Correction Estimates Sample (adjusted): 1985–2012 Included observations: 28 after adjustments Standard errors in parentheses ( ) and t-statistics in brackets [ ]			
Cointegrating equation	**CointEq1**		
LNPIP(−1)	1.000000		
LNCM(−1)	0.173471 (1.02761) [0.16881]		
LNPM(−1)	−2.321904 (1.00064) [−2.32043]		
Error correction	**D(LNPIP)**	**D(LNCM)**	**D(LNPM)**
CointEq1	0.005173 (0.00195) [2.65946]	−0.034788 (0.01104) [−3.15205]	0.005221 (0.00717) [0.72776]
R-squared	0.458899	0.252746	0.361018
Adj. R-squared	0.304299	0.039244	0.178451

Table D10 Vector error correction estimates (series: LNPIP, LNCX, and LNPX)

Sample (adjusted): 1986–2012 Included observations: 27 after adjustments Standard errors in parentheses ( ) and t-statistics in brackets [ ]			
Cointegrating equation	**CointEq1**		
LNPIP(−1)	1.000000		
LNCX(−1)	1.909295 (0.38631) [4.94236]		
LNPX(−1)	−3.053029 (0.37471) [−8.14762]		
Error correction	**D(LNPIP)**	**D(LNCX)**	**D(LNPX)**
CointEq1	−0.000590 (0.00402) [−0.14685]	0.001620 (0.01642) [0.09865]	0.055628 (0.01151) [4.83343]
R-squared	0.360947	0.163093	0.559469
Adj. R-squared	0.169231	−0.087979	0.427310

Table D11 Vector error correction estimates (series: LNSIP, LNCM, and LNPM)

Sample (adjusted): 1985−2012
Included observations: 28 after adjustments
Standard errors in parentheses ( ) and t-statistics in brackets [ ]

Cointegrating equation	CointEq1
LNSIP(−1)	1.000000
LNCM(−1)	0.113645
	(0.48139)
	[0.23608]
LNPM(−1)	−1.492470
	(0.45346)
	[−3.29129]

Error correction	D(LNSIP)	D(LNCM)	D(LNPM)
CointEq1	−0.001256	−0.020447	0.053741
	(0.00430)	(0.02943)	(0.01506)
	[−0.29194]	[−0.69475]	[3.56928]
R-squared	0.339825	−0.072789	0.431817
Adj. R-squared	0.151203	−0.379300	0.269479

Table D12 Vector error correction estimates (series: LNSIP, LNCX, and LNPX)

Sample (adjusted): 1983−2012
Included observations: 30 after adjustments
Standard errors in parentheses ( ) and t-statistics in brackets [ ]

Cointegrating equation	CointEq1
LNSIP(−1)	1.000000
LNCX(−1)	2.386625
	(1.47696)
	[1.61590]
LNPX(−1)	−4.028120
	(1.39236)
	[−2.89303]

Error correction	D(LNSIP)	D(LNCX)	D(LNPX)
CointEq1	3.43E-05	−0.024199	−0.004715
	(0.00195)	(0.00789)	(0.00693)
	[0.01762]	[−3.06751]	[−0.68060]
R-squared	0.112618	0.013651	0.190053
Adj. R-squared	0.010227	−0.100158	0.096598

Table D13 Vector error correction estimates (series: LNTIP, LNCM, and LNPM)

Sample (adjusted): 1986–2012
Included observations: 27 after adjustments
Standard errors in parentheses ( ) and t-statistics in brackets [ ]

Cointegrating equation	CointEq1		
LNTIP(−1)	1.000000		
LNCM(−1)	1.781351		
	(0.49849)		
	[3.57348]		
LNPM(−1)	−3.139817		
	(0.48304)		
	[−6.50016]		
Error correction	**D(LNTIP)**	**D(LNCM)**	**D(LNPM)**
CointEq1	0.001915	−0.036431	0.038550
	(0.00353)	(0.01886)	(0.01270)
	[0.54243]	[−1.93213]	[3.03613]
R-squared	0.239390	0.308818	0.410867
Adj. R-squared	0.011207	0.101463	0.234128

Table D14 Vector error correction estimates (series: LNTIP, LNCX, and LNPX)

Sample (adjusted): 1984–2012
Included observations: 29 after adjustments
Standard errors in parentheses ( ) and t-statistics in brackets [ ]

Cointegrating equation	CointEq1		
LNTIP(−1)	1.000000		
LNCX(−1)	0.536178		
	(0.45904)		
	[1.16805]		
LNPX(−1)	−1.755503		
	(0.43013)		
	[−4.08133]		
Error correction	**D(LNTIP)**	**D(LNCX)**	**D(LNPX)**
CointEq1	0.009697	−0.028588	0.028263
	(0.00700)	(0.03266)	(0.02323)
	[1.38594]	[−0.87522]	[1.21647]
R-squared	0.259517	−0.222548	0.368665
Adj. R-squared	0.057567	−0.555970	0.196482

Appendix E   Results of Granger causality tests

Table E1 **Pairwise Granger causality tests (series: LNTE, LNCM, and LNPM)**

Sample: 1981−2012			
Null hypothesis	**Observations**	**F-statistic**	**Probability**
Lags: 7			
LNCM does not cause LNTE	25	1.43063	0.2931
LNTE does not cause LNCM		1.61416	0.2374
LNPM does not cause LNTE	25	0.32739	0.9241
LNTE does not cause LNPM		0.74877	0.6396
Lags: 8			
LNCM does not cause LNTE	24	1.06510	0.4734
LNTE does not cause LNCM		2.12751	0.1679
LNPM does not cause LNTE	24	0.83518	0.6006
LNTE does not cause LNPM		2.37615	0.1355
Lags: 9			
LNCM does not cause LNTE	23	84.4049	0.0003
LNTE does not cause LNCM		2.66259	0.1794
LNPM does not cause LNTE	23	9.99763	0.0203
LNTE does not cause LNPM		1.21597	0.4574

Table E2 **Pairwise Granger causality tests (series: LNTE, LNCX, and LNPX)**

Sample: 1981−2012			
Null hypothesis	**Observations**	**F-statistic**	**Probability**
Lags: 7			
LNCX does not cause LNTE	25	0.16813	0.9864
LNTE does not cause LNCX		0.55302	0.7777
LNPX does not cause LNTE	25	1.33462	0.3277
LNTE does not cause LNPX		0.77773	0.6200
Lags: 8			
LNCX does not cause LNTE	24	0.12404	0.9957
LNTE does not cause LNCX		0.44163	0.8626
LNPX does not cause LNTE	24	2.46176	0.1262
LNTE does not cause LNPX		1.92331	0.2020

(*Continued*)

Table E2 (Continued)

Sample: 1981–2012			
Null hypothesis	**Observations**	**F-statistic**	**Probability**
Lags: 9			
LNCX does not cause LNTE	23	23.6314	0.0040
LNTE does not cause LNCX		0.36281	0.9049
LNPX does not cause LNTE	23	8.73001	0.0259
LNTE does not cause LNPX		1.46202	0.3794

Table E3 Pairwise Granger causality tests (series: LNUE, LNCM, and LNPM)

Sample: 1981–2012			
Null hypothesis	**Observations**	**F-statistic**	**Probability**
Lags: 5			
LNCM does not cause LNUE	27	1.00059	0.4486
LNUE does not cause LNCM		3.00061	0.0425
LNPM does not cause LNUE	27	0.85274	0.5329
LNUE does not cause LNPM		1.54014	0.2330
Lags: 6			
LNCM does not cause LNUE	26	2.08537	0.1256
LNUE does not cause LNCM		2.47033	0.0810
LNPM does not cause LNUE	26	0.68638	0.6644
LNUE does not cause LNPM		1.22108	0.3563
Lags: 7			
LNCM does not cause LNUE	25	1.55822	0.2530
LNUE does not cause LNCM		2.29711	0.1127
LNPM does not cause LNUE	25	0.44040	0.8556
LNUE does not cause LNPM		1.25513	0.3595
Lags: 8			
LNCM does not cause LNUE	24	1.45973	0.3157
LNUE does not cause LNCM		2.90875	0.0886
LNPM does not cause LNUE	24	0.99263	0.5105
LNUE does not cause LNPM		2.47835	0.1245

(Continued)

Table E3 **(Continued)**

Sample: 1981–2012			
Null hypothesis	**Observations**	**F-statistic**	**Probability**
Lags: 9			
LNCM does not cause LNUE	23	54.2176	0.0008
LNUE does not cause LNCM		3.03474	0.1486
LNPM does not cause LNUE	23	8.45049	0.0275
LNUE does not cause LNPM		1.33732	0.4165

Table E4 **Pairwise Granger causality tests (series: LNUE, LNCX, and LNPX)**

Sample: 1981–2012			
Null hypothesis	**Observations**	**F-statistic**	**Probability**
Lags: 6			
LNCX does not cause LNUE	26	0.29676	0.9277
LNUE does not cause LNCX		0.94116	0.4989
LNPX does not cause LNUE	26	2.80709	0.0561
LNUE does not cause LNPX		1.61497	0.2201
Lags: 7			
LNCX does not cause LNUE	25	0.26755	0.9533
LNUE does not cause LNCX		0.72020	0.6592
LNPX does not cause LNUE	25	1.87025	0.1781
LNUE does not cause LNPX		2.11500	0.1365
Lags: 8			
LNCX does not cause LNUE	24	0.34786	0.9189
LNUE does not cause LNCX		0.60572	0.7515
LNPX does not cause LNUE	24	2.68476	0.1054
LNUE does not cause LNPX		2.96905	0.0847
Lags: 9			
LNCX does not cause LNUE	23	22.7678	0.0043
LNUE does not cause LNCX		0.41187	0.8762
LNPX does not cause LNUE	23	10.5702	0.0183
LNUE does not cause LNPX		1.76034	0.3075

Table E5 Pairwise Granger causality tests (series: LNRE, LNCM, and LNPM)

Sample: 1981–2012			
Null hypothesis	**Observations**	**F-statistic**	**Probability**
Lags: 1			
LNCM does not cause LNRE	31	13.1851	0.0011
LNRE does not cause LNCM		0.94821	0.3385
LNPM does not cause LNRE	31	11.5609	0.0020
LNRE does not cause LNPM		0.03984	0.8432
Lags: 2			
LNCM does not cause LNRE	30	3.88924	0.0338
LNRE does not cause LNCM		0.10764	0.8984
LNPM does not cause LNRE	30	3.53877	0.0443
LNRE does not cause LNPM		0.12946	0.8792
Lags: 3			
LNCM does not cause LNRE	29	2.29889	0.1055
LNRE does not cause LNCM		0.46854	0.7072
LNPM does not cause LNRE	29	2.22964	0.1132
LNRE does not cause LNPM		0.04859	0.9854

Table E6 Pairwise Granger causality tests (series: LNRE, LNCX, and LNPX)

Sample: 1981–2012			
Null hypothesis	**Observations**	**F-statistic**	**Probability**
Lags: 1			
LNCX does not cause LNRE	31	15.5824	0.0005
LNRE does not cause LNCX		1.14360	0.2940
LNPX does not cause LNRE	31	10.9685	0.0026
LNRE does not cause LNPX		0.01525	0.9026
Lags: 2			
LNCX does not cause LNRE	30	4.98793	0.0150
LNRE does not cause LNCX		0.68695	0.5124
LNPX does not cause LNRE	30	3.89419	0.0337
LNRE does not cause LNPX		0.04098	0.9599

(Continued)

Table E6 **(Continued)**

Sample: 1981–2012			
Null hypothesis	**Observations**	**F-statistic**	**Probability**
Lags: 3			
LNCX does not cause LNRE	29	2.38466	0.0967
LNRE does not cause LNCX		0.37789	0.7698
LNPX does not cause LNRE	29	2.42864	0.0924
LNRE does not cause LNPX		0.12245	0.9459
Lags: 4			
LNCX does not cause LNRE	28	1.47754	0.2483
LNRE does not cause LNCX		0.51568	0.7251
LNPX does not cause LNRE	28	1.73714	0.1835
LNRE does not cause LNPX		0.36222	0.8324

Table E7 **Pairwise Granger causality tests (series: LNEAP, LNCM, and LNPM)**

Sample: 1981–2012			
Null hypothesis	**Observations**	**F-statistic**	**Probability**
Lags: 6			
LNCM does not cause LNEAP	26	2.79308	0.0569
LNEAP does not cause LNCM		1.35799	0.3013
LNPM does not cause LNEAP	26	0.81110	0.5796
LNEAP does not cause LNPM		0.52603	0.7791
Lags: 7			
LNCM does not cause LNEAP	25	1.73536	0.2069
LNEAP does not cause LNCM		1.67120	0.2225
LNPM does not cause LNEAP	25	0.42961	0.8627
LNEAP does not cause LNPM		0.70263	0.6714
Lags: 8			
LNCM does not cause LNEAP	24	1.37681	0.3432
LNEAP does not cause LNCM		2.19097	0.1588
LNPM does not cause LNEAP	24	0.98004	0.5172
LNEAP does not cause LNPM		2.05788	0.1787
Lags: 9			
LNCM does not cause LNEAP	23	7.54838	0.0336
LNEAP does not cause LNCM		2.26013	0.2245
LNPM does not cause LNEAP	23	12.4753	0.0135
LNEAP does not cause LNPM		1.05097	0.5220

Table E8 Pairwise Granger causality tests (series: LNEAP, LNCX, and LNPX)

Sample: 1981–2012			
Null hypothesis	**Observations**	**F-statistic**	**Probability**
Lags: 6			
LNCX does not cause LNEAP	26	0.20788	0.9680
LNEAP does not cause LNCX		0.60051	0.7256
LNPX does not cause LNEAP	26	2.10952	0.1221
LNEAP does not cause LNPX		0.40624	0.8620
Lags: 7			
LNCX does not cause LNEAP	25	0.25276	0.9595
LNEAP does not cause LNCX		0.47015	0.8356
LNPX does not cause LNEAP	25	1.37793	0.3116
LNEAP does not cause LNPX		0.64809	0.7098
Lags: 8			
LNCX does not cause LNEAP	24	0.17138	0.9881
LNEAP does not cause LNCX		0.40841	0.8835
LNPX does not cause LNEAP	24	2.37117	0.1361
LNEAP does not cause LNPX		1.57992	0.2801
Lags: 9			
LNCX does not cause LNEAP	23	10.8212	0.0176
LNEAP does not cause LNCX		0.27115	0.9518
LNPX does not cause LNEAP	23	18.7699	0.0063
LNEAP does not cause LNPX		1.20102	0.4628

Table E9 Pairwise Granger causality tests (series: LNPIP, LNCM, and LNPM)

Sample: 1981–2012			
Null hypothesis	**Observations**	**F-statistic**	**Probability**
Lags: 1			
LNCM does not cause LNPIP	31	12.9654	0.0012
LNPIP does not cause LNCM		1.06138	0.3117
LNPM does not cause LNPIP	31	10.5499	0.0030
LNPIP does not cause LNPM		0.47755	0.4952

(Continued)

Table E9 **(Continued)**

Sample: 1981–2012			
Null hypothesis	**Observations**	**F-statistic**	**Probability**
Lags: 2			
LNCM does not cause LNPIP	30	2.42260	0.1092
LNPIP does not cause LNCM		0.17298	0.8422
LNPM does not cause LNPIP	30	2.02632	0.1529
LNPIP does not cause LNPM		0.24592	0.7839
Lags: 3			
LNCM does not cause LNPIP	29	2.20169	0.1165
LNPIP does not cause LNCM		0.18770	0.9036
LNPM does not cause LNPIP	29	1.69249	0.1977
LNPIP does not cause LNPM		0.06908	0.9758
Lags: 4			
LNCM does not cause LNPIP	28	2.67114	0.0638
LNPIP does not cause LNCM		0.29217	0.8794
LNPM does not cause LNPIP	28	2.34798	0.0912
LNPIP does not cause LNPM		0.05731	0.9934
Lags: 5			
LNCM does not cause LNPIP	27	2.20599	0.1045
LNPIP does not cause LNCM		1.43624	0.2646
LNPM does not cause LNPIP	27	1.96703	0.1388
LNPIP does not cause LNPM		0.37847	0.8562

Table E10 **Pairwise Granger causality tests (series: LNPIP, LNCX, and LNPX)**

Sample: 1981–2012			
Null hypothesis	**Observations**	**F-statistic**	**Probability**
Lags: 1			
LNCX does not cause LNPIP	31	14.8959	0.0006
LNPIP does not cause LNCX		1.97950	0.1704
LNPX does not cause LNPIP	31	9.90194	0.0039
LNPIP does not cause LNPX		0.04572	0.8322

(Continued)

Table E10 **(Continued)**

Sample: 1981–2012			
Null hypothesis	**Observations**	**F-statistic**	**Probability**
Lags: 2			
LNCX does not cause LNPIP	30	3.30398	0.0533
LNPIP does not cause LNCX		1.44289	0.2552
LNPX does not cause LNPIP	30	1.52087	0.2381
LNPIP does not cause LNPX		0.01807	0.9821
Lags: 3			
LNCX does not cause LNPIP	29	2.05591	0.1353
LNPIP does not cause LNCX		1.11962	0.3626
LNPX does not cause LNPIP	29	1.20920	0.3297
LNPIP does not cause LNPX		0.00659	0.9992
Lags: 4			
LNCX does not cause LNPIP	28	1.90764	0.1506
LNPIP does not cause LNCX		0.62890	0.6478
LNPX does not cause LNPIP	28	1.16907	0.3557
LNPIP does not cause LNPX		0.08940	0.9847

Table E11 **Pairwise Granger causality tests (series: LNSIP, LNCM, and LNPM)**

Sample: 1981–2012			
Null hypothesis	**Observations**	**F-statistic**	**Probability**
Lags: 1			
LNCM does not cause LNSIP	31	5.65228	0.0245
LNSIP does not cause LNCM		0.59097	0.4485
LNPM does not cause LNSIP	31	3.10762	0.0888
LNSIP does not cause LNPM		0.48519	0.4918
Lags: 2			
LNCM does not cause LNSIP	30	3.19437	0.0582
LNSIP does not cause LNCM		0.02868	0.9718
LNPM does not cause LNSIP	30	2.43258	0.1083
LNSIP does not cause LNPM		0.43955	0.6492

(Continued)

Table E11 (Continued)

Sample: 1981–2012			
Null hypothesis	**Observations**	**F-statistic**	**Probability**
Lags: 3			
LNCM does not cause LNSIP	29	2.74095	0.0676
LNSIP does not cause LNCM		1.08481	0.3762
LNPM does not cause LNSIP	29	2.85255	0.0606
LNSIP does not cause LNPM		0.86851	0.4723
Lags: 4			
LNCM does not cause LNSIP	28	3.27001	0.0336
LNSIP does not cause LNCM		0.71148	0.5942
LNPM does not cause LNSIP	28	1.76828	0.1770
LNSIP does not cause LNPM		1.01171	0.4261

Table E12 Pairwise Granger causality tests (series: LNSIP, LNCX, and LNPX)

Sample: 1981–2012			
Null hypothesis	**Observations**	**F-statistic**	**Probability**
Lags: 1			
LNCX does not cause LNSIP	31	4.66556	0.0395
LNSIP does not cause LNCX		0.40043	0.5320
LNPX does not cause LNSIP	31	2.79011	0.1060
LNSIP does not cause LNPX		0.64835	0.4275
Lags: 2			
LNCX does not cause LNSIP	30	3.01439	0.0672
LNSIP does not cause LNCX		0.04410	0.9569
LNPX does not cause LNSIP	30	2.05415	0.1493
LNSIP does not cause LNPX		0.17633	0.8394
Lags: 3			
LNCX does not cause LNSIP	29	3.10547	0.0473
LNSIP does not cause LNCX		0.28152	0.8382
LNPX does not cause LNSIP	29	2.37498	0.0976
LNSIP does not cause LNPX		0.30602	0.8207

(Continued)

Table E12 (Continued)

Sample: 1981−2012			
Null hypothesis	**Observations**	**F-statistic**	**Probability**
Lags: 4			
LNCX does not cause LNSIP	28	1.94287	0.1446
LNSIP does not cause LNCX		1.57892	0.2206
LNPX does not cause LNSIP	28	1.69927	0.1917
LNSIP does not cause LNPX		0.22228	0.9226
Lags: 5			
LNCX does not cause LNSIP	27	1.41868	0.2704
LNSIP does not cause LNCX		1.26355	0.3268
LNPX does not cause LNSIP	27	1.85857	0.1582
LNSIP does not cause LNPX		1.77791	0.1744
Lags: 6			
LNCX does not cause LNSIP	26	0.87692	0.5377
LNSIP does not cause LNCX		1.44495	0.2709
LNPX does not cause LNSIP	26	2.36397	0.0912
LNSIP does not cause LNPX		1.48329	0.2585
Lags: 7			
LNCX does not cause LNSIP	25	1.00130	0.4827
LNSIP does not cause LNCX		1.27170	0.3526
LNPX does not cause LNSIP	25	4.36192	0.0182
LNSIP does not cause LNPX		1.40042	0.3035
Lags: 8			
LNCX does not cause LNSIP	24	0.90975	0.5563
LNSIP does not cause LNCX		0.83366	0.6015
LNPX does not cause LNSIP	24	3.45204	0.0600
LNSIP does not cause LNPX		2.32165	0.1419

Table E13 **Pairwise Granger causality tests (series: LNTIP, LNCM, and LNPM)**

Sample: 1981–2012			
Null hypothesis	**Observations**	**F-statistic**	**Probability**
Lags: 5			
LNCM does not cause LNTIP	27	0.82896	0.5475
LNTIP does not cause LNCM		1.84379	0.1610
LNPM does not cause LNTIP	27	0.43977	0.8143
LNTIP does not cause LNPM		0.67008	0.6518
Lags: 6			
LNCM does not cause LNTIP	26	1.08337	0.4211
LNTIP does not cause LNCM		2.71986	0.0616
LNPM does not cause LNTIP	26	0.63460	0.7011
LNTIP does not cause LNPM		0.99266	0.4694
Lags: 7			
LNCM does not cause LNTIP	25	0.70343	0.6709
LNTIP does not cause LNCM		2.53125	0.0889
LNPM does not cause LNTIP	25	0.44384	0.8533
LNTIP does not cause LNPM		1.51563	0.2657
Lags: 8			
LNCM does not cause LNTIP	24	0.53457	0.8005
LNTIP does not cause LNCM		2.72012	0.1025
LNPM does not cause LNTIP	24	0.39083	0.8942
LNTIP does not cause LNPM		1.52761	0.2950
Lags: 9			
LNCM does not cause LNTIP	23	12.6032	0.0133
LNTIP does not cause LNCM		4.72890	0.0745
LNPM does not cause LNTIP	23	1.10593	0.4992
LNTIP does not cause LNPM		1.42332	0.3904

Table E14 Pairwise Granger causality tests (series: LNTIP, LNCX, and LNPX)

Sample: 1981–2012			
Null hypothesis	**Observations**	**F-statistic**	**Probability**
Lags: 1			
LNCX does not cause LNTIP	31	0.15276	0.6989
LNTIP does not cause LNCX		2.03500	0.1648
LNPX does not cause LNTIP	31	3.18135	0.0853
LNTIP does not cause LNPX		0.02185	0.8835
Lags: 2			
LNCX does not cause LNTIP	30	0.01600	0.9841
LNTIP does not cause LNCX		0.78647	0.4664
LNPX does not cause LNTIP	30	1.80752	0.1849
LNTIP does not cause LNPX		0.48185	0.6233
Lags: 3			
LNCX does not cause LNTIP	29	0.02966	0.9929
LNTIP does not cause LNCX		0.33864	0.7976
LNPX does not cause LNTIP	29	1.52759	0.2353
LNTIP does not cause LNPX		0.64986	0.5914
Lags: 4			
LNCX does not cause LNTIP	28	0.12609	0.9712
LNTIP does not cause LNCX		0.85422	0.5088
LNPX does not cause LNTIP	28	0.95297	0.4555
LNTIP does not cause LNPX		0.53307	0.7130

Appendix F   Impulse responses function

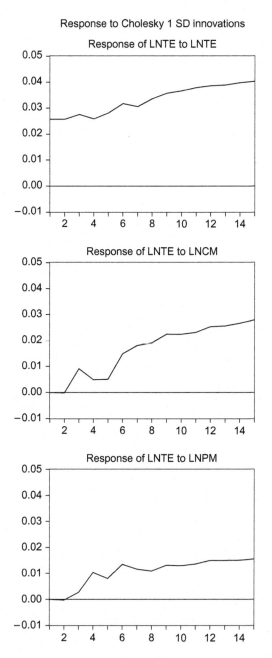

Figure F1 Impulse response function (between LNTE, LNCM, and LNPM).

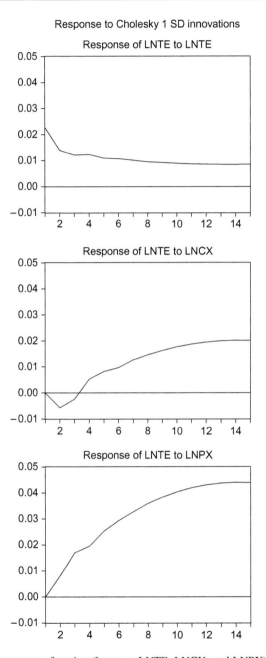

Figure F2 Impulse response function (between LNTE, LNCX, and LNPX).

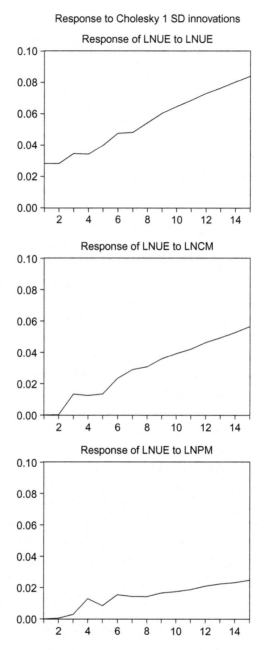

Figure F3 Impulse response function (between LNUE, LNCM, and LNPM).

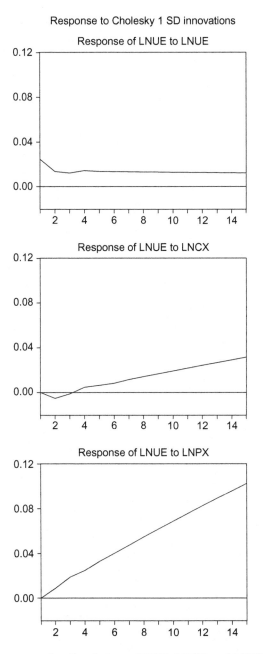

Figure F4 Impulse response function (between LNUE, LNCX, and LNPX).

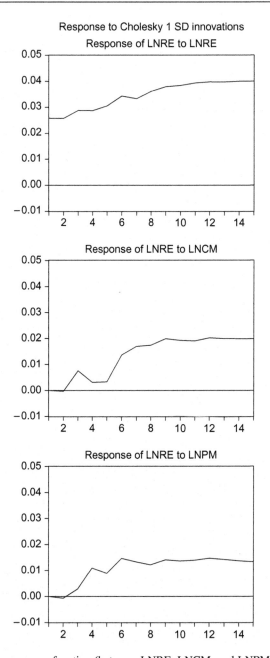

Figure F5 Impulse response function (between LNRE, LNCM, and LNPM).

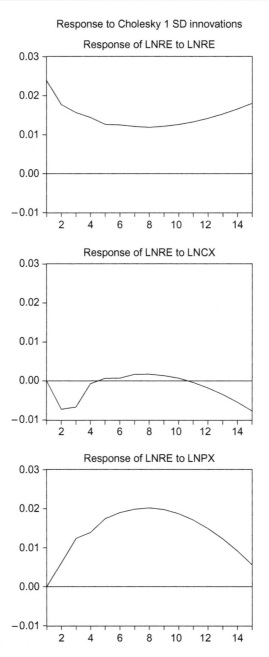

Figure F6 Impulse response function (between LNRE, LNCX, and LNPX).

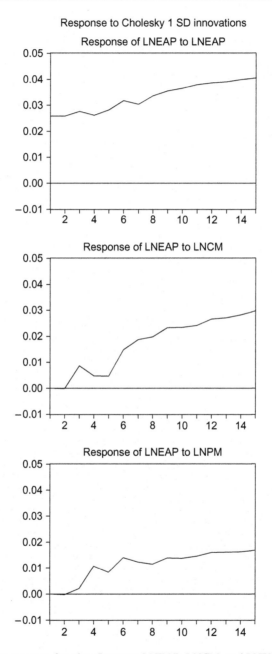

Figure F7 Impulse response function (between LNEAP, LNCM, and LNPM).

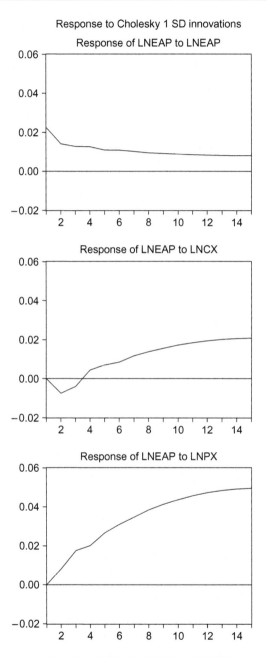

Figure F8 Impulse response function (LNEAP, LNCX, and LNPX).

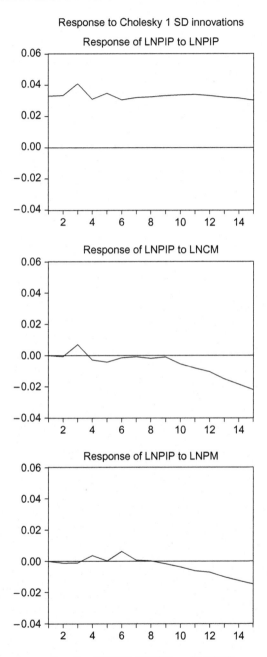

Figure F9 Impulse response function (LNPIP, LNCM, and LNPM).

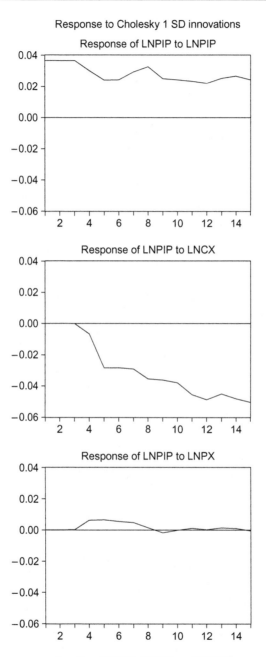

Figure F10 Impulse response function (LNPIP, LNCX, and LNPX).

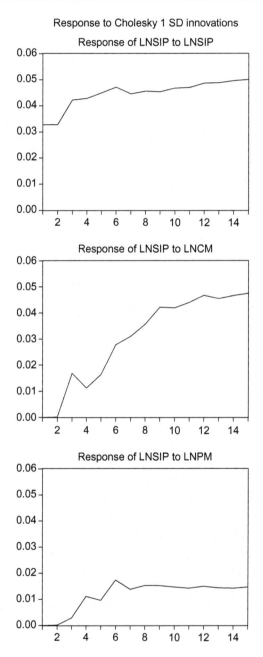

Figure F11 Impulse response function (between LNSIP, LNCM, and LNPM).

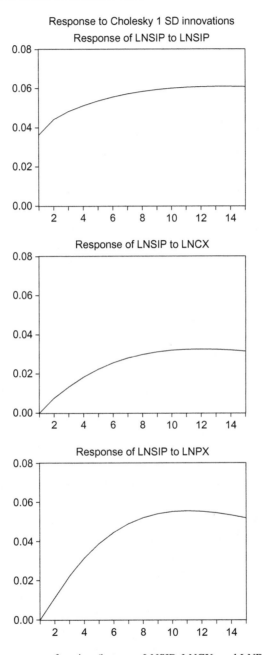

Figure F12 Impulse response function (between LNSIP, LNCX, and LNPX).

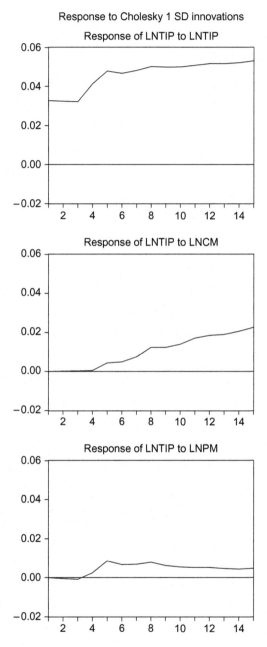

Figure F13 Impulse response function (between LNTIP, LNCM, and LNPM).

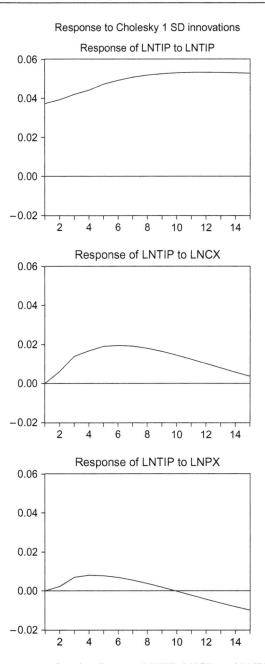

Figure F14 Impulse response function (between LNTIP, LNCX, and LNPX).

Appendix G   Results of variance decomposition

Table G1 **Decomposition of LNTE (Cholesky ordering: LNTE, LNCM, and LNPM)**

Period	SE	LNTE	LNCM	LNPM
1	0.025697	100.0000	0.000000	0.000000
2	0.036341	99.99128	0.002013	0.006703
3	0.046576	95.84042	3.825477	0.334108
4	0.054482	92.56677	3.603022	3.830213
5	0.062019	91.94650	3.445756	4.607742
6	0.072483	86.42883	6.742986	6.828181
7	0.081543	82.31871	10.24799	7.433300
8	0.090884	79.91309	12.66174	7.425169
9	0.101036	77.13097	15.17857	7.690454
10	0.110531	75.41397	16.78722	7.798810
11	0.119878	74.09300	17.99050	7.916493
12	0.129323	72.57952	19.27681	8.143663
13	0.138261	71.41935	20.28424	8.296410
14	0.147078	70.42387	21.19694	8.379180
15	0.155810	69.45112	22.08952	8.459357

Table G2 **Decomposition of LNTE (Cholesky ordering: LNTE, LNCX, and LNPX)**

Period	SE	LNTE	LNCX	LNPX
1	0.022671	100.0000	0.000000	0.000000
2	0.028421	87.63826	4.057135	8.304605
3	0.035328	68.45745	3.100353	28.44220
4	0.042529	55.60882	3.683851	40.70733
5	0.051357	42.62735	5.050450	52.32220
6	0.060892	33.41084	6.108512	60.48065
7	0.070993	26.60514	7.653478	65.74138
8	0.081458	21.56042	9.045431	69.39415
9	0.091972	17.91379	10.22752	71.85869
10	0.102385	15.20962	11.24148	73.54890
11	0.112559	13.17553	12.06825	74.75622
12	0.122376	11.63197	12.74491	75.62313
13	0.131754	10.44602	13.29273	76.26125
14	0.140625	9.529525	13.72673	76.74375
15	0.148941	8.820016	14.06520	77.11478

Table G3 **Decomposition of LNUE (Cholesky ordering: LNUE, LNCM, and LNPM)**

Period	SE	LNUE	LNCM	LNPM
1	0.028236	100.0000	0.000000	0.000000
2	0.039918	99.98748	0.001504	0.011014
3	0.054520	93.77701	5.944538	0.278454
4	0.066804	88.68364	7.420735	3.895622
5	0.079364	88.03188	8.090037	3.878085
6	0.096663	83.55152	11.29501	5.153471
7	0.112695	79.72272	14.89085	5.386432
8	0.129579	77.83635	16.89481	5.268838
9	0.148279	75.98545	18.74807	5.266474
10	0.167330	74.58719	20.20221	5.210605
11	0.186616	73.48751	21.32302	5.189470
12	0.206702	72.36143	22.38981	5.248766
13	0.226901	71.38883	23.29350	5.317675
- 14	0.247466	70.54347	24.11169	5.344840
15	0.268530	69.71734	24.89925	5.383406

Table G4 **Decomposition of LNUE (Cholesky ordering: LNUE, LNCX, and LNPX)**

Period	SE	LNUE	LNCX	LNPX
1	0.024382	100.0000	0.000000	0.000000
2	0.029671	88.09613	3.019739	8.884131
3	0.037182	66.76102	2.028663	31.21032
4	0.047108	50.88158	2.260633	46.85779
5	0.059432	37.20505	2.563007	60.23195
6	0.073463	27.66333	2.950136	69.38653
7	0.089212	20.98607	3.680162	75.33377
8	0.106454	16.25697	4.350678	79.39235
9	0.124918	12.89274	4.930519	82.17674
10	0.144511	10.42738	5.454051	84.11857
11	0.165124	8.580419	5.911213	85.50837
12	0.186656	7.170924	6.310012	86.51906
13	0.209032	6.073691	6.659531	87.26678
14	0.232187	5.205051	6.966578	87.82837
15	0.256063	4.507081	7.237946	88.25497

Table G5 **Decomposition of LNRE (Cholesky ordering: LNRE, LNCM, and LNPM)**

Period	SE	LNRE	LNCM	LNPM
1	0.025774	100.0000	0.000000	0.000000
2	0.036410	99.95521	0.009012	0.035777
3	0.047099	97.04930	2.571174	0.379524
4	0.056296	93.88942	2.096560	4.014016
5	0.064722	93.22347	1.844028	4.932506
6	0.075942	88.10710	4.590443	7.302453
7	0.085664	84.33296	7.525279	8.141761
8	0.095363	82.40792	9.400542	8.191536
9	0.105478	80.28153	11.24243	8.476045
10	0.114713	79.09152	12.32860	8.579878
11	0.123567	78.32811	13.00564	8.666256
12	0.132185	77.49468	13.70189	8.803436
13	0.140190	76.93970	14.20715	8.853145
14	0.147775	76.57467	14.60096	8.824368
15	0.154960	76.30696	14.92869	8.764349

Table G6 **Decomposition of LNRE (Cholesky ordering: LNRE, LNCX, and LNPX)**

Period	SE	LNRE	LNCX	LNPX
1	0.023819	100.0000	0.000000	0.000000
2	0.031161	90.67578	5.409709	3.914509
3	0.037614	79.56432	6.885853	13.54983
4	0.042620	73.38994	5.392525	21.21754
5	0.047752	65.45894	4.315294	30.22577
6	0.052889	58.93893	3.535353	37.52572
7	0.057793	53.74816	3.045012	43.20683
8	0.062389	49.75690	2.688540	47.55456
9	0.066575	47.03031	2.401661	50.56803
10	0.070292	45.40061	2.163984	52.43541
11	0.073547	44.72651	1.979502	53.29398
12	0.076394	44.90166	1.889452	53.20889
13	0.078943	45.79684	1.963088	52.24008
14	0.081363	47.25963	2.296638	50.44373
15	0.083877	49.08621	2.997896	47.91590

Table G7 **Decomposition of LNEAP (Cholesky ordering: LNEAP, LNCM, and LNPM)**

Period	SE	LNEAP	LNCM	LNPM
1	0.025797	100.0000	0.000000	0.000000
2	0.036482	99.99374	0.001641	0.004621
3	0.046597	96.36873	3.422595	0.208677
4	0.054688	92.78341	3.246095	3.970495
5	0.062254	92.07170	3.060399	4.867902
6	0.072799	86.33957	6.395128	7.265304
7	0.081998	81.76187	10.26100	7.977134
8	0.091518	79.11736	12.91256	7.970078
9	0.101840	76.03407	15.67562	8.290306
10	0.111554	74.09518	17.47678	8.428042
11	0.121152	72.62338	18.78803	8.588587
12	0.130887	70.92456	20.22410	8.851342
13	0.140169	69.58833	21.36872	9.042954
14	0.149329	68.45050	22.39634	9.153165
15	0.158452	67.32903	23.41250	9.258468

Table G8 **Decomposition of LNEAP (Cholesky ordering: LNEAP, LNCX, and LNPX)**

Period	LNEAP	LNCX	LNPX
1	0.022508	0.000000	0.000000
2	0.014118	−0.007508	0.008147
3	0.012797	−0.004010	0.017581
4	0.012653	0.004318	0.020135
5	0.010939	0.007000	0.026678
6	0.010887	0.008500	0.030991
7	0.010234	0.011704	0.034686
8	0.009466	0.013789	0.038401
9	0.009161	0.015581	0.041286
10	0.008770	0.017218	0.043719
11	0.008450	0.018425	0.045774
12	0.008253	0.019406	0.047314
13	0.008092	0.020132	0.048454
14	0.008004	0.020578	0.049201
15	0.007983	0.020799	0.049560

Table G9 **Decomposition of LNPIP (Cholesky ordering: LNPIP, LNCM, and LNPM)**

Period	SE	LNPIP	LNCM	LNPM
1	0.032980	100.0000	0.000000	0.000000
2	0.046967	99.91776	0.017657	0.064581
3	0.062701	98.66856	1.266355	0.065085
4	0.070096	98.50260	1.176136	0.321260
5	0.078369	98.51148	1.230935	0.257582
6	0.084362	98.12719	1.091311	0.781496
7	0.090260	98.35129	0.961050	0.687660
8	0.095933	98.50543	0.885362	0.609209
9	0.101551	98.63029	0.798521	0.571189
10	0.107210	98.39815	0.970944	0.630911
11	0.112939	97.73546	1.399480	0.865056
12	0.118418	96.79621	2.064970	1.138822
13	0.124059	94.92509	3.367513	1.707399
14	0.129966	92.41381	5.105336	2.480859
15	0.136041	89.28255	7.274237	3.443217

Table G10 **Decomposition of LNPIP (Cholesky ordering: LNPIP, LNCX, and LNPX)**

Period	SE	LNPIP	LNCX	LNPX
1	0.036625	100.0000	0.000000	0.000000
2	0.051783	99.99971	6.60E-08	0.000293
3	0.063407	99.99915	1.92E-07	0.000851
4	0.070766	98.33571	0.896028	0.768258
5	0.080223	85.49629	13.25517	1.248540
6	0.088648	77.49762	21.10093	1.401442
7	0.097912	72.43633	26.18589	1.377772
8	0.109131	67.22289	31.65136	1.125745
9	0.117670	62.31321	36.69523	0.991555
10	0.125990	58.06287	41.07202	0.865107
11	0.135989	52.76838	46.48283	0.748788
12	0.146133	47.95414	51.39736	0.648499
13	0.155006	45.25449	54.16196	0.583548
14	0.164501	42.79858	56.68013	0.521294
15	0.173771	40.29604	59.23551	0.468445

Table G11 **Decomposition of LNSIP (Cholesky ordering: LNSIP, LNCM, and LNPM)**

Period	SE	LNSIP	LNCM	LNPM
1	0.032782	100.0000	0.000000	0.000000
2	0.046374	99.99835	0.000470	0.001176
3	0.064984	93.09750	6.705351	0.197147
4	0.079431	91.43856	6.476986	2.084454
5	0.093209	89.63023	7.797041	2.572728
6	0.109475	83.50557	12.11913	4.375300
7	0.122980	79.29771	15.97793	4.724354
8	0.136789	75.21233	19.72098	5.066689
9	0.150936	70.81074	24.00722	5.182035
10	0.164156	67.99676	26.82168	5.181564
11	0.176929	65.62038	29.27171	5.107907
12	0.189979	63.49826	31.45336	5.048385
13	0.201883	62.09319	32.93151	4.975298
14	0.213558	60.90291	34.20595	4.891144
15	0.224940	59.86349	35.30199	4.834522

Table G12 **Decomposition of LNSIP (Cholesky ordering: LNSIP, LNCX, and LNPX)**

Period	SE	LNSIP	LNCX	LNPX
1	0.036344	100.0000	0.000000	0.000000
2	0.058764	94.70203	1.684929	3.613036
3	0.080314	86.73891	3.660533	9.600557
4	0.101947	79.02142	5.505155	15.47343
5	0.123586	72.57348	7.017522	20.40900
6	0.144930	67.47086	8.214677	24.31446
7	0.165694	63.52058	9.151821	27.32760
8	0.185660	60.49225	9.885538	29.62221
9	0.204680	58.18653	10.46179	31.35168
10	0.222662	56.44582	10.91572	32.63846
11	0.239565	55.14906	11.27367	33.57727
12	0.255382	54.20376	11.55540	34.24084
13	0.270132	53.53885	11.77586	34.68529
14	0.283854	53.09917	11.94651	34.95433
15	0.296601	52.84135	12.07623	35.08242

Table G13 **Decomposition of LNTIP (Cholesky ordering: LNTIP, LNCM, and LNPM)**

Period	SE	LNTIP	LNCM	LNPM
1	0.032708	100.0000	0.000000	0.000000
2	0.046046	99.98866	0.000927	0.010410
3	0.056171	99.96726	0.002678	0.030065
4	0.069739	99.85647	0.006512	0.137019
5	0.085154	98.63668	0.263500	1.099825
6	0.097499	98.23860	0.449251	1.312144
7	0.109259	97.73060	0.828431	1.440970
8	0.121152	96.67061	1.729367	1.600026
9	0.131786	96.08192	2.342340	1.575737
10	0.141759	95.49058	2.998988	1.510436
11	0.151676	94.66701	3.896223	1.436764
12	0.161401	93.87244	4.755750	1.371813
13	0.170615	93.19746	5.499628	1.302909
14	0.179670	92.49033	6.275178	1.234489
15	0.188788	91.69724	7.121008	1.181748

Table G14 **Decomposition of LNTIP (Cholesky ordering: LNTIP, LNCX, and LNPX)**

Period	SE	LNTIP	LNCX	LNPX
1	0.037347	100.0000	0.000000	0.000000
2	0.054584	98.59323	1.240884	0.165883
3	0.070603	94.28178	4.665750	1.052467
4	0.085309	91.34442	7.061777	1.593802
5	0.099687	89.41155	8.825484	1.762968
6	0.113100	88.43357	9.827772	1.738662
7	0.125600	88.10761	10.29336	1.599031
8	0.137156	88.22057	10.36310	1.416337
9	0.147847	88.60803	10.15753	1.234436
10	0.157764	89.14640	9.769335	1.084267
11	0.167007	89.74426	9.269980	0.985757
12	0.175677	90.33538	8.714082	0.950534
13	0.183862	90.87377	8.142495	0.983734
14	0.191644	91.32965	7.584858	1.085490
15	0.199089	91.68614	7.061639	1.252216

Vertical specialization and accelerating poverty reduction: comparing impacts of conventional trade and processing trade patterns on income in China

5

5.1 Introduction

The increase of vertically specialized trade in manufacturing has been a feature of China's economy over the past decades. Increased vertically specialized trade in China stands out strongly in the data of imports and exports by processing trade. China's processing trade is characterized by production fragmentation, including intermediate goods that move across borders multiple times before export processing of the final product is undertaken.

Inclusive growth requires rapid and sustained poverty reduction that allows people to benefit from enlarging the size of the economy. Accelerating poverty reduction is unquestionably necessary for inclusive growth, but for this to be sustainable in the long-term, it should be arguably more general and inclusive of the poor, the nearly poor, middle income groups, and even the rich (Klasen, 2010: 2). This conceptualization has been focusing on what extent of growth was increasing income and estimating whether and why poverty was reduced in an absolute or relative definition.

Taking international production fragmentation into account has important implications for China's poverty reduction policy. The Customs in China classify each import and export transaction into processing and nonprocessing categories. Evidence in China Statistical Yearbook (2013) suggests that China is a major player in vertical specialization. Imported intermediate inputs for processing trade purposes are eligible for import tax rebates. When China's foreign trade in intermediate inputs is prevalent, huge amounts of imports and exports by processing trade take place where the parts and components, raw and auxiliary materials, accessories, and packaging materials are imported from abroad free of duty.

This chapter is organized as follows: Section 5.2 presents trade and income in the literature review. Section 5.3 is a description of data and methodology. The different effects on income are obtained under two different trade patterns by comparison in Section 5.4. We finally draw some conclusions and implications for policy in Section 5.5.

5.2 Trade and income in the economic literature

The link between trade and income is at the heart of much of trade theory and applied trade policy analysis. Among the many channels through which trade may affect income, the most important is the Stolper-Samuelson effect. According to the principal explanations of comparative advantage theory, because people with relatively abundant production factors benefit from expanded trade opportunities, a labor-abundant developing country would show higher returns to laborers and lower returns to capitalists and, consequently, lower income inequality as a result of international trade liberalization (Stolper and Samuelson, 1941).

Helpman et al. (2015) focus on dispersion in wages within sector-occupation combinations and find that a high initial level of openness is suggestive of a decrease, rather than an increase, in wage inequality. This is in contrast with the neoclassical approach to trade and inequality, which emphasizes wage changes across occupations through intersectoral reallocations (the Stolper-Samuelson effect; Shepherd, 2013).

The wage and income effects of vertical specialization have become increasingly important from a policy point of view because they are closely linked to the concepts of poverty reduction and economic upgrading within China with a substantial inequality and income gap between the urban rich and rural poor presence.

Recent advances in microtheoretical foundations aim to distinguish between the income effect of trade in intermediate and final goods and highlight the pro-competitive effects, emphasizing access to a more diverse set of imported intermediate inputs. Dai et al. (2011) show that it is important to distinguish between traditional exporters and export processors that simply assemble tariff-free imported intermediates into final goods for export. Whereas traditional exporters in China tend to pay higher wages than other firms, export processors tend to pay lower wages and are less productive than nonexporters. Wei and Wu (2001) show that trade openness and urban−rural income inequality data covering the period 1988−1993 tend to be negatively associated when the former is measured as export values divided by GDP. Mah (2013) examines the effect of trade liberalization and expansion of foreign direct investment in-flows, together with the pursuit of decentralization, on China's income inequality between 1985 and 2007. The empirical evidence shows that trade liberalization has led to the higher income inequality in China, discrediting the Stolper-Samuelson theorem in international trade.

Ultimately, the relation between income and trade is an empirical matter. This chapter aims to contribute additional evidence in this respect by focusing on links between various income indicators and various trade indicators.

5.3 Methodology and data

The Vector Autoregression (VAR) is an *ad hoc* dynamic multivariate model, treating simultaneous sets of variables equally, with each endogenous variable regressed on its own lags and the lags of all other variables in a finite-order system (Sims, 1980; Sun et al., 2010). If all variables are integrated with order 1, with the cointegration relationships among them existing, then they can be simulated by the Vector Error Correction Model (VECM) to estimate the variance decomposition functions and impulse response.

Has the vertically specialized trade growth in China been pro-poor? How have the gains from conventional trade and processing trade growth been distributed to households at different levels of income? Has the pro-poor vertically specialized trade growth been absolute or relative? With an absolute approach, the vertically specialized trade growth is considered to be pro-poor if it reduces absolute poverty. In contrast, the vertically specialized trade growth is defined as pro-poor under a relative approach if the vertically specialized trade growth benefits the poor proportionately more than the nonpoor.

Under the *absolute* definition, processing trade growth is considered to be pro-poor as long as people (including the poor, the near-poor, middle income groups, and even the rich) benefit in absolute terms, as reflected in the ratio of total wages of employed persons by registration status to Gross Domestic Products or index of average money wage of the urban units of employment.

In contrast, in the *relative* definition, processing trade growth is "pro-poor" if the incomes of rural poor people grow faster than those of the urban residents (ie, inequality declines). In short, the vertically specialized trade is about raising the pace of wage growth and enlarging the size of the income of all stripes of society. The employing ratio of per capita annual disposable income of urban households and per capita annual net income of rural households is the indicator of China's income gap between the urban rich and rural poor, and the difference between Engel's coefficient of rural households (%) and Engel's coefficient of urban households (%) is an indicator of rural poverty and economic disparity in China.

All data were obtained from the database of China Statistical Yearbook and China Trade and External Economics Statistical Yearbook published by National Bureau of Statistics of China; the sample covers annual observations from 1981 to 2012. All variables are used and transformed into a natural logarithm. This study used the variable groups in Table A1 to find the relationship.

LN CM = natural logarithm of indices of imports by conventional trade (CM);
LN PM = natural logarithm of indices of imports by processing trade (PM);
LN CX = natural logarithm of indices of exports by conventional trade (CX);
LN PX = natural logarithm of indices of exports by processing trade (PX);
LNRWG = natural logarithm of the ratio of total wages of employed persons by registration status to Gross Domestic Products;
LNMWI = natural logarithm of index of average money wage of the urban units employment;
LNURG = natural logarithm of the ratio of per capita annual disposable income of urban households to per capita annual net income of rural households;
LNUREG = natural logarithm of Engel's coefficient of rural households (%) minus Engel's coefficient of urban households (%).

5.4 Relation between vertically specialized trade and income in China

5.4.1 Unit root test

The augmented Dickey Fuller (ADF) test for unit roots was conducted for all the time series used for the study. Table B1 shows the result of unit root tests using the ADF unit root test at the first difference level. The null hypothesis of nonstationarity is performed at the 1%, the 5% and 10% significance levels. In Table B1, the result of the ADF test illustrates that all the data series are nonstationary at level. However, the result of the ADF test on the first difference strongly supports that all data series are stationary after the first difference at the 10%, 5%, or 1% significance levels. The ADF results show that all the variable series were integrated series of order I (1).

5.4.2 Cointegration test

Cointegration means economic variables share the same stochastic trend so that they are combined together in the long-term. Even if they deviate from each other in the short-term, they tend to come back to the trend in the long-term. A necessary condition for the cointegration test is that all the variables should be integrated at the same order or contain a deterministic trend (Engle and Granger, 1991). The unit root test results in Table B1 show that all the time series are founded to be integrated with I(1) during 1981−2012. Therefore, these time series in the period are valid in the cointegration test. Once the variables are cointegrated, the short-term changes can be explained through the vector error correction model (Engle and Granger, 1987). Following the cointegration test, the VECM was used to analyze the causality within the eight variable groups.

The results of trace statistic and the results of maximum eigen statistics are shown in Tables C1−C8. Trace statistics and maximum eigen statistics values help to find the rank(s) that shows the number of vector(s) containing long-term relations. It is evident that the null hypothesis of no rank is rejected. Therefore, the results of both trace and max-eigen statistics confirm that cointegration vectors exist in the model. This means the long-term relationship prevails among the variables. In summary, the Johansen cointegration test results show the variable groups in Table A1 are cointegrated and had a long-term equilibrium relationship during 1981 to 2012.

To distinguish the importance of vertically specialized trade for poverty reduction, it compares the effects of indices of imports and exports by conventional trade and indices of imports and exports by processing trade on the ratio of total wages of employed persons to Gross Domestic Products, index of average money wage of the urban units employment, the ratio of per capita annual disposable income of urban households to per capita annual net income of rural households, the difference between Engel's coefficient of rural households (%), and Engel's coefficient of urban households (%).

Following Johansen's technique, the normalized long-term cointegration relationships and the comparison coefficients are shown in Tables C1–C8. The normalized long-term cointegration relationships are very revealing. The observed signs are as anticipated. Moreover, the long-term relationships are also as expected, given the intrinsic interdependence between the variables.

From Tables C1–C8, we can obtain the following equations for the long-term:

1. The ratio of total wages of employed persons to Gross Domestic Products, indices of imports and exports by conventional trade, and indices of imports and exports by processing trade:

$$\text{LNRWG} = -1.532159\text{LNCM} + 0.716853\text{LNPM} \tag{5.1}$$
$$\underset{(0.15880)}{} \qquad \underset{(0.16434)}{}$$

$$\text{LNRWG} = -1.407763\text{LNCX} + 0.627587\text{LNPX} \tag{5.2}$$
$$\underset{(0.21445)}{} \qquad \underset{(0.19178)}{}$$

Results from Eqs. (5.1) and (5.2) show the 1% increase in imports by conventional trade (LNCM) will have a negative impact of 1.532159% on the ratio of total wages of employed persons to Gross Domestic Products (LNRWG) and the 1% increase in imports by processing trade (LNPM) will have a positive impact of 0.716853% on the ratio of total wages of employed persons to Gross Domestic Products (LNRWG). The 1% increase in exports by conventional trade (LNCX) will have a negative impact of 1.407763% on the ratio of total wages of employed persons to Gross Domestic Products (LNRWG) and the 1% increase in exports by processing trade (LNPX) will have a positive impact of 0.627587% on the ratio of total wages of employed persons to Gross Domestic Products (LNRWG).

Eqs. (5.1) and (5.2) show that the increase in imports and exports by processing trade could increase the ratio of total wages of employed persons to Gross Domestic Products, and imports and exports by conventional trade decrease the ratio of total wages of employed persons to Gross Domestic Products in the long-term. This provides support for evidence of the foreign trade and vertically specialized trade channels.

2. Index of average money wage of the urban units employment, indices of imports and exports by conventional trade, and indices of imports and exports by processing trade:

$$\text{LNMWI} = 0.810124\text{LNCM} + 1.403220\text{LNPM} \tag{5.3}$$
$$\underset{(0.32330)}{} \qquad \underset{(0.46529)}{}$$

$$\text{LNMWI} = 0.016166\text{LNCX} + 0.099563\text{LNPX} \tag{5.4}$$
$$\underset{(0.07131)}{} \qquad \underset{(0.06061)}{}$$

From Eqs. (5.3) and (5.4), we observe that the 1% increase in imports by conventional trade will have a positive impact of 0.810124% on the index of the average money wage of the urban employment units (MWI) and that the 1% increase in imports by processing trade will have a positive impact of 1.403220% on the index of the average money wage of the urban employment units (MWI). The 1% increase in exports by conventional trade will have a positive impact of 0.016166% on the index of the average money wage of the urban units of employment (MWI) and that the 1% increase in exports by processing trade will have a positive impact of 0.099563% on the index of the average money wage of the urban employment units (MWI).

Eqs. (6.3) and (6.4) demonstrate that the increase in imports and exports by processing trade can cause the increase in the index of the average money wage of the urban units of employment in the long-term; this confirms the existence of the vertical specialization channel.

3. The ratio of per capita annual disposable income of urban households to per capita annual net income of rural households, indices of imports and exports by conventional trade, and indices of imports and exports by processing trade:

$$\text{LNURG} = \underset{(0.31599)}{1.299683\text{LNCM}} - \underset{(0.35094)}{1.068640\text{LNPM}} \tag{5.5}$$

$$\text{LNURG} = \underset{(0.22000)}{1.547222\text{LNCX}} - \underset{(0.15643)}{0.936869\text{LNPX}} \tag{5.6}$$

Eqs. (5.5) and (5.6) show that the 1% increase in imports by conventional trade will have a positive impact of 1.299683% on the ratio of per capita annual disposable income of urban households to per capita annual net income of rural households (URG) and the 1% increase in imports by processing trade will have a negative impact of 1.068640% on the ratio of per capita annual disposable income of urban households to per capita annual net income of rural households (URG). The 1% increase in exports by conventional trade will have a positive impact of 1.547222% on the ratio of per capita annual disposable income of urban households to per capita annual net income of rural households (URG) and the 1% increase in exports by processing trade will have a negative impact of 0.936869% on the ratio of per capita annual disposable income of urban households to per capita annual net income of rural households (URG).

Eqs. (5.5) and (5.6) demonstrate that the increase in imports and exports by processing trade can cause a reduction in the ratio of per capita annual disposable income of urban households to per capita annual net income of rural households in the long-term; this again confirms the existence of the vertical specialization channel in lower rural poverty and economic disparity in China.

4. The difference between Engel's coefficient of rural households and Engel's coefficient of urban households (UREG), indices of imports and exports by conventional trade, and indices of imports and exports by processing trade:

$$\text{LNUREG} = \underset{(1.63934)}{7.208469\text{LNCM}} - \underset{(1.77051)}{2.461847\text{LNPM}} \tag{5.7}$$

$$\text{LNUREG} = \underset{(1.74130)}{-0.983457\text{LNCX}} - \underset{(1.38545)}{9.521662\text{LNPX}} \tag{5.8}$$

Furthermore, from Eqs. (5.7) and (5.8), we observe that the 1% increase in LNCM will have a positive impact of 7.208469% on LNUREG, the 1% increase in imports by processing trade (LNPM) will have a negative impact of 2.461847%, the 1% increase in exports by conventional trade will have a negative impact of 0.983457% on the difference between Engel's coefficient of rural households (%) and Engel's coefficient of urban households (%), and the 1% increase in exports by processing trade will have a negative impact of 9.521662% on the difference between Engel's coefficient of rural households (%) and Engel's coefficient of urban households (%).

Eqs. (5.7) and (5.8) suggest that imports and exports by processing trade are the sources of reducing rural poverty and economic disparity in China.

These equations show that the vertical specialization variables (imports and exports by processing trade) have important effects on the accelerating poverty reduction that connect the vertically specialized trade policy variables with the poverty reduction variables (RWG, MWI, URG, and UREG). These long-term equations support the existence of the vertical specialization channel in the trade policy transmission process in China.

Proposition 1. The contribution and importance of imports and exports by conventional trade for increasing the ratio of total wages of employed persons to Gross Domestic Products are lower than that by processing trade.

Proposition 2. The contribution and importance of imports and exports by conventional trade for increasing the index of average money wage of the urban units of employment (MWI) are lower than that by processing trade.

Proposition 3. The contribution and importance of imports and exports by conventional trade for reducing the ratio of per capita annual disposable income of urban households to per capita annual net income of rural households are lower than that by processing trade.

Proposition 4. The contribution and importance of imports and exports by conventional trade for reducing the difference between Engel's coefficient of rural households (%) and Engel's coefficient of urban households (%) are lower than that by processing trade.

5.4.3   Vector error correction model

ECM is used to estimate the short-term and long-term impacts across a variety of variables, and the ECM coefficients show the speed with which the system converges to equilibrium. When the first difference variables are confirmed as having stationarity, ECM can be regressed, in which vecm-1 is one difference error correction item whose coefficient represents the impact of the last period's error correction on this period's variable. The results of VECM are reported in Tables D1–D8.

In Table D2, for D(LNPX), the coefficient of error correction term is -0.897512. It shows that if a deviation from the long-term happens as a shock, then the adjustment speed toward long-term equilibrium will be 0.897512 and there will be full adjustment of deviation.

In Table D4, for D(LNPX), the coefficient of error correction term is -0.906215. It shows that if a deviation from the long-term happens as a shock, then the adjustment speed toward long-term equilibrium will be 0.906215 and there will be full adjustment of deviation.

In Table D5, for D(LNPM), the coefficient of error correction term is -0.431067. It shows that if a deviation from the long-term happens as a shock, then the adjustment speed toward long-term equilibrium will be 0.431067 and there will be full adjustment of deviation.

In Table D6, for D(LNPX), the coefficient of error correction term is -0.231962. It shows that if a deviation from the long-term happens as a shock, then the adjustment speed toward long-term equilibrium will be 0.231962 and there will be full adjustment of deviation.

In Table D7, for D(LNPX), the coefficient of error correction term is -0.068278. It shows that if a deviation from the long-term happens as a shock, then the adjustment speed toward long-term equilibrium will be 0.068278 and there will be full adjustment of deviation.

In Table D8, for D(LNPX), the coefficient of error correction term is -0.214089. It shows that if a deviation from the long-term happens as a shock, then the adjustment speed toward long-term equilibrium will be 0.214089 and there will be full adjustment of deviation.

5.4.4   Granger causality tests

In Table E1, when one lag is applied, the hypothesis that LNCM does not involve Granger causality of LNRWG can be rejected at the 5% level of significance, and the hypothesis that LNRWG does not involve Granger causality of LNCM can be rejected at the 5% level of significance. Thus, we found bidirectional causality running from LNCM to LNRWG. It also reveals unidirectional causality running from LNRWG to LNPM when one lag and five lags are applied at the 5% level of significance.

In Table E2, when one lag, two lags, and five lags are applied, the hypothesis that LNRWG does not involve Granger causality of LNCX can be rejected at the 5% and 10% levels of significance. Thus, we found unidirectional causality running from LNRWG to LNCX. It also reveals unidirectional causality running from LNRWG to LNPX when one lag and five lags are applied at the 5% and 10% levels of significance.

The results in Table E3 indicate the existence of unidirectional causality running from LNMWI to LNCM when two and three lags are applied at the 10% level of significance. The results in Table E4 indicate the existence of unidirectional causality running from LNCX to LNMWI when nine lags are applied at the 10% level of significance.

The results in Table E5 indicate the existence of unidirectional causality running from LNURG to LNPM when one lag, two lags, and three lags are applied at the 5% and 10% levels of significance. It also reveals unidirectional causality running from LNCM to LNURG when one lag is applied at the 5% level of significance, and unidirectional causality running from LNURG to LNCM when four lags are applied at the 5% level of significance.

The results in Table E6 indicate the existence of unidirectional causality running from LNPX to LNURG when two lags are applied at the 5% level of significance. It also indicates the existence of unidirectional causality running from LNURG to LNPX when one lag, four lags, and five lags are applied at the 5% and 10% levels of significance. We also found unidirectional causality running from LNURG to LNCX when one lag and two lags are applied at the 5% and 10% levels of significance.

The results in Table E7 indicate the existence of unidirectional causality running from LNPM to LNUREG when one lag and two lags are applied at the 10% level of significance. It also reveals the existence of bidirectional causality running from LNCM to LNUREG when four lags are applied at the 10% level of significance.

The results in Table E8 indicate the existence of bidirectional causality running from LNPX to LNUREG when five lags are applied at the 5% level of significance.

5.4.5 Impulse response function

Finally, to scrutinize the behavior of each variable once confronted with an increase in a single specific variable, as well as the duration of its effect, the impulse response functions (IRFs) are exhibited. The impulse-response function curves simulated by the analytic method are shown in Figs. F1−F8. How a one-time positive shock of 1 standard deviation (SD) (±2 SE innovations) to the conventional trade and processing trade endures on the income in China is shown. We consider the response of four variables to 1 SD innovation of conventional trade and processing trade.

By observing Fig. F1, we find that the LNRWG increases quickly at the early time of the LNCM shock. When it arrives at 17, the LNRWG will be negative. By contrast, the LNRWG decreases quickly at the early time of the LNPM shock. When it arrives at 17, the LNRWG will be positive. From Fig. F2, following an exports by conventional trade shock (an innovation in LNCX), the ratio of total wages of employed persons to Gross Domestic Products variable (LNRWG) declines immediately (negative change rate). By contrast, following an exports by processing trade shock (an innovation in LNPX), the ratio of total wages of employed persons to Gross Domestic Products variable (LNRWG) increases immediately (positive change rate). Therefore, we should conclude that the effects of the trade policy shocks are transmitted through the mutual effects of the conventional trade channel and processing trade channel based on these results in this case. The increase of the LNRWG after the LNPM and LNPX shocks indicates possible evidence of a vertical specialization channel in China's trade policy transmission.

From Figs. F3 and F4, following a positive processing trade shock (an innovation in growth in LNPM and LNPX), the LNMWI increases after period 12 (positive change rates); hence, there is an increase in the index of the average money wage of the urban units of employment (MWI) in the long-term.

In Figs. F5 and F6, following an imports and exports by conventional trade shock (an innovation in LNCM and LNCX), the ratio of per capita annual disposable income of urban households to per capita annual net income of rural households variable (LNURG) increases immediately (positive change rate). By contrast, following an imports and exports by processing trade shock (an innovation in LNPM and LNPX), the ratio of per capita annual disposable income of urban households to per capita annual net income of rural households variable (LNURG) declines immediately (negative change rate). This suggests the existence of the vertical specialization channel in China's trade policy transmission; the narrowing of China's income gap between the urban rich and rural poor is caused by the increase in the processing trade, not by the increase in the conventional trade.

In Fig. F7, following an imports by conventional trade shock (an innovation in LNCM), the LNUREG variable increases immediately (positive change rate). By contrast, following an imports by processing trade shock (an innovation in LNPM), the LNUREG variable declines immediately (negative change rate). In Fig. F8, following a positive export by processing trade shock (an innovation in LNPX), the LNUREG declines in the long-term; thus, the declines in LNUREG could be caused by the increase in LNPX.

In sum, by computing the impulse responses functions in the VAR model, we can identify the existence of the vertical specialization channel and conventional trade channel in China's trade policy transmission process. Furthermore, we can conclude that the effects of trade policy shock on poverty reduction through vertical specialization and conventional trade channels are different when we use indicators under the *absolute* and *relative* definitions, respectively. The results support the argument that the trade policy does have impacts on the poverty reduction activities in the long-term, especially in an expansionary vertical special trade operation.

5.4.6   Variance decomposition

The variance decomposition functions are reported in Tables G1–G8.

In Table G1, LNRWG, LNCM, and LNPM are the contribution of the innovation to forecasting variance, respectively, which sum to 100. It can be seen from Table G1 that, at the end of the forecast period, LNPM explains approximately 25.68901% of the forecast error variance, supporting the evidence for the vertical specialization channel, which reflects that a positive trade policy of increasing import tax rebates of imported intermediate inputs for processing trade purposes has greater influences on the ratio of total wages of employed persons by registration status to Gross Domestic Products than a trade policy of increasing the imports by conventional trade does in China. In Table G2, LNPX contributes to the forecasted variance decomposition of LNRWG, which helps trace the effects of the vertical specialization channel.

The variance decompositions in Tables G3 and G4 show that imports and exports by processing trade contribute to the forecasted variance of LNMWI (1.306911 and 61.26843, respectively, at the end of the period), and this supports the effects of trade through the vertical specialization channel in China. Also, comparing the variance decompositions in Table G4, we find that LNPX provides more contributions to LNMWI than LNCX does.

The variance decompositions in Tables G5 and G6 show that imports and exports by processing trade contribute to the forecasted variance of LNURG (8.673855 and 30.02671, respectively, at period 32). This supports the effects of trade policy through the vertical specialization channel in China.

Moreover, the variance decomposition functions in Tables G7 and G8 show that LNPM and LNPX contribute much to the forecasted variance of LNUREG (3.181293 and 11.32686, respectively, at period 32), supporting the evidence for the vertical specialization channel.

In sum, the results of variance decompositions in Tables G1–G8 also support the existence of accelerating poverty reduction effects of vertical specialization trade policy because imports and exports by processing trade provide diverse contributions to the variance decomposition of LNRWG, LNMWI, LNURG, and LNUREG.

Given the effects of foreign trade and processing trade on the ratio of total wages of employed persons by registration status to Gross Domestic Products, index of average money wage of the urban units of employment, the ratio of per capita annual disposable income of urban households to per capita annual net income of rural households, and the difference between Engel's coefficient of rural households (%) and Engel's coefficient of urban households (%) implied by the aforementioned results, China's policy not only targets foreign trade openness but also aims to promote vertical specialization trade, thereby achieving acceleration of poverty reduction and sustainable growth.

5.5   Concluding remarks and policy implications

Given that poverty reduction involves absolute and relative poverty definition, it is important to break out aggregate results like these. The evidence generally suggests that vertical specialization participation can have a positive impact on poverty reduction in China. And there is also significant evidence that trade openness—including through imports and exports by processing trade—is associated with poverty reduction that tends to increase the ratio of total wages of employed persons to Gross Domestic Products and the index of average money wage of the urban units of employment. However, the ratio of per capita annual disposable income of urban households to per capita annual net income of rural households and the difference between Engel's coefficient of rural households and Engel's coefficient of urban households might narrow under pressures exerted by vertical specialization participation.

This chapter has found evidence regarding the income and poverty reduction effects of vertical specialization in China by focusing on econometric studies. Due to the relative importance of imports and exports by processing trade compared with conventional trade in China, it highlights the fact that the connection between wages and vertically specialized trade is likely to be complex and highly case-specific. Therefore, trade protectionism not only harms access to a broader and less costly variety of imported inputs but also thwarts income, undermining poverty reduction as a result. If the evidence from China is generalizable, then imports and exports by processing trade might accelerate poverty reduction under the absolute and relative definitions.

The Chinese case examined by this chapter highlights the importance of integrating into vertical specialization within a global production network as a determinant of increasing income and poverty reduction policies. For other developing countries interested in dealing with absolute and relative wages, inequality and the income gap between the urban rich and rural poor presence, and learning from China's experience, it will be important for future research to examine whether vertically specialized trade generally has these kinds of implications, or whether there is something special about the tax rebate policy of imported intermediate inputs for processing trade purposes that drives the results.

Furthermore, we found a strong positive link between income and processing trade in China that will contribute to increased income levels. All these results point to the importance for China to be able to integrate into vertical specialization. The Chinese case makes clear that maintaining open markets for intermediate inputs and final goods is crucial to accelerating poverty reduction. Therefore, policies in areas such as tax rebates for imported intermediates and relatively undistorted other incentives are important complements to openness in this regard.

Vertical specialization raises questions for trade policy in several ways. When accounting for the fact that wage and income can increase through imports of intermediate inputs from abroad, public policymakers cannot look at imports and exports by processing trade with the traditional mercantilist approach.

Thus, the empirical results of this study yield strong support for the hypothesis of a positive link between vertical specialization and income in China and emphasize the need to facilitate imports and exports of intermediate inputs.

Appendix A   Variables grouping

Table A1 **Variable grouping**

Group number	Variables	Sample range
1	LNRWG, LNCM, and LNPM	1981−2012
2	LNRWG, LNCX, and LNPX	1981−2012
3	LNMWI, LNCM, and LNPM	1981−2012
4	LNMWI, LNCX, and LNPX	1981−2012
5	LNURG, LNCM, and LNPM	1981−2012
6	LNURG, LNCX, and LNPX	1981−2012
7	LNUREG, LNCM, and LNPM	1981−2012
8	LNUREG, LNCX, and LNPX	1981−2012

Note: PM is indices of imports by processing trade, preceding year = 100; CM is indices of imports by conventional trade, preceding year = 100; PX is indices of exports by processing trade, preceding year = 100; CX is indices of exports by conventional trade, preceding year = 100; RWG indicates ratio of total wages of employed persons by registration status to Gross Domestic Products, or total wages of employed persons by registration status/Gross Domestic Products; MWI indicates index of average money wage of the urban units employment. Preceding year = 100; URG is the ratio of per capita annual disposable income of urban households to per capita annual net income of rural households, or indicates per capita annual disposable income of urban households/ per capita annual net income of rural households; Engel's coefficient of rural households (%) minus Engel's coefficient of urban households (%) is UREG.

Appendix B   The results of unit root tests

Table B1 **Augmented Dickey Fuller test of unit roots for all variables**

S\No.	Variables	Test type (C, T, P)	ADF test statistic	Order of integration
1	LNCM	(0,0,0)	0.192686	I(1)
2	D(LNCM)	(0,0,0)	−6.190714*	I(0)
3	LNPM	(0,0,0)	−0.233714	I(1)
4	D(LNPM)	(0,0,0)	−5.684092*	I(0)
7	LNCX	(0,0,0)	0.586035	I(1)
8	D(LNCX)	(0,0,0)	−8.757645*	I(0)
9	LNPX	(0,0,0)	−0.047070	I(1)
10	D(LNPX)	(0,0,0)	−9.234865*	I(0)
13	LNRWG	(0,0,0)	0.371444	I(1)
14	D(LNRWG)	(0,0,0)	−3.390663*	I(0)
15	LNMWI	(0,0,0)	0.309756	I(1)
16	D(LNMWI)	(0,0,0)	−5.691336*	I(0)
17	LNURG	(0,0,0)	0.889761	I(0)
18	D(LNURG)	(0,0,0)	−3.799002*	I(1)
19	LNUREG	(0,0,0)	−0.936238	I(0)
20	D(LNUREG)	(0,0,0)	−7.487101*	I(1)

Note: C, T, and P in test type stand for constant, trend, and lag orders, respectively. At three remarkable levels, when the ADF value is greater than the critical value, the corresponding series has a unit root. D stands for the first differential of the variables.
*denote the rejection of the null hypothesis of unit root at 1% significance level.

Appendix C   Results of cointegration tests

Table C1 Cointegration test result (series: LNRWG, LNCM, and LNPM)

Sample (adjusted): 1984−2012 Included observations: 29 after adjustments Trend assumption: linear deterministic trend Lags interval (in first differences): 1−2				
Unrestricted cointegration rank test (trace)				
Hypothesized number of CE(s)	**Eigenvalue**	**Trace statistic**	**0.05 Critical value**	**Probability[a]**
None[b] At most 1 At most 2	0.692203 0.292172 0.062665	46.06892 11.89781 1.876732	29.79707 15.49471 3.841466	0.0003 0.1619 0.1707
Trace test indicates 1 cointegrating equation at the 0.05 level				
Unrestricted cointegration rank test (maximum eigenvalue)				
Hypothesized number of CE(s)	**Eigenvalue**	**Max-eigen statistic**	**0.05 Critical value**	**Probability[a]**
None[b] At most 1 At most 2	0.692203 0.292172 0.062665	34.17111 10.02108 1.876732	21.13162 14.26460 3.841466	0.0004 0.2105 0.1707
Max-eigenvalue test indicates 1 cointegrating equation at the 0.05 level				
1 Cointegrating equation		**Log likelihood**		**112.1971**
Normalized cointegrating coefficients (standard error in parentheses)				
LNRWG 1.000000	**LNCM** 1.532159 (0.15880)	**LNPM** −0.716853 (0.16434)		

[a]MacKinnon−Haug−Michelis (1999) *P* values.
[b]Rejection of the hypothesis at the 0.05 level.

Table C2 Cointegration test result (series: LNRWG, LNCX, and LNPX)

Sample (adjusted): 1987−2012
Included observations: 26 after adjustments
Trend assumption: Linear deterministic trend
Lags interval (in first differences): 1−5

Unrestricted cointegration rank test (trace)

Hypothesized number of CE(s)	Eigenvalue	Trace statistic	0.05 Critical value	Probability[a]
None[b]	0.744418	51.65131	29.79707	0.0000
At most 1[b]	0.459352	16.18175	15.49471	0.0394
At most 2	0.007361	0.192090	3.841466	0.6612

Trace test indicates 2 cointegrating equations at the 0.05 level

Unrestricted cointegration rank test (maximum eigenvalue)

Hypothesized number of CE(s)	Eigenvalue	Max-eigen statistic	0.05 Critical value	Probability[a]
None[b]	0.744418	35.46956	21.13162	0.0003
At most 1[b]	0.459352	15.98966	14.26460	0.0264
At most 2	0.007361	0.192090	3.841466	0.6612

Max-eigenvalue test indicates 2 cointegrating equations at the 0.05 level

1 Cointegrating equation	Log likelihood	145.1494

Normalized cointegrating coefficients (standard error in parentheses)

LNRWG	LNCX	LNPX
1.000000	1.407763	−0.627587
	(0.21445)	(0.19178)

[a]MacKinnon−Haug−Michelis (1999) *P* values.
[b]Rejection of the hypothesis at the 0.05 level.

Table C3 Cointegration test result (series: LNMWI, LNCM, and LNPM)

Sample (adjusted): 1985–2012
Included observations: 28 after adjustments
Trend assumption: Linear deterministic trend
Lags interval (in first differences): 2–3

Unrestricted cointegration rank test (trace)

Hypothesized number of CE(s)	Eigenvalue	Trace statistic	0.05 Critical value	Probability[a]
None[b]	0.490564	33.56349	29.79707	0.0176
At most 1	0.315830	14.67886	15.49471	0.0661
At most 2[b]	0.134715	4.051485	3.841466	0.0441

Trace test indicates 1 cointegrating equation at the 0.05 level

Unrestricted cointegration rank test (maximum eigenvalue)

Hypothesized number of CE(s)	Eigenvalue	Max-eigen statistic	0.05 Critical value	Probability[a]
None	0.490564	18.88463	21.13162	0.1002
At most 1	0.315830	10.62737	14.26460	0.1739
At most 2[b]	0.134715	4.051485	3.841466	0.0441

Max-eigenvalue test indicates no cointegration at the 0.05 level

1 Cointegrating equation		Log likelihood	91.43503

Normalized cointegrating coefficients (standard error in parentheses)

LNMWI	LNCM	LNPM
1.000000	−0.810124	−1.403220
	(0.32330)	(0.46529)

[a]MacKinnon–Haug–Michelis (1999) P values.
[b]Rejection of the hypothesis at the 0.05 level.

Table C4 Cointegration test result (series: LNMWI, LNCX, and LNPX)

Sample (adjusted): 1986–2012
Included observations: 27 after adjustments
Trend assumption: Linear deterministic trend
Lags interval (in first differences): 1–4

Unrestricted cointegration rank test (trace)

Hypothesized number of CE(s)	Eigenvalue	Trace statistic	0.05 Critical value	Probability[a]
None[b]	0.616691	51.41170	29.79707	0.0001
At most 1[b]	0.597896	25.52101	15.49471	0.0011
At most 2	0.033601	0.922822	3.841466	0.3367

Trace test indicates 2 cointegrating equations at the 0.05 level

Unrestricted cointegration rank test (maximum eigenvalue)

Hypothesized number of CE(s)	Eigenvalue	Max-eigen statistic	0.05 Critical value	Probability[a]
None[b]	0.616691	25.89069	21.13162	0.0099
At most 1[b]	0.597896	24.59819	14.26460	0.0009
At most 2	0.033601	0.922822	3.841466	0.3367

Max-eigenvalue test indicates 2 cointegrating equations at the 0.05 level

1 Cointegrating equation(s)		Log likelihood	131.3797

Normalized cointegrating coefficients (standard error in parentheses)

LNMWI	LNCX	LNPX
1.000000	−0.016166	−0.099563
	(0.07131)	(0.06061)

[a]MacKinnon–Haug–Michelis (1999) *P* values.
[b]Rejection of the hypothesis at the 0.05 level.

Table C5 Cointegration test result (series: LNURG, LNCM, and LNPM)

Sample (adjusted): 1984−2012
Included observations: 29 after adjustments
Trend assumption: Linear deterministic trend
Lags interval (in first differences): 1−2

Unrestricted cointegration rank test (trace)

Hypothesized number of CE(s)	Eigenvalue	Trace statistic	0.05 Critical value	Probability[a]
None[b]	0.537839	37.13437	29.79707	0.0060
At most 1	0.327481	14.75095	15.49471	0.0645
At most 2	0.105892	3.245934	3.841466	0.0716

Trace test indicates 1 cointegrating equation at the 0.05 level

Unrestricted cointegration rank test (maximum eigenvalue)

Hypothesized number of CE(s)	Eigenvalue	Max-eigen statistic	0.05 Critical value	Probability[a]
None[b]	0.537839	22.38342	21.13162	0.0332
At most 1	0.327481	11.50501	14.26460	0.1307
At most 2	0.105892	3.245934	3.841466	0.0716

Max-eigenvalue test indicates 1 cointegrating equation at the 0.05 level

1 Cointegrating equation(s)		Log likelihood	93.57150

Normalized cointegrating coefficients (standard error in parentheses)

LNURG	LNCM	LNPM
1.000000	−1.299683	1.068640
	(0.31599)	(0.35094)

[a]MacKinnon−Haug−Michelis (1999) P values.
[b]Rejection of the hypothesis at the 0.05 level.

Table C6 Cointegration test result (series: LNURG, LNCX, and LNPX)

Sample (adjusted): 1984−2012
Included observations: 29 after adjustments
Trend assumption: linear deterministic trend
Lags interval (in first differences): 1−2

Unrestricted cointegration rank test (trace)

Hypothesized number of CE(s)	Eigenvalue	Trace statistic	0.05 Critical value	Probability[a]
None[b]	0.470864	35.06204	29.79707	0.0113
At most 1[b]	0.331937	16.60327	15.49471	0.0339
At most 2[b]	0.155620	4.905440	3.841466	0.0268

Trace test indicates 3 cointegrating equations at the 0.05 level

Unrestricted cointegration rank test (maximum eigenvalue)

Hypothesized number of CE(s)	Eigenvalue	Max-eigen statistic	0.05 Critical value	Probability[a]
None	0.470864	18.45877	21.13162	0.1136
At most 1	0.331937	11.69783	14.26460	0.1225
At most 2[b]	0.155620	4.905440	3.841466	0.0268

Max-eigenvalue test indicates no cointegration at the 0.05 level

1 Cointegrating equation	Log likelihood	118.0396

Normalized cointegrating coefficients (standard error in parentheses)

LNURG	LNCX	LNPX
1.000000	−1.547222	0.936869
	(0.22000)	(0.15643)

[a]MacKinnon−Haug−Michelis (1999) P values.
[b]Rejection of the hypothesis at the 0.05 level.

Table C7 Cointegration test result (series: LNUREG, LNCM, and LNPM)

Sample (adjusted): 1984−2012
Included observations: 29 after adjustments
Trend assumption: Linear deterministic trend
Lags interval (in first differences): 1−2

Unrestricted cointegration rank test (trace)

Hypothesized number of CE(s)	Eigenvalue	Trace statistic	0.05 Critical value	Probability[a]
None[b]	0.515548	41.37801	29.79707	0.0015
At most 1[b]	0.396501	20.36064	15.49471	0.0085
At most 2[b]	0.178876	5.715345	3.841466	0.0168

Trace test indicates 3 cointegrating equations at the 0.05 level

Unrestricted cointegration rank test (maximum eigenvalue)

Hypothesized number of CE(s)	Eigenvalue	Max-eigen statistic	0.05 Critical value	Probability[a]
None	0.515548	21.01736	21.13162	0.0519
At most 1[b]	0.396501	14.64530	14.26460	0.0435
At most 2[b]	0.178876	5.715345	3.841466	0.0168

Max-eigenvalue test indicates no cointegration at the 0.05 level

1 Cointegrating equation		Log likelihood	17.51068

Normalized cointegrating coefficients (standard error in parentheses)

LNUREG	LNCM	LNPM
1.000000	−7.208469	2.461847
	(1.63934)	(1.77051)

[a]MacKinnon−Haug−Michelis (1999) P values.
[b]Rejection of the hypothesis at the 0.05 level.

Table C8 Cointegration test result (series: LNUREG, LNCX, and LNPX)

Sample (adjusted): 1987–2012
Included observations: 26 after adjustments
Trend assumption: Linear deterministic trend
Lags interval (in first differences): 1–5

Unrestricted cointegration rank test (trace)

Hypothesized number of CE(s)	Eigenvalue	Trace statistic	0.05 Critical value	Probability[a]
None[b]	0.574680	34.31430	29.79707	0.0141
At most 1	0.371413	12.08653	15.49471	0.1528
At most 2	0.000586	0.015230	3.841466	0.9016

Trace test indicates 1 cointegrating equation at the 0.05 level

Unrestricted cointegration rank test (maximum eigenvalue)

Hypothesized number of CE(s)	Eigenvalue	Max-eigen statistic	0.05 Critical value	Probability[a]
None[b]	0.574680	22.22777	21.13162	0.0349
At most 1	0.371413	12.07130	14.26460	0.1080
At most 2	0.000586	0.015230	3.841466	0.9016

Max-eigenvalue test indicates 1 cointegrating equation at the 0.05 level

1 Cointegrating equation(s):	Log likelihood	66.26449

Normalized cointegrating coefficients (standard error in parentheses)

LNUREG	LNCX	LNPX
1.000000	0.983457	9.521662
	(1.74130)	(1.38545)

[a]MacKinnon–Haug–Michelis (1999) P values.
[b]Rejection of the hypothesis at the 0.05 level.

Appendix D   Results of vector error correction model

Table D1 Vector error correction estimates (series: LNRWG, LNCM, and LNPM)

Sample (adjusted): 1984–2012 Included observations: 29 after adjustments Standard errors in parentheses ( ) and t-statistics in brackets [ ]			
Cointegrating equation	**CointEq1**		
LNRWG(−1) LNCM(−1) LNPM(−1) C	1.000000 1.532159 (0.15880) [9.64857] −0.716853 (0.16434) [−4.36201] −1.794624		
Error correction	**D(LNRWG)**	**D(LNCM)**	**D(LNPM)**
CointEq1	0.123961 (0.05152) [2.40625]	−0.796707 (0.35860) [−2.22170]	0.516494 (0.23863) [2.16445]

Table D2 Vector error correction estimates (series: LNRWG, LNCX, and LNPX)

Sample (adjusted): 1987–2012 Included observations: 26 after adjustments Standard errors in parentheses ( ) and t-statistics in brackets [ ]			
Cointegrating equation	**CointEq1**		
LNRWG(−1) LNCX(−1) LNPX(−1) C	1.000000 1.407763 (0.21445) [6.56465] −0.627587 (0.19178) [−3.27248] −1.593921		
Error correction	**D(LNRWG)**	**D(LNCX)**	**D(LNPX)**
CointEq1	−0.220683 (0.14291) [−1.54418]	−1.704394 (0.79481) [−2.14441]	−0.897512 (0.50758) [−1.76821]

Table D3 Vector error correction estimates (series: LNMWI, LNCM, and LNPM)

Sample (adjusted): 1985–2012
Included observations: 28 after adjustments
Standard errors in parentheses ( ) and t-statistics in brackets [ ]

Cointegrating equation	CointEq1		
LNMWI(−1)	1.000000		
LNCM(−1)	−0.810124		
	(0.32330)		
	[−2.50579]		
LNPM(−1)	−1.403220		
	(0.46529)		
	[−3.01577]		
C	5.826925		
Error correction	**D(LNMWI)**	**D(LNCM)**	**D(LNPM)**
CointEq1	−0.045108	0.490942	0.326718
	(0.03848)	(0.15642)	(0.10969)
	[−1.17226]	[3.13855]	[2.97848]

Table D4 Vector error correction estimates (series: LNMWI, LNCX, and LNPX)

Sample (adjusted): 1986–2012
Included observations: 27 after adjustments
Standard errors in parentheses ( ) and t-statistics in brackets [ ]

Cointegrating equation	CointEq1		
LNMWI(−1)	1.000000		
LNCX(−1)	−0.016166		
	(0.07131)		
	[−0.22668]		
LNPX(−1)	−0.099563		
	(0.06061)		
	[−1.64277]		
C	−4.188740		
Error correction	**D(LNMWI)**	**D(LNCX)**	**D(LNPX)**
CointEq1	−0.944977	−1.576769	−0.906215
	(0.20966)	(1.58801)	(1.21205)
	[−4.50718]	[−0.99292]	[−0.74767]

Table D5 Vector error correction estimates (series: LNURG, LNCM, and LNPM)

Sample (adjusted): 1984–2012
Included observations: 29 after adjustments
Standard errors in parentheses ( ) and t-statistics in brackets [ ]

Cointegrating equation	CointEq1
LNURG(−1)	1.000000
LNCM(−1)	−1.299683
	(0.31599)
	[−4.11300]
LNPM(−1)	1.068640
	(0.35094)
	[3.04512]
C	0.075616

Error correction	D(LNURG)	D(LNCM)	D(LNPM)
CointEq1	−0.126207	0.178095	−0.431067
	(0.05536)	(0.27081)	(0.15079)
	[−2.27967]	[0.65765]	[−2.85877]

Table D6 Vector error correction estimates (series: LNURG, LNCX, and LNPX)

Sample (adjusted): 1984–2012
Included observations: 29 after adjustments
Standard errors in parentheses ( ) and t-statistics in brackets [ ]

Cointegrating equation	CointEq1
LNURG(−1)	1.000000
LNCX(−1)	−1.547222
	(0.22000)
	[−7.03295]
LNPX(−1)	0.936869
	(0.15643)
	[5.98919]
C	1.838115

Error correction	D(LNURG)	D(LNCX)	D(LNPX)
CointEq1	−0.207605	0.543941	−0.231962
	(0.09582)	(0.38566)	(0.32727)
	[−2.16654]	[1.41041]	[−0.70878]

Table D7 Vector error correction estimates (series: LNUREG, LNCM, and LNPM)

Sample (adjusted): 1984–2012
Included observations: 29 after adjustments
Standard errors in parentheses ( ) and t-statistics in brackets [ ]

Cointegrating equation	CointEq1		
LNUREG(−1)	1.000000		
LNCM(−1)	−7.208469		
	(1.63934)		
	[−4.39719]		
LNPM(−1)	2.461847		
	(1.77051)		
	[1.39047]		
C	20.86536		
Error correction	**D(LNUREG)**	**D(LNCM)**	**D(LNPM)**
CointEq1	−0.240222	0.076561	−0.068278
	(0.17998)	(0.04746)	(0.03211)
	[−1.33474]	[1.61325]	[−2.12606]

Table D8 Vector error correction estimates (series: LNUREG, LNCX, and LNPX)

Sample (adjusted): 1987–2012
Included observations: 26 after adjustments
Standard errors in parentheses ( ) and t-statistics in brackets [ ]

Cointegrating equation	CointEq1		
LNUREG(−1)	1.000000		
LNCX(−1)	0.983457		
	(1.74130)		
	[0.56478]		
LNPX(−1)	9.521662		
	(1.38545)		
	[6.87262]		
C	−52.26679		
Error correction	**D(LNUREG)**	**D(LNCX)**	**D(LNPX)**
CointEq1	−0.258603	−0.266926	−0.214089
	(0.35237)	(0.10273)	(0.07100)
	[−0.73389]	[−2.59825]	[−3.01553]

Appendix E   Results of Granger causality tests

Table E1 **Results of Granger causality tests (series: LNRWG, LNCM, and LNPM)**

Sample: 1981–2012			
Null hypothesis	**Observations**	**F-statistic**	**Probability**
Lags: 1			
LNCM does not cause LNRWG	31	6.76914	0.0147
LNRWG does not cause LNCM		5.67424	0.0242
LNPM does not cause LNRWG	31	0.11234	0.7400
LNRWG does not cause LNPM		5.94601	0.0213
Lags: 2			
LNCM does not cause LNRWG	30	4.21855	0.0264
LNRWG does not cause LNCM		4.32896	0.0243
LNPM does not cause LNRWG	30	0.40005	0.6745
LNRWG does not cause LNPM		1.59508	0.2229
Lags: 3			
LNCM does not cause LNRWG	29	3.27657	0.0402
LNRWG does not cause LNCM		2.18654	0.1183
LNPM does not cause LNRWG	29	0.89631	0.4587
LNRWG does not cause LNPM		1.37501	0.2765
Lags: 4			
LNCM does not cause LNRWG	28	2.49700	0.0772
LNRWG does not cause LNCM		1.47100	0.2502
LNPM does not cause LNRWG	28	0.39076	0.8126
LNRWG does not cause LNPM		2.08420	0.1230
Lags: 5			
LNCM does not cause LNRWG	27	1.72729	0.1855
LNRWG does not cause LNCM		2.78673	0.0538
LNPM does not cause LNRWG	27	0.69463	0.6350
LNRWG does not cause LNPM		2.64433	0.0631

Table E2 Results of Granger causality tests (series: LNRWG, LNCX, and LNPX)

Sample: 1981–2012			
Null hypothesis	**Observations**	**F-statistic**	**Probability**
Lags: 1			
LNCX does not cause LNRWG	31	0.03587	0.8511
LNRWG does not cause LNCX		5.63971	0.0246
LNPX does not cause LNRWG	31	0.22867	0.6362
LNRWG does not cause LNPX		7.35100	0.0113
Lags: 2			
LNCX does not cause LNRWG	30	0.24636	0.7835
LNRWG does not cause LNCX		3.10245	0.0626
LNPX does not cause LNRWG	30	0.78312	0.4679
LNRWG does not cause LNPX		1.56197	0.2295
Lags: 3			
LNCX does not cause LNRWG	29	0.67678	0.5755
LNRWG does not cause LNCX		1.11353	0.3649
LNPX does not cause LNRWG	29	1.25758	0.3132
LNRWG does not cause LNPX		1.21669	0.3271
Lags: 4			
LNCX does not cause LNRWG	28	0.65211	0.6324
LNRWG does not cause LNCX		1.24348	0.3262
LNPX does not cause LNRWG	28	0.72820	0.5837
LNRWG does not cause LNPX		1.30917	0.3022
Lags: 5			
LNCX does not cause LNRWG	27	1.62463	0.2102
LNRWG does not cause LNCX		0.99262	0.4529
LNPX does not cause LNRWG	27	0.76376	0.5890
LNRWG does not cause LNPX		2.30189	0.0934

Table E3 Results of Granger causality tests (series: LNMWI, LNCM, and LNPM)

Sample: 1981–2012			
Null hypothesis:	Observations	F-statistic	Probability
Lags: 1			
LNCM does not cause LNMWI	31	0.42096	0.5217
LNMWI does not cause LNCM		0.00065	0.9799
LNPM does not cause LNMWI	31	0.04400	0.8354
LNMWI does not cause LNPM		0.59061	0.4486
Lags: 2			
LNCM does not cause LNMWI	30	0.47089	0.6299
LNMWI does not cause LNCM		2.54109	0.0989
LNPM does not cause LNMWI	30	0.61971	0.5462
LNMWI does not cause LNPM		0.04202	0.9589
Lags: 3			
LNCM does not cause LNMWI	29	0.55367	0.6511
LNMWI does not cause LNCM		2.77543	0.0654
LNPM does not cause LNMWI	29	0.05252	0.9837
LNMWI does not cause LNPM		1.10487	0.3683

Table E4 Results of Granger causality tests (series: LNMWI, LNCX, and LNPX)

Sample: 1981−2012			
Null hypothesis	**Observations**	**F-statistic**	**Probability**
Lags: 1			
LNCX does not cause LNMWI	31	0.12836	0.7228
LNMWI does not cause LNCX		0.42367	0.5204
LNPX does not cause LNMWI	31	0.03335	0.8564
LNMWI does not cause LNPX		0.76979	0.3877
Lags: 2			
LNCX does not cause LNMWI	30	0.10845	0.8976
LNMWI does not cause LNCX		0.04594	0.9552
LNPX does not cause LNMWI	30	0.71685	0.4981
LNMWI does not cause LNPX		0.17344	0.8418
Lags: 3			
LNCX does not cause LNMWI	29	0.09974	0.9593
LNMWI does not cause LNCX		0.39198	0.7600
LNPX does not cause LNMWI	29	0.08752	0.9661
LNMWI does not cause LNPX		0.71000	0.5564
Lags: 4			
LNCX does not cause LNMWI	28	0.38691	0.8153
LNMWI does not cause LNCX		0.30463	0.8713
LNPX does not cause LNMWI	28	1.17747	0.3522
LNMWI does not cause LNPX		0.83184	0.5215
Lags: 9			
LNCX does not cause LNMWI	23	4.54772	0.0794
LNMWI does not cause LNCX		0.58888	0.7663
LNPX does not cause LNMWI	23	0.47613	0.8367
LNMWI does not cause LNPX		0.83851	0.6225

Table E5 **Results of Granger causality tests (series: LNURG, LNCM, and LNPM)**

Sample: 1981–2012			
Null hypothesis	Observations	F-statistic	Probability
Lags: 1			
LNCM does not cause LNURG	31	3.34422	0.0781
LNURG does not cause LNCM		1.00975	0.3236
LNPM does not cause LNURG	31	0.31866	0.5769
LNURG does not cause LNPM		4.68741	0.0391
Lags: 2			
LNCM does not cause LNURG	30	1.16680	0.3277
LNURG does not cause LNCM		0.96942	0.3931
LNPM does not cause LNURG	30	0.51767	0.6022
LNURG does not cause LNPM		3.91562	0.0332
Lags: 3			
LNCM does not cause LNURG	29	0.70456	0.5595
LNURG does not cause LNCM		0.46532	0.7094
LNPM does not cause LNURG	29	0.48277	0.6976
LNURG does not cause LNPM		2.48957	0.0869
Lags: 4			
LNCM does not cause LNURG	28	0.50630	0.7317
LNURG does not cause LNCM		3.06378	0.0418
LNPM does not cause LNURG	28	0.19894	0.9358
LNURG does not cause LNPM		1.87729	0.1560

Table E6 Results of Granger causality tests (series: LNURG, LNCX, and LNPX)

Sample: 1981–2012			
Null hypothesis	**Observations**	**F-statistic**	**Probability**
Lags: 1			
LNCX does not cause LNURG	31	0.15325	0.6984
LNURG does not cause LNCX		7.25206	0.0118
LNPX does not cause LNURG	31	0.05988	0.8085
LNURG does not cause LNPX		5.44290	0.0271
Lags: 2			
LNCX does not cause LNURG	30	0.27067	0.7651
LNURG does not cause LNCX		5.88768	0.0080
LNPX does not cause LNURG	30	5.04212	0.0145
LNURG does not cause LNPX		2.41490	0.1099
Lags: 3			
LNCX does not cause LNURG	29	0.13192	0.9400
LNURG does not cause LNCX		1.78978	0.1785
LNPX does not cause LNURG	29	2.30465	0.1048
LNURG does not cause LNPX		2.17811	0.1193
Lags: 4			
LNCX does not cause LNURG	28	0.28280	0.8855
LNURG does not cause LNCX		1.86632	0.1580
LNPX does not cause LNURG	28	1.59756	0.2158
LNURG does not cause LNPX		2.66451	0.0642
Lags: 5			
LNCX does not cause LNURG	27	0.30963	0.9000
LNURG does not cause LNCX		1.49783	0.2454
LNPX does not cause LNURG	27	1.48013	0.2508
LNURG does not cause LNPX		3.53825	0.0241

Table E7 **Results of Granger causality tests (series: LNUREG, LNCM, and LNPM)**

Sample: 1981–2012			
Null hypothesis	Observations	F-statistic	Probability
Lags: 1			
LNCM does not cause LNUREG	31	1.04547	0.3153
LNUREG does not cause LNCM		0.88326	0.3553
LNPM does not cause LNUREG	31	4.07827	0.0531
LNUREG does not cause LNPM		1.37453	0.2509
Lags: 2			
LNCM does not cause LNUREG	30	0.94484	0.4022
LNUREG does not cause LNCM		0.96777	0.3937
LNPM does not cause LNUREG	30	2.77493	0.0816
LNUREG does not cause LNPM		1.58484	0.2249
Lags: 3			
LNCM does not cause LNUREG	29	0.79175	0.5115
LNUREG does not cause LNCM		2.28248	0.1072
LNPM does not cause LNUREG	29	1.17627	0.3414
LNUREG does not cause LNPM		1.35745	0.2817
Lags: 4			
LNCM does not cause LNUREG	28	2.27310	0.0992
LNUREG does not cause LNCM		2.31206	0.0950
LNPM does not cause LNUREG	28	0.76932	0.5584
LNUREG does not cause LNPM		1.55968	0.2256
Lags: 5			
LNCM does not cause LNUREG	27	3.14050	0.0366
LNUREG does not cause LNCM		1.81903	0.1659
LNPM does not cause LNUREG	27	0.71844	0.6190
LNUREG does not cause LNPM		2.11444	0.1165

Table E8 Results of Granger causality tests (series: LNUREG, LNCX, and LNPX)

Sample: 1981–2012			
Null hypothesis	**Observations**	**F-statistic**	**Probability**
Lags: 1			
LNCX does not cause LNUREG	31	0.07432	0.7872
LNUREG does not cause LNCX		1.57716	0.2195
LNPX does not cause LNUREG	31	1.95918	0.1726
LNUREG does not cause LNPX		1.83532	0.1863
Lags: 2			
LNCX does not cause LNUREG	30	0.01741	0.9828
LNUREG does not cause LNCX		1.46888	0.2494
LNPX does not cause LNUREG	30	1.88810	0.1723
LNUREG does not cause LNPX		0.26553	0.7689
Lags: 3			
LNCX does not cause LNUREG	29	0.16643	0.9179
LNUREG does not cause LNCX		0.46444	0.7100
LNPX does not cause LNUREG	29	0.99279	0.4145
LNUREG does not cause LNPX		1.11030	0.3662
Lags: 4			
LNCX does not cause LNUREG	28	0.16060	0.9557
LNUREG does not cause LNCX		0.58750	0.6756
LNPX does not cause LNUREG	28	1.10124	0.3846
LNUREG does not cause LNPX		1.04154	0.4119
Lags: 5			
LNCX does not cause LNUREG	27	0.49291	0.7769
LNUREG does not cause LNCX		0.43537	0.8174
LNPX does not cause LNUREG	27	3.16457	0.0356
LNUREG does not cause LNPX		3.04854	0.0404

Appendix F   Impulse response function

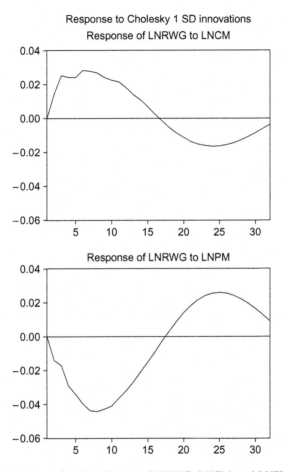

Figure F1 Impulse response function (between LNRWG, LNCM, and LNPM).

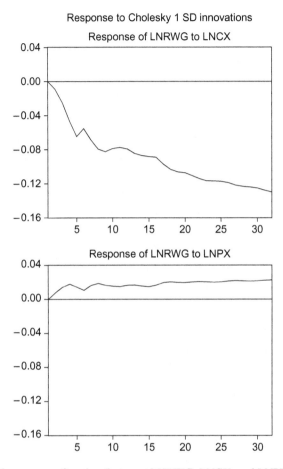

Figure F2 Impulse response function (between LNRWG, LNCX, and LNPX).

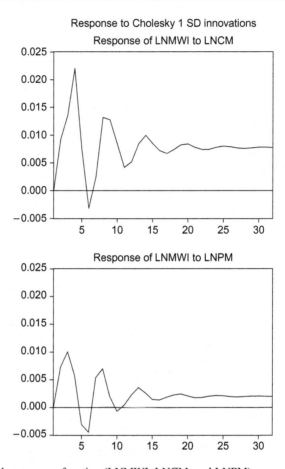

Figure F3 Impulse response function (LNMWI, LNCM, and LNPM).

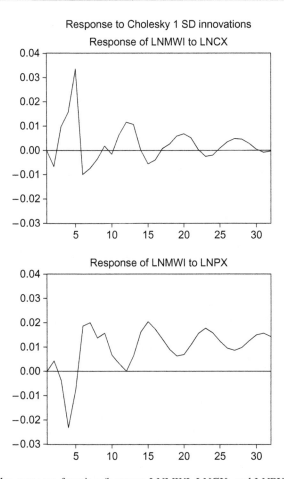

Figure F4 Impulse response function (between LNMWI, LNCX, and LNPX).

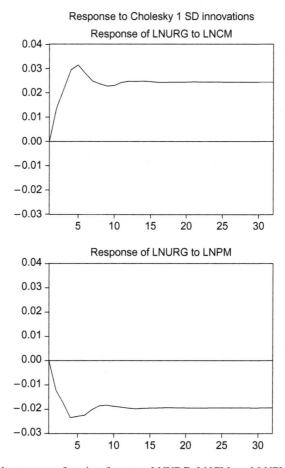

Figure F5 Impulse response function (between LNURG, LNCM, and LNPM).

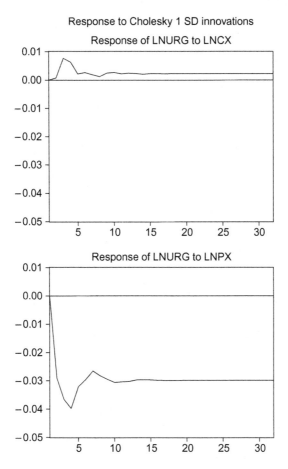

Figure F6 Impulse response function (between LNURG, LNCX, and LNPX).

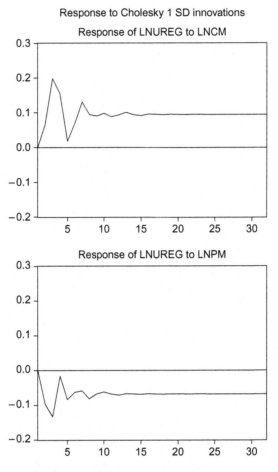

Figure F7 Impulse response function (between LNUREG, LNCM, and LNPM).

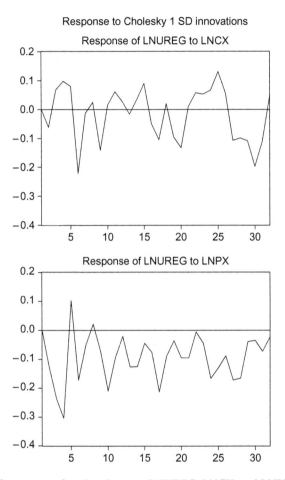

Figure F8 Impulse response function (between LNUREG, LNCX, and LNPX).

Appendix G   Results of variance decomposition

Table   G1 Decomposition   of   LNRWG   (Cholesky   ordering:
LNRWG, LNCM, and LNPM)

Period	SE	LNRWG	LNCM	LNPM
1	0.030177	100.0000	0.000000	0.000000
2	0.047735	82.24825	9.065477	8.686271
3	0.072546	74.61842	15.99200	9.389579
4	0.100167	72.29786	14.22992	13.47222
5	0.124760	70.86821	12.91516	16.21663
6	0.149195	68.89586	12.64351	18.46063
7	0.172181	67.57549	12.11072	20.31379
8	0.191697	66.54358	11.73387	21.72255
9	0.207681	65.89415	11.34912	22.75672
10	0.220652	65.28182	11.09679	23.62139
11	0.230203	64.71151	11.07544	24.21305
12	0.236961	64.26393	11.04293	24.69315
13	0.241210	63.93120	10.98811	25.08069
14	0.243448	63.64690	10.98818	25.36492
15	0.244382	63.46260	10.98228	25.55512
16	0.244591	63.37703	10.97271	25.65026
17	0.244688	63.38978	10.96871	25.64151
18	0.245205	63.47616	10.97346	25.55037
19	0.246539	63.61584	10.98027	25.40389
20	0.248903	63.77840	10.98028	25.24132
21	0.252259	63.91555	10.98827	25.09618
22	0.256459	64.02128	10.98428	24.99444
23	0.261194	64.08105	10.96697	24.95198
24	0.266082	64.08327	10.95438	24.96234
25	0.270819	64.04207	10.93829	25.01964
26	0.275097	63.96719	10.92120	25.11161
27	0.278695	63.86827	10.90886	25.22287
28	0.281522	63.76166	10.89603	25.34231
29	0.283547	63.65654	10.88577	25.45769
30	0.284835	63.56348	10.87837	25.55815
31	0.285528	63.49122	10.87164	25.63714
32	0.285800	63.44380	10.86719	25.68901

Table G2 Decomposition of LNRWG (Cholesky Ordering: LNRWG, LNCX, and LNPX)

Period	SE	LNRWG	LNCX	LNPX
1	0.033677	100.0000	0.000000	0.000000
2	0.051669	94.80424	3.041155	2.154601
3	0.077731	84.27551	11.46180	4.262695
4	0.112319	72.83736	22.56285	4.599788
5	0.165124	71.41257	25.72587	2.861557
6	0.207160	74.46113	23.46336	2.075514
7	0.247834	74.05891	24.04986	1.891235
8	0.288795	72.90947	25.27505	1.815474
9	0.329921	72.72616	25.63146	1.642383
10	0.366929	73.15893	25.33913	1.501937
11	0.403271	73.94267	24.67722	1.380109
12	0.436451	74.30952	24.36997	1.320514
13	0.470050	74.48206	24.25381	1.264128
14	0.504076	74.73287	24.07405	1.193079
15	0.539370	75.17618	23.70751	1.116315
16	0.573480	75.54307	23.38604	1.070889
17	0.608452	75.62027	23.32335	1.056373
18	0.644495	75.59993	23.35629	1.043788
19	0.681688	75.67022	23.31203	1.017748
20	0.718485	75.79443	23.21389	0.991682
21	0.755235	75.87586	23.15336	0.970778
22	0.791517	75.88770	23.15823	0.954063
23	0.827893	75.91005	23.15611	0.933837
24	0.863749	75.98459	23.10322	0.912185
25	0.899047	76.07919	23.02687	0.893939
26	0.933531	76.13926	22.97855	0.882195
27	0.967913	76.16837	22.95931	0.872315
28	1.002169	76.21015	22.92955	0.860300
29	1.036278	76.27543	22.87767	0.846897
30	1.069947	76.33475	22.82961	0.835642
31	1.103450	76.36940	22.80378	0.826815
32	1.136800	76.39113	22.79001	0.818854

Table G3 Decomposition of LNMWI (Cholesky Ordering: LNMWI, LNCM, and LNPM)

Period	SE	LNMWI	LNCM	LNPM
1	0.044720	100.0000	0.000000	0.000000
2	0.065639	96.78844	1.989955	1.221609
3	0.075894	92.64539	4.690028	2.664582
4	0.081209	85.71450	11.45746	2.828037
5	0.084136	85.77483	11.45835	2.766819
6	0.088163	86.65657	10.56507	2.778360
7	0.094757	88.06410	9.212196	2.723705
8	0.101042	87.32558	9.804490	2.869932
9	0.105416	86.85396	10.47429	2.671749
10	0.108377	86.93876	10.52949	2.531748
11	0.111480	87.51501	10.09096	2.394032
12	0.115174	88.06415	9.655476	2.280379
13	0.119406	88.30394	9.484516	2.211542
14	0.123170	88.30762	9.568270	2.124110
15	0.126315	88.41787	9.549328	2.032807
16	0.129231	88.61228	9.434780	1.952942
17	0.132320	88.86237	9.255538	1.882090
18	0.135546	89.06138	9.117726	1.820898
19	0.138743	89.17443	9.056812	1.768755
20	0.141713	89.24907	9.033832	1.717098
21	0.144512	89.35463	8.979496	1.665872
22	0.147275	89.48228	8.899054	1.618670
23	0.150077	89.60714	8.815817	1.577045
24	0.152869	89.70267	8.757399	1.539927
25	0.155590	89.77527	8.719679	1.505053
26	0.158213	89.84557	8.683563	1.470868
27	0.160777	89.92478	8.636990	1.438227
28	0.163322	90.00423	8.587499	1.408276
29	0.165855	90.07539	8.543704	1.380903
30	0.168352	90.13590	8.508906	1.355193
31	0.170798	90.19121	8.478230	1.330556
32	0.173196	90.24637	8.446718	1.306911

Table   G4 **Decomposition   of   LNMWI   (Cholesky   Ordering: LNMWI, LNCX, and LNPX)**

Period	SE	LNMWI	LNCX	LNPX
1	0.023263	100.0000	0.000000	0.000000
2	0.028174	91.97133	5.676798	2.351875
3	0.030236	81.00937	15.39300	3.597622
4	0.042783	47.79732	21.17784	31.02484
5	0.054971	29.19884	50.13862	20.66254
6	0.059020	25.74736	46.35434	27.89830
7	0.062769	22.77272	42.39442	34.83286
8	0.064505	21.99974	40.46155	37.53871
9	0.067238	22.68934	37.31341	39.99725
10	0.067864	23.05405	36.68036	40.26559
11	0.068235	22.80911	37.14313	40.04776
12	0.069359	22.48485	38.75509	38.76007
13	0.070534	21.89132	39.77050	38.33817
14	0.072389	20.79692	37.75829	41.44479
15	0.075447	19.20749	35.31496	45.47755
16	0.077617	18.41107	33.63899	47.94994
17	0.078921	18.29896	32.54690	49.15414
18	0.079537	18.17665	32.15237	49.67098
19	0.080005	17.96470	32.31533	49.71997
20	0.080631	17.77036	32.53399	49.69566
21	0.081567	17.41031	32.19242	50.39727
22	0.083054	16.79258	31.05187	52.15555
23	0.084996	16.10303	29.73827	54.15870
24	0.086546	15.68167	28.73656	55.58177
25	0.087500	15.48666	28.12652	56.38681
26	0.088109	15.31666	27.89673	56.78661
27	0.088667	15.12476	27.84961	57.02563
28	0.089341	14.91196	27.70104	57.38701
29	0.090270	14.61099	27.23807	58.15094
30	0.091515	14.22278	26.50436	59.27286
31	0.092880	13.85918	25.73982	60.40100
32	0.094012	13.60651	25.12506	61.26843

Table G5 **Decomposition of LNURG (Cholesky Ordering: LNURG, LNCM, and LNPM)**

Period	SE	LNURG	LNCM	LNPM
1	0.042807	100.0000	0.000000	0.000000
2	0.073114	97.40899	1.198551	1.392460
3	0.094249	95.37948	2.085237	2.535286
4	0.107948	93.86114	1.737124	4.401732
5	0.116929	92.37908	1.482878	6.138040
6	0.122993	91.58097	1.341801	7.077230
7	0.127534	91.19603	1.248569	7.555398
8	0.131190	90.98868	1.181835	7.829482
9	0.134191	90.87056	1.135735	7.993707
10	0.136653	90.78272	1.101317	8.115960
11	0.138652	90.70226	1.073848	8.223894
12	0.140261	90.63243	1.052245	8.315320
13	0.141554	90.57599	1.035144	8.388861
14	0.142599	90.53146	1.021531	8.447009
15	0.143447	90.49689	1.010744	8.492362
16	0.144137	90.46995	1.002157	8.527891
17	0.144700	90.44846	0.995262	8.556276
18	0.145159	90.43106	0.989701	8.579238
19	0.145534	90.41691	0.985202	8.597889
20	0.145840	90.40538	0.981552	8.613065
21	0.146089	90.39601	0.978587	8.625404
22	0.146293	90.38839	0.976177	8.635429
23	0.146460	90.38221	0.974215	8.643578
24	0.146596	90.37717	0.972618	8.650212
25	0.146707	90.37307	0.971315	8.655620
26	0.146798	90.36972	0.970253	8.660031
27	0.146872	90.36698	0.969386	8.663633
28	0.146933	90.36475	0.968678	8.666574
29	0.146983	90.36292	0.968099	8.668977
30	0.147024	90.36143	0.967627	8.670940
31	0.147057	90.36022	0.967241	8.672544
32	0.147084	90.35922	0.966925	8.673855

Table G6 Decomposition of LNURG (Cholesky Ordering: LNURG, LNCX, and LNPX)

Period	SE	LNURG	LNCX	LNPX
1	0.035870	100.0000	0.000000	0.000000
2	0.067200	81.26237	0.012034	18.72559
3	0.095625	75.49548	0.643761	23.86076
4	0.116183	71.41499	0.729058	27.85595
5	0.128938	70.57546	0.620756	28.80379
6	0.138542	69.92710	0.574157	29.49875
7	0.147484	70.21491	0.523047	29.26204
8	0.156447	70.27225	0.470932	29.25682
9	0.165596	70.27772	0.442567	29.27972
10	0.174634	70.18960	0.421570	29.38883
11	0.183075	70.11355	0.397998	29.48845
12	0.190958	70.01062	0.381888	29.60749
13	0.198448	69.98058	0.367275	29.65215
14	0.205628	69.95513	0.352269	29.69261
15	0.212600	69.93238	0.340667	29.72695
16	0.219406	69.91203	0.330825	29.75715
17	0.226013	69.89212	0.321386	29.78649
18	0.232427	69.86764	0.313493	29.81887
19	0.238663	69.84971	0.306459	29.84383
20	0.244730	69.83392	0.299743	29.86634
21	0.250648	69.81928	0.293813	29.88691
22	0.256434	69.80675	0.288472	29.90478
23	0.262094	69.79536	0.283468	29.92118
24	0.267635	69.78400	0.278943	29.93706
25	0.273064	69.77387	0.274803	29.95133
26	0.278387	69.76454	0.270921	29.96454
27	0.283608	69.75575	0.267341	29.97691
28	0.288736	69.74772	0.264026	29.98826
29	0.293774	69.74029	0.260915	29.99879
30	0.298727	69.73324	0.258018	30.00874
31	0.303599	69.72667	0.255311	30.01801
32	0.308395	69.72053	0.252763	30.02671

Table G7 Decomposition of LNUREG (Cholesky Ordering: LNUREG, LNCM, and LNPM)

Period	SE	LNUREG	LNCM	LNPM
1	0.727778	100.0000	0.000000	0.000000
2	0.800565	97.83086	0.693290	1.475849
3	0.909047	91.45241	5.278309	3.269284
4	0.992673	90.37744	6.853102	2.769459
5	1.036763	90.49630	6.315400	3.188296
6	1.110786	91.00834	5.895905	3.095757
7	1.186239	90.65318	6.390358	2.956458
8	1.243111	90.47539	6.403504	3.121107
9	1.294121	90.44988	6.399027	3.151091
10	1.349925	90.47767	6.415821	3.106505
11	1.402293	90.54148	6.345187	3.113336
12	1.451474	90.51855	6.338431	3.143019
13	1.501030	90.48317	6.381448	3.135380
14	1.547435	90.48397	6.375930	3.140096
15	1.592146	90.49236	6.355467	3.152176
16	1.636824	90.49179	6.359019	3.149193
17	1.680026	90.48806	6.359889	3.152049
18	1.721702	90.48559	6.355518	3.158895
19	1.762677	90.48313	6.356666	3.160206
20	1.802761	90.48311	6.355222	3.161672
21	1.841823	90.48308	6.351837	3.165087
22	1.880177	90.48132	6.351664	3.167021
23	1.917780	90.48003	6.351453	3.168521
24	1.954576	90.47946	6.349787	3.170748
25	1.990731	90.47874	6.348860	3.172400
26	2.026268	90.47798	6.348304	3.173716
27	2.061159	90.47734	6.347349	3.175313
28	2.095474	90.47665	6.346632	3.176715
29	2.129248	90.47603	6.346081	3.177892
30	2.162485	90.47552	6.345361	3.179117
31	2.195219	90.47500	6.344730	3.180268
32	2.227478	90.47448	6.344227	3.181293

Table G8 **Decomposition of LNUREG (Cholesky ordering: LNUREG, LNCX, and LNPX)**

Period	SE	LNUREG	LNCX	LNPX
1	0.528413	100.0000	0.000000	0.000000
2	0.717326	96.03396	0.738957	3.227078
3	0.877755	89.49837	1.088431	9.413204
4	1.054414	83.54841	1.610147	14.84144
5	1.089221	83.15992	2.049629	14.79045
6	1.161744	79.35548	5.424029	15.22049
7	1.176820	79.67441	5.298769	15.02682
8	1.199754	80.37042	5.140453	14.48913
9	1.251848	80.36101	5.980658	13.65833
10	1.312707	79.56666	5.451255	14.98209
11	1.369858	80.57159	5.203309	14.22510
12	1.427800	82.05861	4.826522	13.11486
13	1.474913	82.43637	4.535555	13.02807
14	1.523950	82.80998	4.297788	12.89223
15	1.560393	83.19294	4.428141	12.37891
16	1.594004	83.57053	4.338968	12.09050
17	1.640180	82.39162	4.503896	13.10449
18	1.658813	82.48280	4.417380	13.09982
19	1.684348	82.64523	4.603206	12.75157
20	1.712464	82.29952	5.052372	12.64811
21	1.738367	82.52035	4.906151	12.57350
22	1.778907	83.20315	4.788849	12.00800
23	1.826705	83.92630	4.624322	11.44937
24	1.887092	84.03924	4.455687	11.50507
25	1.943845	84.05180	4.653128	11.29508
26	1.979622	84.34332	4.565612	11.09107
27	2.011632	83.82189	4.703705	11.47441
28	2.030155	83.20979	4.855038	11.93517
29	2.038824	83.03181	5.097403	11.87079
30	2.056681	82.37527	5.930369	11.69436
31	2.073216	82.24265	6.124607	11.63274
32	2.102194	82.66822	6.004921	11.32686

Vertical specialization and lowering environmental damage: comparing impacts of conventional trade and processing trade patterns on energy consumption in China

6

6.1 Introduction

The increase of vertical specialization in a variety of industries has been a salient feature of the Chinese economy during the past decades. Vertical specialization is characterized by a fragmentation of production and assembly processes across customs borders. China's Customs Statistics (CCS) distinguishes between imports and exports linked to conventional trade and processing trade. Imports and exports by processing trade do rely on a production network in which parts and components move across customs borders multiple times during the process of assembly and production. This fragmentation of production and expansion of imports and exports by processing trade in China has had a marked effect on energy consumption. The types of trade patterns as well as where these trade patterns are placed are shifting at an ever-increasing rate. The expansion of vertical specialization trade has occurred at the same time as a massive shift in the size and composition of Chinese energy consumption. Following the adoption of an open-door policy in 1978 and the entry into the WTO in 2001, creating a shock with imports and exports by processing trade on a scale unlike anything experienced before, the Chinese economy is increasing its role in global trade of intermediate goods, which is a widely used indication of vertical specialization participation.

Increasing participation in vertical specialization has benefits for lowering environment damage in China. Vertical specialization—linked transactions and FDI (foreign direct investment) typically come with quality control systems and prevailing global environmental standards that can exceed those in conventional trade.

Imports and exports by processing trade can achieve greater success in lowering environmental damage by combing domestic and foreign intermediate inputs and creating opportunities for fast technological learning and skill acquisition that leverage energy consumption in China. The success of vertical specialization in lowering environmental damage, especially compared with conventional trade, relies heavily on these interlinkages with more efficient geographical allocation of industrial activities and increased the availability of a variety of energy-saving intermediate goods in the developed world.

The purpose of this chapter is to provide econometric evidence for the links between vertical specialization and energy consumption while focusing on China to investigate four questions concerning lowering the environmental damage impacts of vertical specialization in the Chinese economy:

1. Are the imports and exports by conventional trade associated with stronger total energy consumption compared with processing trade?
2. Are the imports and exports by conventional trade associated with stronger relative demand for coal consumption compared with processing trade?
3. Are the imports and exports by conventional trade associated with stronger relative demand for petroleum consumption compared with processing trade?
4. Are the imports and exports by conventional trade associated with stronger relative demand for natural gas consumption compared with processing trade?
5. Are the imports and exports by conventional trade associated with the higher hydro power, nuclear power, and other power consumption compared with processing trade?

6.2   International trade and energy consumption

The increase of energy consumption is a major threat to the environment of China. The expansion in foreign trade poses questions about its impact on pollution. The rapid economic growth and expansion of the process of integrating into globalization of China compel intensive use of energy, resulting in more residue and waste being released in nature that could lead to environmental degradation. It is implied that the benefits of achieving energy consumption efficiency are limited to lowering environmental damage, but there are benefits to inclusive growth in China. Energy consumption efficiency refers to achieving value for the existing energy consumption. The benefits of promoting energy consumption efficiency include reduction in greenhouse gas emissions, environmental sustainability, and sustainable economic development (Adom, 2015). The energy intensity has been used as a proxy measure for energy efficiency. Most of the previous studies utilized CO_2 emission as an indicator of the environmental damage (Al-Mulali and Ozturk, 2015). Moreover, the most common macroeconomic variables that are used as the main factors of the environmental damage are GDP growth, energy consumption, trade openness, foreign direct investment, financial development, and urbanization (Al-Mulali and Ozturk, 2015).

The literature on the relationship between trade, energy consumption, and carbon emissions, which are considered a proxy variable for environmental quality (Soytas et al., 2007), mainly focuses on the testing of the existence of the causal relationships between trade growth and energy consumption. More trade involving goods necessitates more energy to produce and transport these goods from one country to another. The use of more energy implies more production of goods, and the excess of production in some countries is exported to importing countries (Ben Jebli and

Ben Youssef, 2015). It was found that trade openness has positive short-term and long-term impacts on CO_2 in newly industrialized countries (Hossain, 2011). Sadorsky (2011) found a Granger causality running from exports to energy consumption and a bidirectional causality between imports and energy consumption in the short-term by using panel cointegration techniques for eight Middle Eastern countries. In another work using a sample of seven South American countries, Sadorsky (2012) concluded that environmental policies made to reduce energy consumption will reduce trade. Erkan et al. (2010) showed cointegration between exports and energy use in Turkey, whereas energy use for exports involves a Granger causality. Similarly, in Malaysia, exports and energy generation do not seem to involve Granger causalties (Lean and Smyth 2010a,b; Shahbaz et al., 2013). According to the studies by Fisher-Vanden et al. (2004), Cole (2006), and Shen (2007), trade openness promotes energy efficiency in China. Shen (2007) argues that the declining positive role of foreign trade is due to the changing composition of foreign trade. In addition, exports are deemed important factors that increased pollution levels in China (Michieka et al., 2013). Andersson et al. (2009) showed that foreign trade plays an important role in determining the level of CO_2 in the transport sector and greater emissions are attributed to exports than to imports of China.

6.3 Empirical evidence of the impact of vertical specialization trade policy on energy consumption

6.3.1 Methodology and data

Variables groups are tested with different diagnostics to perform time series analyses. First, the order of integration in the data is tested by using the augmented Dicky Fuller (ADF) unit root test; if the unit root is present, then stationarity is achieved by the first difference of the data. Having established the order of integration, it next tests for cointegration by applying the Johansen cointegration method. Then, a vector error correction model (VECM) is used to assess the short-term relationship between the variables. Finally, the results are verified through impulse response functions and variance decomposition.

It attempts to trace the long-term equilibrium relationship as well as the short-term relationship among imports by conventional trade (CM), imports by processing trade (PM), exports by conventional trade (CX), exports by processing trade (PX), total energy consumption (TEC), coal consumption (CEC), petroleum consumption (PEC), natural gas consumption (NEC), hydro power, nuclear power, and other power consumption (HEC) using the time series framework. All these variables are used and transformed into natural logarithm form. All data have been obtained from the database of China Statistical Yearbook, China Trade and External Economic Statistical Yearbook, and China Energy Statistical Yearbook published by National Bureau of Statistics of China; the sample covers annual observations from 1981 to 2012. This study used the variables groups in Table A1 to find the relationship.

LN CM = natural logarithm of imports by conventional trade (CM),
LN PM = natural logarithm of imports by processing trade (PM),
LN PX = natural logarithm of exports by processing trade (PX),
LN CX = natural logarithm of exports by conventional trade (CX),
LNTEC = natural logarithm of total energy consumption (TEC),
LNCEC = natural logarithm of coal consumption (CEC),
LNPEC = natural logarithm of petroleum consumption (PEC),
LNNEC = natural logarithm of natural gas consumption (NEC),
LNHEC = natural logarithm of hydro power, nuclear power, and other power consumption (HEC).

6.3.2   Unit root test for stationarity

The augmented Dickey Fuller (ADF) test for unit roots was conducted for all time series used for the study. Table A1 shows the result of unit root tests by using the ADF unit root test at the first difference level. The null hypothesis of nonstationary is performed at the 1%, 5%, and 10% significance levels. In Table B1, the results of the ADF test illustrate that all the nonstationarity data series are performed at the 1%, 5%, or 10% significance levels. The ADF results show that all variable series were integrated with series of order I (1).

6.3.3   Results of Johansen's cointegration tests

Cointegration means economic variables share the same stochastic trend, so they are combined together in the long-term. Even if they deviate from each other in the short-term, they tend to return to the trend in the long-term. A necessary condition for the cointegration test is that all the variables should be integrated at the same order or should contain a deterministic trend (Engle and Granger, 1991). The unit root test results show that all the time series of imports by conventional trade, imports by processing trade, exports by conventional trade, exports by processing trade, total energy consumption, coal consumption, petroleum consumption, natural gas consumption, hydro power, nuclear power, and other power consumption are integrated at the first difference but are not integrated in level form during 1981 to 2012. Therefore, the time series in this period are valid in the cointegration test. Once the variables are cointegrated, the short-term changes can be explained through the vector error correction model (Engle and Granger, 1987). Following the cointegration test, the VECM was used to analyze the causality within the 10 variable groups.

Results of trace statistics and the results of maximum Eigen (max-Eigen) statistics are shown in Tables C1−C10. Trace statistics and maximum Eigen statistics values help to find the rank(s), which shows the number of vector(s) containing long-term relations. It is evident that the null hypothesis of no rank is rejected. Therefore, the results of both trace and max-Eigen statistics confirm that cointegration vectors exist in the model. This means that the long-term relationship prevails among the variables. In summary, the Johansen cointegration test results show that the 10 variable groups in Table A1 are cointegrated and have a long-term equilibrium relationship during 1981 to 2012.

To distinguish the importance of vertical specialization trade for lowering environmental damage, we compare the effects of imports and exports by conventional trade and of imports and exports by processing trade, on total energy consumption (TEC), coal consumption (CEC), petroleum consumption (PEC), natural gas consumption (NEC), hydro power, nuclear power, and other power consumption (HEC) based on coal equivalent calculations.

Following Johansen's technique, the normalized long-term cointegration relationships and the comparison coefficients are shown in Tables C1−C10. The normalized long-term cointegration relationships are very revealing. The observed signs are as anticipated. Moreover, the long-term relationships are also as expected, given the intrinsic interdependence between the variables.

1. Total energy consumption, imports and exports by conventional trade, and imports and exports by processing trade:

$$LNTEC = \underset{(0.10025)}{0.226749LNCM} - \underset{(0.07126)}{0.023184LNPM} \tag{6.1}$$

$$LNTEC = \underset{(0.02784)}{0.34258LNCX} + \underset{(0.01819)}{0.074873LNPX} \tag{6.2}$$

We can see from the results of Eqs. (6.1) and (6.2) that the 1% increase in imports by conventional trade (LNCM) will have a positive impact of 0.226749% on total energy consumption (LNTEC), the 1% increase in imports by processing trade (LNPM) will have a negative impact of 0.023184% on total energy consumption (LNTEC), the 1% increase in exports by conventional trade (LNCX) will have a positive impact of 0.34258% on total energy consumption (LNTEC), and the 1% increase in exports by processing trade (LNPX) will have a positive impact of 0.074873% on total energy consumption (LNTEC).

2. Coal consumption, imports and exports by conventional trade, and imports and exports by processing trade:

$$LNCEC = \underset{(0.01942)}{0.2142LNCM} + \underset{(0.01352)}{0.102244LNPM} \tag{6.3}$$

$$LNCEC = \underset{(1.63052)}{7.063753LNCX} - \underset{(1.63938)}{6.248154LNPX} \tag{6.4}$$

We can see from the results of Eqs. (6.3) and (6.4) that the 1% increase in imports by conventional trade (LNCM) will have a positive impact of 0.2142% on coal consumption (LNCEC), the 1% increase in imports by processing trade (LNPM) will have a positive impact of 0.102244% on coal consumption (LNCEC), the 1% increase in exports by conventional trade (LNCX) will have a positive impact of 7.063753% on coal consumption (LNECE), and the 1% increase in exports by processing trade (LNPX) will have a negative impact of 6.248154% on coal consumption (LNCEC).

3. Petroleum consumption, imports and exports by conventional trade, and imports and exports by processing trade:

$$LNPEC = \underset{(0.35925)}{0.570064LNCM} - \underset{(0.32590)}{0.734653\ LNPM} \tag{6.5}$$

$$LNPEC = \underset{(1.60520)}{12.82947} + \underset{(0.38579)}{0.091567LNCX} - \underset{(0.30056)}{0.191082LNPX} \tag{6.6}$$

Eq. (6.5) reveals that the 1% increase in imports by conventional trade (LNCM) will have a positive impact of 0.570064% on petroleum consumption (LNPEC) and the 1% increase in imports by processing trade (LNPM) will have a negative impact of 0.734653% on petroleum consumption. Eq. (,6.6) reveals that the 1% increase in exports by conventional trade (LNCX) will have a positive impact of 0.091567% on petroleum consumption (LNPEC) and the 1% increase in exports by processing trade (LNPX) will have negative impact of 0.191082% on petroleum consumption (LNPEC).

4. Natural gas consumption, imports and exports by conventional trade, and imports and exports by processing trade:

$$LNNEC = \underset{(0.19777)}{3.733538} + \underset{(0.03741)}{0.75606LNCM} - \underset{(0.01988)}{0.04464LNPM} \tag{6.7}$$

$$LNNEC = \underset{(3.68489)}{-3.093962LNCX} - \underset{(1.96437)}{5.252946LNPX} \tag{6.8}$$

Eq. (6.7) reveals that the 1% increase in imports by conventional trade (LNCM) will have a positive impact of 0.75606% on natural gas consumption (LNNEC) and the 1% increase in imports by conventional trade (LNPM) will have a negative impact of 0.04464% on natural gas consumption (LNNEC). Eq. (6.8) reveals that the 1% increase in exports by conventional trade (LNCX) will have a negative impact of 3.093962% on natural gas consumption (LNNEC) and the 1% increase in exports by processing trade (LNPX) will have a negative impact of 5.252946% on natural gas consumption (LNNEC).

5. Hydro power, nuclear power, and other power consumption, imports and exports by conventional trade, and imports and exports by processing trade:

$$LNHEC = \underset{(0.37786)}{7.556833} + \underset{(0.09096)}{0.246857LNCM} - \underset{(0.06802)}{0.008056LNPM} \tag{6.9}$$

$$LNHEC = \underset{(0.08310)}{0.500451LNCX} - \underset{(0.06012)}{0.088039LNPX} \tag{6.10}$$

Eq. (6.9) reveals that the 1% increase in imports by conventional trade (LNCM) will have a positive impact of 0.246857% on hydro power, nuclear power, and other power consumption (LNHEC) and that the 1% rise in imports by processing trade (LNPM) will have a negative impact of 0.008056% on hydro power, nuclear power, and other power consumption (LNHEC). Eq. (6.10) reveals that the 1% increase in imports by conventional trade (LNCX) will have a positive impact of 0.500451% on hydro power, nuclear power, and other power consumption (LNHEC), and that the 1% increase in exports by processing trade (LNPX) will have a negative impact of 0.088039% on hydro power, nuclear power, and other power consumption.

In fact, these equations reveal the contribution of the vertical specialization variables (imports and exports by processing trade) to lowering energy consumption, which connects the vertically specialized trade policy variables with the coal equivalent calculation variables (TEC, CEC, PEC, NEC, and HEC). These long-term equations support the existence of a vertical specialization channel in the trade policy transmission process in China.

Proposition 1. The contribution and importance of conventional trade on lowering total energy consumption are lower than that of processing trade.
Proposition 2. The contribution and importance of conventional trade on lowering coal consumption are lower than that of processing trade.
Proposition 3. The contribution and importance of conventional trade on lowering petroleum consumption are lower than that of processing trade.
Proposition 4. The contribution and importance of conventional trade on lowering natural gas consumption are lower than that of processing trade.
Proposition 5. The contribution and importance of conventional trade on lowering hydro power, nuclear power, and other power consumption are lower than that of processing trade.

6.3.4   The vector error correction model (VECM)

The results of VECM are reported in Tables D1–D10. The ECM coefficients show the speed with which the system converges to equilibrium.

In Tables D1, D3, D5, D7, and D9, for D(LNPM), the coefficient of error correction terms, respectively, are -0.254983, -1.004778, -0.086632, -0.861449, and -0.350071. This shows that if a deviation from the long-term happens as a shock, then the adjustment speed toward long-term equilibrium will be 25.4983%, 100.4778%, 8.6632%, 86.1449%, 35.0071%, and full adjustment of deviation, respectively.

In Tables D6, D8, and D10, for D(LNPX), the coefficient of error correction terms, respectively, are -0.103394, -0.011891, and -0.408697. This shows that if a deviation from the long-term happens as a shock, then the adjustment speed toward long-term equilibrium will be 10.3394%, 1.1891%, and 40.8697%, respectively.

6.3.5   Granger causality tests

If a cointegration vector exists between the variables, then there is causality between these variables in at least one direction. Table E1 reports the causality test results for LNTEC, LNCM, and LNPM. When nine lags are applied, the hypothesis that LNPM does not involve a Granger causality in LNTEC can be rejected at a 10% level of significance, and the hypothesis that LNTEC does not involve a Granger causality in LNPM can be rejected at a 5% level of significance. Thus, we found bidirectional causality from LNPM to LNTEC. When one lag is applied, the hypothesis that LNCM does not involve Granger causality in LNTEC can be rejected at a 5% level of significance. Thus, we found unidirectional causality from

LNCM to LNTEC. When five lags and six lags are applied, the hypothesis that LNTEC does not involve Granger causality in LNCM can be rejected at a 10% level of significance. Thus, we found unidirectional causality from LNTEC to LNCM.

In Table E2, when two lags and five lags are applied, the hypothesis that LNTEC does not involve Granger causality in LNPX can be rejected at a 5% level of significance. Thus, we found unidirectional causality from LNTEC to LNPX. When one lag, two lags, three lags, four lags, and five lags are applied, the hypothesis that LNTEC does not involve Granger causality in LNCX can be rejected at 10%, 5%, and 1% levels of significance. Thus, we found unidirectional causality from LNTEC to LNCX.

In Table E3, when three lags, four lags, and five lags are applied, the hypothesis that LNPM does not involve Granger causality in LNCEC can be rejected at a 10% level of significance and that LNCEC does not involve Granger causality in LNPM can be rejected at a 5% level of significance. Thus, we found bidirectional causality from LNPM to LNCEC.

From Table E4, when three lags are applied, the hypothesis that LNPX does not involve Granger causality in LNCEC can be rejected at a 10% level of significance. Thus, we found unidirectional causality from LNPX to LNCEC. When two lags and five lags are applied, we find unidirectional causality from LNCEC to LNPX at 10% and 1% levels of significance, respectively. When two lags, three lags, four lags, and five lags are applied, we find bidirectional causality from LNCX to LNCEC at a 10% level of significance.

In Table E5, when one lag is applied, we find unidirectional causality from LNPM to LNPEC at a 10% level of significance, and unidirectional causality from LNPEC to LNCM at a 10% level of significance.

In Table E6, when one lag and eight lags are applied, we find unidirectional causality from LNPX to LNPEC at 10% and 5% levels of significance, respectively. When seven lags are applied, we find bidirectional causality from LNPX to LNPEC at a 10% level of significance. When one lag and two lags are applied, we find unidirectional causality from LNPEC to LNCX at a 5% level of significance.

In Table E7, when one lag is applied, we find unidirectional causality from LNPM to LNNEC at a 10% level of significance, respectively. When one lag, two lags, three lags, and four lags are applied, we find bidirectional causality from LNCM to LNNEC at a 1% level of significance.

In Table E8, when one lag is applied, we find unidirectional causality from LNCX to LNNEC at a 5% level of significance. When two lags are applied, we find unidirectional causality from LNNEC to LNPX at a 10% level of significance.

In Table E9, when one lag is applied, we find bidirectional causality running from LNCM to LNHEC at 5% and 10% levels of significance. When five lags and six lags are applied, we find unidirectional causality from LNHEC to LNCM at a 5% level of significance.

In Table E10, when one lag and two lags are applied, we find unidirectional causality from LNCX to LNHEC at 5% and 10% levels of significance.

6.3.6 Impulse response function

Impulse-response function curves simulated by analytic method are shown in Figs. F1−F10. These indicate how a one-time positive shock of 1 standard deviation (SD) (±2 SE innovations) to the conventional trade and processing trade endures regarding the energy consumption of China. We consider the response of five variables to 1 SD in the innovation of conventional trade and processing trade.

In Fig. F1, following a shock by imports by conventional trade (an innovation in LNCM), the LNTEC decreases quickly (negative change rate). After a shock by imports by processing trade (an innovation in LNPM), the LNTEC increases quickly (positive change rate).

In Figs. F2, F6, F8, and F10, after a shock by exports by conventional trade (an innovation in LNCX), the energy consumption variables (LNTEC, LNPEC, LNNEC, and LNHEC) increase quickly (positive change rate). After a shock by exports by processing trade (an innovation in LNPX), the energy consumption variables (LNTEC, LNPEC, LNNEC, and LNHEC) decrease quickly (negative change rate). Therefore, we should conclude that the effects of the trade policy shocks are transmitted through the mutual effects of the conventional trade channel and processing trade channel based on these results in this case.

Fig. F4 illustrates that the response of the LNCEC to a 1 SD shock on LNCX and LNPX is positive and powerful, with a persistent effect. However, the influence of LNPM is lower than that of LNCM from period one to period eight.

In Figs. F7 and F8, following a shock in conventional trade (an innovation in LNCM or LNCX), the energy consumption variables (LNNEC) increase quickly (positive change rate); following a shock in processing trade (an innovation in LNPM or LNPX), the energy consumption variables (LNNEC) decrease quickly (negative change rate).

Fig. F9 illustrates that the response of the LNHEC to a 1 SD shock in LNCM and LNPM is positive and powerful, with a persistent effect. However, the influence of LNPM is lower than that of LNCM.

6.3.7 Variance decomposition

The forecast error variance decomposition follows. It aims to capture the intensity of the response of a variable in the face of shocks suffered by the other variables. Tables G1−G10 reveal the percentages of the forecast error variances of all variables generated by a shock in each of the other variables.

In Tables G1−G10, the first columns are the periods that are set to a maximum of 15. The data in the SE (standard error) column are the forecasting variances of various periods, which are caused by the change of the present value or future value.

In Tables G1, G3, G7, and G9, it can be seen that the impact of a shock to LNPM on the energy consumption variables (LNTEC, LNCEC, LNNEC, and LNHEC) is relatively low when compared with the impact of a shock to LNCM on the energy consumption variables (LNTEC, LNCEC, LNNEC, and LNHEC).

In Tables G2 and G8, it can be seen that the impact of a shock to LNPX on the energy consumption variables (LNTEC and LNHEC) is relatively lower than that of the LNCX. For example, in Table G2, at the end of the forecast period, LNCX explains approximately 30% of the forecast error variance. This is approximately 27% higher than in the LNPX case.

In Tables G4, G6, and G10, it can be seen that the impact of a shock to LNCX on the energy consumption variables (LNCEC, LNPEC, and LNHEC) is relatively low when compared with the impact of a shock to LNPX on the energy consumption variables (LNCEC, LNPEC, and LNHEC). For example, in Table G4, at the end of the forecast period, LNCX explains approximately 10% of the forecast error variance. This is approximately 5% lower than in the LNPX case.

In Table G5, during the fifteenth forecast period, LNPM explains approximately 1.2% of the forecast error variance. This is approximately 0.4% higher than in the LNCM case.

6.4   Concluding remarks and policy implications

The environmental damage impacts of assembly operations, which have relatively low energy consumption, are different from those of ordinary trade, which tend to be associated with stronger relative demand for energy consumption and higher environmental damage. By disaggregating the total imports and exports into conventional trade and processing trade, we estimate the different effects of two types of trade patterns on total energy consumption (TEC), coal consumption (CEC), petroleum consumption (PEC), natural gas consumption (NEC), and hydro power, nuclear power, and other power consumption (HEC), and seek more evidence for the lower impact of vertical specialization on environmental damage based on processing trade rather than conventional trade.

This study shows that total energy consumption effect, coal consumption, petroleum consumption, natural gas consumption effect, and hydro power, nuclear power, and other power consumption effect of processing trade are lower than that of conventional trade. In other words, while imports and exports by processing trade were becoming increasingly important for lowering environmental damage in China, the relative importance of imports and exports by conventional trade was declining. This could signal that some of the resources freed up in the economy are being allocated to the vertically specialized trade, thus stimulating the lower environmental damage in China during the transition to inclusive growth in China.

The fact that processing trade tends to lower total energy consumption could be a factor tending to decrease environmental damage. This would have stronger effects on trade policies designed to promote inclusive growth in China.

From a policy point of view, the findings suggest that vertically specialized trade in comparison with ordinary trade have considerable potential to lower environmental damage, which would increase the contribution of trade to inclusive growth in China. The fact that foreign-invested enterprises tend to increase the relative demand for trade in intermediate inputs could be a factor tending to decrease total energy consumption. This would have stronger effects in pursuing development in a scientific way and is designed to promote inclusive growth and development in China.

A second policy implication is that the place a Chinese enterprise within a vertical specialization is likely to be a crucial determinant of lowering environment damage effects of vertical specialization participation. China's processing trade enterprises involved primarily in simple assembly tasks are likely to see different total energy consumption from those involved in offshored research and development activities. Policies that are designed to help China's processing trade enterprises—in a nondistortionary way—move through vertical specialization to positions of higher value added are likely to help promote the upgrading and transformation effects of vertical specialization participation, which can provide firms with the foundation they need to successfully grow in inclusive growth activities.

Appendix A   Variables grouping

Table A1 **Variables grouping**

Group number	Variables	Sample range
1	LNTEC, LNCM, LNPM	1981−2012
2	LNTEC, LNCX, LNPX	1981−2012
3	LNCEC, LNCM, LNPM	1981−2012
4	LNCEC, LNCX, LNPX	1981−2012
5	LNPEC, LNCM, LNPM	1981−2012
6	LNNPEC, LNCX, LNPX	1981−2012
7	LNNEC, LNCM, LNPM	1981−2012
8	LNNEC, LNCX, LNPM	1981−2012
9	LNHEC, LNCM, LNPM	1981−2012
10	LNHEC, LNCX, LNPM	1981−2012

Note: PM is imports by processing trade, CM is imports by conventional trade, PX is exports by processing trade, CX is exports by conventional trade, TEC stands for total energy consumption (10^4 tee), CEC stands for coal consumption (10^4 tee), PEC stands for petroleum consumption (10^4 tee), NEC stands for natural gas consumption (10^4 tee), HEC stands for hydro power, nuclear power, and other power consumption (10^4 tee) based on coal equivalent calculations.

Appendix B   The results of unit root tests

Table B1 Augmented Dickey-Fuller test on unit roots for all variables

S\No.	Variables	Test type (C,T,P)	ADF test statistic	Order of integration
1	LNPM	(C,T,0)	−1.261698	I(1)
2	D(LNPM)	(C,T,0)	−4.351388*	I(0)
3	LNCM	(C,T,0)	−1.265244	I(1)
4	D(LNCM)	(C,T,0)	−4.968410*	I(0)
5	LNPX	(C,T,0)	−1.034865	I(1)
6	D(LNPX)	(C,T,0)	−4.158776**	I(0)
7	LNCX	(C,T,0)	−1.780058	I(1)
8	D(LNCX)	(C,T,0)	−6.235275*	I(0)
9	LNTEC	(C,0,0)	0.081939	I(1)
10	D(LNTEC)	(C,0,0)	−2.877573***	I(0)
11	LNCEC	(C,T,1)	−2.769063	I(1)
12	D(LNCEC)	(C,T,4)	−3.256449***	I(0)
13	LNPEC	(C,0,0)	0.958557	I(1)
14	D(LNPEC)	(C,0,0)	−5.560215*	I(0)
15	LNNEC	(C,0,0)	5.070995	I(1)
16	D(LNNEC)	(C,0,0)	−3.141941**	I(0)
17	LNHEC	(C,0,0)	1.022355	I(1)
18	D(LNHEC)	(C,0,0)	−5.647126*	I(0)

Note: C, T, and P in test type stand for constant, trend, and lag orders, respectively. At three remarkable levels, when the ADF value is greater than the critical value, the corresponding series has a unit root. D stands for the first differential of the variables.
***, **, and *denote the rejection of the null hypothesis of the unit root at 10%, 5%, and 1% significance levels, respectively.

Appendix C   Results of cointegration tests

Table C1 **Cointegration test result (series: LNTEC, LNCM, and LNPM)**

Sample (adjusted): 1982−2012
Included observations: 31 after adjustments
Trend assumption: Linear deterministic trend
Series: LNTEC, LNCM, LNPM
Lags interval (in first differences): No lags

Unrestricted cointegration rank test (trace)

Hypothesized number of CE(s)	Eigenvalue	Trace statistic	0.05 critical value	Probability[a]
None[b]	0.475659	35.75178	29.79707	0.0092
At most 1[b]	0.397785	15.73780	15.49471	0.0460
At most 2	0.000530	0.016430	3.841466	0.8979

Trace test indicates 2 cointegrating equations at the 0.05 level

Unrestricted cointegration rank test (maximum eigenvalue)

Hypothesized number of CE(s)	Eigenvalue	Max-eigen statistic	0.05 critical value	Probability[a]
None	0.475659	20.01398	21.13162	0.0711
At most 1[b]	0.397785	15.72137	14.26460	0.0292
At most 2	0.000530	0.016430	3.841466	0.8979

Max-eigenvalue test indicates no cointegration at the 0.05 level

1 cointegrating equation		Log likelihood	106.1012

Normalized cointegrating coefficients (standard error in parentheses)

LNTEC	LNCM	LNPM
1.000000	− 0.226749	0.023184
	(0.10025)	(0.07126)

[a]MacKinnon−Haug−Michelis (1999) P values.
[b]Rejection of the hypothesis at the 0.05 level.

Table C2 Cointegration test result (series: LNTEC, LNCX, and LNPX)

Sample (adjusted): 1985–2012
Included observations: 28 after adjustments
Trend assumption: Linear deterministic trend
Lags interval (in first differences): 2–3

Unrestricted cointegration rank test (trace)

Hypothesized number of CE(s)	Eigenvalue	Trace statistic	0.05 critical value	Probability[a]
None[b]	0.570460	38.49067	29.79707	0.0039
At most 1	0.410070	14.82954	15.49471	0.0628
At most 2	0.001874	0.052509	3.841466	0.8187

Trace test indicates 1 cointegrating equation at the 0.05 level

Unrestricted cointegration rank test (maximum eigenvalue)

Hypothesized number of CE(s)	Eigenvalue	Max-eigen statistic	0.05 critical value	Probability[a]
None[b]	0.570460	23.66112	21.13162	0.0215
At most 1[b]	0.410070	14.77703	14.26460	0.0415
At most 2	0.001874	0.052509	3.841466	0.8187

Max-eigenvalue test indicates 2 cointegrating equations at the 0.05 level

1 cointegrating equation(s)	Log likelihood	119.5273

Normalized cointegrating coefficients (standard error in parentheses)

LNTEC	LNCX	LNPX
1.000000	− 0.342580	− 0.074873
	(0.02784)	(0.01819)

[a]MacKinnon–Haug–Michelis (1999) P values.
[b]Rejection of the hypothesis at the 0.05 level.

Table C3 Cointegration test result (series: LNCEC, LNCM, and LNPM)

Sample (adjusted): 1984–2012
Included observations: 29 after adjustments
Trend assumption: Linear deterministic trend
Lags interval (in first differences): 1–2

Unrestricted cointegration rank test (trace)

Hypothesized number of CE(s)	Eigenvalue	Trace statistic	0.05 critical value	Probability[a]
None[b]	0.694014	52.56396	29.79707	0.0000
At most 1[b]	0.460934	18.22166	15.49471	0.0189
At most 2	0.010361	0.302041	3.841466	0.5826

Trace test indicates 2 cointegrating equations at the 0.05 level

Unrestricted cointegration rank test (maximum eigenvalue)

Hypothesized number of CE(s)	Eigenvalue	Max-eigen statistic	0.05 critical value	Probability[a]
None[b]	0.694014	34.34230	21.13162	0.0004
At most 1[b]	0.460934	17.91962	14.26460	0.0126
At most 2	0.010361	0.302041	3.841466	0.5826

Max-eigenvalue test indicates 2 cointegrating equations at the 0.05 level

1 cointegrating equation		Log likelihood		129.0974

Normalized cointegrating coefficients (standard error in parentheses)

LNCEC	LNCM	LNPM
1.000000	− 0.214200	− 0.102244
	(0.01942)	(0.01352)

[a]MacKinnon–Haug–Michelis (1999) P values.
[b]Rejection of the hypothesis at the 0.05 level.

Table C4 **Cointegration test result (series: LNCEC, LNCX, and LNPX)**

Sample (adjusted): 1985−2012
Included observations: 28 after adjustments
Trend assumption: No deterministic trend
Lags interval (in first differences): 1−3

Unrestricted cointegration rank test (trace)

Hypothesized number of CE(s)	Eigenvalue	Trace statistic	0.05 critical value	Probability[a]
None[b]	0.503991	30.00358	24.27596	0.0085
At most 1	0.306154	10.37108	12.32090	0.1038
At most 2	0.004879	0.136947	4.129906	0.7601

Trace test indicates 1 cointegrating equation at the 0.05 level

Unrestricted cointegration rank test (maximum eigenvalue)

Hypothesized number of CE(s)	Eigenvalue	Max-eigen statistic	0.05 critical value	Probability[a]
None[b]	0.503991	19.63251	17.79730	0.0262
At most 1	0.306154	10.23413	11.22480	0.0743
At most 2	0.004879	0.136947	4.129906	0.7601

Max-eigenvalue test indicates 1 cointegrating equation at the 0.05 level

1 cointegrating equation		Log likelihood	127.1842

Normalized cointegrating coefficients (standard error in parentheses)		
LNCEC 1.000000	LNCX − 7.063753 (1.63052)	LNPX 6.248154 (1.63938)

[a]MacKinnon−Haug−Michelis (1999) P values.
[b]Rejection of the hypothesis at the 0.05 level.

Table C5 Cointegration test result (series: LNPEC, LNCM, and LNPM)

Sample (adjusted): 1985−2012
Included observations: 28 after adjustments
Trend assumption: Linear deterministic trend
Lags interval (in first differences): 2−3

Unrestricted cointegration rank test (trace)

Hypothesized number of CE(s)	Eigenvalue	Trace statistic	0.05 critical value	Probability[a]
None[b]	0.447115	31.79208	29.79707	0.0291
At most 1	0.359730	15.19911	15.49471	0.0554
At most 2	0.092408	2.714899	3.841466	0.0994

Trace test indicates 1 cointegrating equation at the 0.05 level

Unrestricted cointegration rank test (maximum eigenvalue)

Hypothesized number of CE(s)	Eigenvalue	Max-eigen statistic	0.05 critical value	Probability[a]
None	0.447115	16.59297	21.13162	0.1921
At most 1	0.359730	12.48421	14.26460	0.0938
At most 2	0.092408	2.714899	3.841466	0.0994

Max-eigenvalue test indicates no cointegration at the 0.05 level

1 cointegrating equation		Log likelihood	108.3669

Normalized cointegrating coefficients (standard error in parentheses)

LNPEC	LNCM	LNPM
1.000000	− 0.570064 (0.35925)	0.734653 (0.32590)

[a]MacKinnon−Haug−Michelis (1999) *P* values.
[b]Rejection of the hypothesis at the 0.05 level.

Table C6 Cointegration test result (series: LNPEC, LNCX, and LNPX)

| Sample (adjusted): 1985−2012 |
| Included observations: 28 after adjustments |
| Trend assumption: No deterministic trend (restricted constant) |
| Lags interval (in first differences): 2−3 |

Unrestricted cointegration rank test (trace)

Hypothesized number of CE(s)	Eigenvalue	Trace statistic	0.05 critical value	Probability[a]
None[b]	0.522845	48.04617	35.19275	0.0013
At most 1[b]	0.465309	27.32855	20.26184	0.0045
At most 2*	0.295279	9.798674	9.164546	0.0379

Trace test indicates 3 cointegrating equations at the 0.05 level

Unrestricted cointegration rank test (maximum eigenvalue)

Hypothesized number of CE(s)	Eigenvalue	Max-eigen statistic	0.05 critical value	Probability[a]
None	0.522845	20.71761	22.29962	0.0819
At most 1[b]	0.465309	17.52988	15.89210	0.0274
At most 2[b]	0.295279	9.798674	9.164546	0.0379

Max-eigenvalue test indicates no cointegration at the 0.05 level

1 cointegrating equation		Log likelihood	106.0075	

Normalized cointegrating coefficients (standard error in parentheses)

LNPEC	LNCX	LNPX	C
1.000000	− 0.091567 (0.38579)	0.191082 (0.30056)	−12.82947(1.60520)

[a]MacKinnon−Haug−Michelis (1999) P values.
[b]Rejection of the hypothesis at the 0.05 level.

Table C7 Cointegration test result (series: LNNEC, LNCM, and LNPM)

Sample (adjusted): 1984–2012
Included observations: 29 after adjustments
Trend assumption: No deterministic trend (restricted constant)
Lags interval (in first differences): 1–2

Unrestricted cointegration rank test (trace)

Hypothesized number of CE(s)	Eigenvalue	Trace statistic	0.05 critical value	Probability[a]
None[b]	0.677355	54.84985	35.19275	0.0001
At most 1[b]	0.463240	22.04493	20.26184	0.0281
At most 2	0.128871	4.000986	9.164546	0.4120

Trace test indicates 2 cointegrating equations at the 0.05 level

Unrestricted cointegration rank test (maximum eigenvalue)

Hypothesized number of CE(s)	Eigenvalue	Max-eigen statistic	0.05 critical value	Probability[a]
None[b]	0.677355	32.80492	22.29962	0.0012
At most 1[b]	0.463240	18.04394	15.89210	0.0226
At most 2	0.128871	4.000986	9.164546	0.4120

Max-eigenvalue test indicates 2 cointegrating equations at the 0.05 level

1 cointegrating equation		Log likelihood	102.9774

Normalized cointegrating coefficients (standard error in parentheses)

LNNEC	LNCM	LNPM	C
1.000000	− 0.756060	0.044640	−3.733538
	(0.03741)	(0.01988)	(0.19777)

[a]MacKinnon–Haug–Michelis (1999) P values.
[b]Rejection of the hypothesis at the 0.05 level.

Table C8 Cointegration test result (series: LNNEC, LNCX, and LNPX)

Sample (adjusted): 1985−2012
Included observations: 28 after adjustments
Trend assumption: Linear deterministic trend
Lags interval (in first differences): 2−3

Unrestricted cointegration rank test (trace)

Hypothesized number of CE(s)	Eigenvalue	Trace statistic	0.05 critical value	Probability[a]
None[b]	0.626342	41.12162	29.79707	0.0017
At most 1	0.382658	13.55804	15.49471	0.0959
At most 2	0.001882	0.052746	3.841466	0.8183

Trace test indicates 1 cointegrating equation at the 0.05 level

Unrestricted cointegration rank test (maximum eigenvalue)

Hypothesized number of CE(s)	Eigenvalue	Max-eigen statistic	0.05 critical value	Probability[a]
None[b]	0.626342	27.56358	21.13162	0.0054
At most 1	0.382658	13.50529	14.26460	0.0656
At most 2	0.001882	0.052746	3.841466	0.8183

Max-eigenvalue test indicates 1 cointegrating equation at the 0.05 level

1 cointegrating equation		Log likelihood	108.1472

Normalized cointegrating coefficients (standard error in parentheses)

LNNEC	LNCX	LNPX
1.000000	3.093962 (3.68489)	5.252946 (1.96437)

[a]MacKinnon−Haug−Michelis (1999) P values.
[b]Rejection of the hypothesis at the 0.05 level.

Table C9 Cointegration test result (series: LNHEC, LNCM, and LNPM)

Date: 08/15/15 Time: 11:14
Sample (adjusted): 1985–2012
Included observations: 28 after adjustments
Trend assumption: No deterministic trend (restricted constant)
Series: LNHEC, LNCM, LNPM
Lags interval (in first differences): 2–3

Unrestricted cointegration rank test (trace)

Hypothesized number of CE(s)	Eigenvalue	Trace statistic	0.05 critical value	Probability[a]
None[b]	0.620098	46.50162	35.19275	0.0020
At most 1	0.427348	19.40202	20.26184	0.0653
At most 2	0.126679	3.792655	9.164546	0.4439

Trace test indicates 1 cointegrating equation at the 0.05 level

Unrestricted cointegration rank test (maximum eigenvalue)

Hypothesized number of CE(s)	Eigenvalue	Max-eigen statistic	0.05 critical value	Probability[a]
None[b]	0.620098	27.09960	22.29962	0.0099
At most 1	0.427348	15.60936	15.89210	0.0553
At most 2	0.126679	3.792655	9.164546	0.4439

Max-eigenvalue test indicates 1 cointegrating equation at the 0.05 level

1 cointegrating equation		Log likelihood	85.78374

Normalized cointegrating coefficients (standard error in parentheses)

LNHEC	LNCM	LNPM	C
1.000000	− 0.246857 (0.09096)	0.008056 (0.06802)	− 7.556833 (0.37786)

[a]MacKinnon-Haug-Michelis (1999) P values.
[b]Rejection of the hypothesis at the 0.05 level.

Table C10 Cointegration test result (series: LNHEC, LNCX, and LNPX)

Sample (adjusted): 1985–2012
Included observations: 28 after adjustments
Trend assumption: Linear deterministic trend
Lags interval (in first differences): 2–3

Unrestricted cointegration rank test (Trace)

Hypothesized number of CE(s)	Eigenvalue	Trace statistic	0.05 critical value	Probability[a]
None[b]	0.467475	32.75919	29.79707	0.0221
At most 1	0.407995	15.11569	15.49471	0.0570
At most 2	0.015485	0.436963	3.841466	0.5086

Trace test indicates 1 cointegrating equation at the 0.05 level

Unrestricted cointegration rank test (maximum eigenvalue)

Hypothesized number of CE(s)	Eigenvalue	Max-eigen statistic	0.05 critical value	Probability[a]
None	0.467475	17.64350	21.13162	0.1438
At most 1[b]	0.407995	14.67873	14.26460	0.0430
At most 2	0.015485	0.436963	3.841466	0.5086

Max-eigenvalue test indicates no cointegration at the 0.05 level

1 cointegrating equation(s)	Log likelihood	96.21255

Normalized cointegrating coefficients (standard error in parentheses)

LNHEC	LNCX	LNPX
1.000000	− 0.500451	0.088039
	(0.08310)	(0.06012)

[a]MacKinnon-Haug-Michelis (1999) *P* values.
[b]Rejection of the hypothesis at the 0.05 level.

Appendix D   Results of vector error correction model

Table D1 Vector error correction estimates (series: LNTEC, LNCM, and LNPM)

Sample (adjusted): 1982−2012 Included observations: 31 after adjustments Standard errors in parentheses ( ) and t-statistics in brackets [ ]			
Cointegrating eq	**CointEq1**		
LNTEC(−1) LNCM(−1) LNPM(−1) C	1.000000 − 0.226749 (0.10025) [−2.26184] 0.023184 (0.07126) [0.32533] − 10.45598		
Error correction	**D(LNTEC)**	**D(LNCM)**	**D(LNPM)**
CointEq1 C R-squared Adj. R-squared	0.001645 (0.01992) [0.08258] 0.058252 (0.00593) [9.82270] 0.000235 − 0.034240	0.191373 (0.11158) [1.71507] 0.126323 (0.03322) [3.80229] 0.092090 0.060782	−0.254983 (0.06589) [−3.86954] 0.186075 (0.01962) [9.48406] 0.340509 0.317768

Table D2 Vector error correction estimates (series: LNTEC, LNCX, and LNPX)

Sample (adjusted): 1985−2012
Included observations: 28 after adjustments
Standard errors in parentheses ( ) and t-statistics in brackets [ ]

Cointegrating eq	CointEq1		
LNTEC(−1)	1.000000		
LNCX(−1)	− 0.342580		
	(0.02784)		
	[−12.3054]		
LNPX(−1)	− 0.074873		
	(0.01819)		
	[− 4.11646]		
C	− 9.030403		

Error correction	D(LNTEC)	D(LNCX)	D(LNPX)
CointEq1	− 0.198147	1.010130	1.332756
	(0.15728)	(0.63158)	(0.54570)
	[−1.25982]	[1.59937]	[2.44227]
R-squared	0.226848	0.288503	0.425054
Adj. R-squared	− 0.043755	0.039479	0.223823

Table D3 Vector error correction estimates (series: LNCEC, LNCM, and LNPM)

Sample (adjusted): 1984−2012
Included observations: 29 after adjustments
Standard errors in parentheses ( ) and t-statistics in brackets [ ]

Cointegrating eq	CointEq1		
LNCEC(−1)	1.000000		
LNCM(−1)	−0.214200		
	(0.01942)		
	[−11.0319]		
LNPM(−1)	− 0.102244		
	(0.01352)		
	[−7.56392]		
C	− 9.464211		

Error correction	D(LNCEC)	D(LNCM)	D(LNPM)
CointEq1	−0.285204	−0.622331	−1.004778
	(0.07638)	(0.39050)	(0.26065)
	[−3.73388]	[−1.59367]	[−3.85485]
R-squared	0.732322	0.644040	0.680829
Adj. R-squared	0.643096	0.525387	0.574439

Table D4 Vector error correction estimates (series: LNCEC, LNCX, and LNPX)

Sample (adjusted): 1985−2012
Included observations: 28 after adjustments
Standard errors in parentheses ( ) and t-statistics in brackets [ ]

Cointegrating eq	CointEq1		
LNCEC(−1)	1.000000		
LNCX(−1)	− 7.063753		
	(1.63052)		
	[−4.33221]		
LNPX(−1)	6.248154		
	(1.63938)		
	[3.81128]		
Error correction	**D(LNCEC)**	**D(LNCX)**	**D(LNPX)**
CointEq1	− 0.001306	0.025923	0.004708
	(0.00233)	(0.00732)	(0.00801)
	[−0.56155]	[3.54340]	[0.58809]
R-squared	0.606804	0.647157	0.542703
Adj. R-squared	0.410207	0.470736	0.314055

Table D5 Vector error correction estimates (series: LNPEC, LNCM, and LNPM)

Sample (adjusted): 1985−2012
Included observations: 28 after adjustments
Standard errors in parentheses ( ) and t-statistics in brackets [ ]

Cointegrating eq	CointEq1		
LNPEC(−1)	1.000000		
LNCM(−1)	− 0.570064		
	(0.35925)		
	[−1.58683]		
LNPM(−1)	0.734653		
	(0.32590)		
	[2.25421]		
C	−11.08489		
Error correction	**D(LNPEC)**	**D(LNCM)**	**D(LNPM)**
CointEq1	0.006947	0.020157	− 0.086632
	(0.01116)	(0.05298)	(0.03180)
	[0.62266]	[0.38044]	[−2.72424]
R-squared	0.196068	0.359046	0.532795
Adj. R-squared	− 0.085309	0.134712	0.369274

Table D6 Vector error correction estimates (series: LNPEC, LNCX, and LNPX)

Sample (adjusted): 1985–2012 Included observations: 28 after adjustments Standard errors in parentheses ( ) and t-statistics in brackets [ ]			
Cointegrating eq	**CointEq1**		
LNPEC(−1) LNCX(−1) LNPX(−1) C	1.000000 − 0.091567 (0.38579) [− 0.23735] 0.191082 (0.30056) [0.63576] − 12.82947 (1.60520) [−7.99242]		
Error correction	**D(LNPEC)**	**D(LNCX)**	**D(LNPX)**
CointEq1 R-squared Adj. R-squared	− 0.042289 (0.01098) [−3.85015] 0.094249 − 0.164537	− 0.053712 (0.04170) [−1.28818] 0.170037 − 0.067096	− 0.103394 (0.03387) [−3.05230] 0.407083 0.237678

Table D7 Vector error correction estimates (series: LNNEC, LNCM, and LNPM)

Sample (adjusted): 1984–2012
Included observations: 29 after adjustments
Standard errors in parentheses ( ) and t-statistics in brackets [ ]

Cointegrating eq	CointEq1		
LNNEC(−1)	1.000000		
LNCM(−1)	− 0.756060		
	(0.03741)		
	[−20.2122]		
LNPM(−1)	0.044640		
	(0.01988)		
	[2.24512]		
C	− 3.733538		
	(0.19777)		
	[−18.8785]		

Error correction	D(LNNEC)	D(LNCM)	D(LNPM)
CointEq1	− 0.454425	− 0.901418	− 0.861449
	(0.08349)	(0.38820)	(0.22598)
	[−5.44259]	[−2.32205]	[−3.81207]
R-squared	0.756885	0.244045	0.484452
Adj. R-squared	0.690581	0.037875	0.343848

Table D8 Vector error correction estimates (series: LNNEC, LNCX, and LNPX)

Sample (adjusted): 1985−2012
Included observations: 28 after adjustments
Standard errors in parentheses ( ) and t-statistics in brackets [ ]

Cointegrating eq	CointEq1		
LNNEC(−1)	1.000000		
LNCX(−1)	3.093962		
	(3.68489)		
	[0.83963]		
LNPX(-1)	5.252946		
	(1.96437)		
	[2.67411]		
C	− 64.90378		

Error correction	D(LNNEC)	D(LNCX)	D(LNPX)
CointEq1	0.001603	0.001140	− 0.011891
	(0.00200)	(0.00513)	(0.00379)
	[0.80223]	[0.22236]	[−3.13779]
R-squared	0.541416	0.210994	0.533676
Adj. R-squared	0.380911	− 0.065158	0.370463

Table D9 Vector error correction estimates (series: LNHEC, LNCM, and LNPM)

Sample (adjusted): 1985−2012
Included observations: 28 after adjustments
Standard errors in parentheses ( ) and t-statistics in brackets [ ]

Cointegrating eq	CointEq1		
LNHEC(−1)	1.000000		
LNCM(−1)	− 0.246857		
	(0.09096)		
	[−2.71401]		
LNPM(−1)	0.008056		
	(0.06802)		
	[0.11845]		
C	− 7.556833		
	(0.37786)		
	[−19.9988]		

Error correction	D(LNHEC)	D(LNCM)	D(LNPM)
CointEq1	0.039591	0.015811	− 0.350071
	(0.04796)	(0.14511)	(0.07327)
	[0.82552]	[0.10896]	[−4.77788]
R-squared	0.254931	0.179136	0.576500
Adj. R-squared	0.042055	− 0.055397	0.455500

Table D10 **Vector error correction estimates (series: LNHEC, LNCX, and LNPX)**

Vector Error Correction Estimates Date: 08/21/15 Time: 23:02 Sample (adjusted): 1985–2012 Included observations: 28 after adjustments Standard errors in parentheses ( ) and t-statistics in brackets [ ]			
Cointegrating eq	**CointEq1**		
LNHEC(−1) LNCX(−1) LNPX(−1) C	1.000000 − 0.500451 (0.08310) [−6.02218] 0.088039 (0.06012) [1.46442] − 6.225060		
Error correction	**D(LNHEC)**	**D(LNCX)**	**D(LNPX)**
CointEq1 R-squared Adj. R-squared	− 0.110057 (0.10324) [−1.06603] 0.197465 − 0.083423	0.021269 (0.21829) [0.09743] 0.223293 − 0.048555	− 0.408697 (0.18334) [−2.22920] 0.406961 0.199398

Appendix E   Results of Granger causality tests

Table E1 Pairwise Granger causality tests (series: LNTEC, LNCM, and LNPM)

Sample: 1981–2012			
Null hypothesis	Observations	F-Statistic	Probability
Lags: 1			
LNCM does not cause LNTEC	31	5.38325	0.0278
LNTEC does not cause LNCM		1.15722	0.2912
LNPM does not cause LNTEC	31	0.02729	0.8700
LNTEC does not cause LNPM		0.00080	0.9776
Lags: 2			
LNCM does not cause LNTEC	30	1.22713	0.3102
LNTEC does not cause LNCM		0.23816	0.7898
LNPM does not cause LNTEC	30	0.26418	0.7700
LNTEC does not cause LNPM		2.96531	0.0699
Lags: 3			
LNCM does not cause LNTEC	29	1.64015	0.2089
LNTEC does not cause LNCM		1.69533	0.1971
LNPM does not cause LNTEC	29	0.90094	0.4565
LNTEC does not cause LNPM		3.10613	0.0473
Lags: 4			
LNCM does not cause LNTEC	28	2.14188	0.1151
LNTEC does not cause LNCM		1.17964	0.3513
LNPM does not cause LNTEC	28	1.02474	0.4199
LNTEC does not cause LNPM		3.10695	0.0399
Lags: 5			
LNCM does not cause LNTEC	27	1.69995	0.1917
LNTEC does not cause LNCM		2.88895	0.0480
LNPM does not cause LNTEC	27	1.40952	0.2734
LNTEC does not cause LNPM		8.36492	0.0005
Lags: 6			
LNCM does not cause LNTEC	26	0.90686	0.5193
LNTEC does not cause LNCM		2.46049	0.0819
LNPM does not cause LNTEC	26	0.49776	0.7992
LNTEC does not cause LNPM		9.55409	0.0004

(Continued)

Table E1 (Continued)

Sample: 1981–2012			
Null hypothesis	**Observations**	**F-Statistic**	**Probability**
Lags: 7			
LNCM does not cause LNTEC	25	0.45588	0.8453
LNTEC does not cause LNCM		1.45074	0.2864
LNPM does not cause LNTEC	25	0.71457	0.6631
LNTEC does not cause LNPM		10.1157	0.0008
Lags: 8			
LNCM does not cause LNTEC	24	0.79151	0.6278
LNTEC does not cause LNCM		1.70942	0.2470
LNPM does not cause LNTEC	24	1.64659	0.2625
LNTEC does not cause LNPM		8.40406	0.0055
Lags: 9			
LNCM does not cause LNTEC	23	0.88258	0.6000
LNTEC does not cause LNCM		2.44517	0.2019
LNPM does not cause LNTEC	23	5.15482	0.0646
LNTEC does not cause LNPM		10.9068	0.0173

Table E2 Pairwise Granger causality tests (series: LNTEC, LNCX, and LNPX)

Sample: 1981−2012			
Null hypothesis	Observations	F-Statistic	Probability
Lags: 1			
LNCX does not cause LNTEC	31	2.33732	0.1375
LNTEC does not cause LNCX		3.75220	0.0629
LNPX does not cause LNTEC	31	0.19086	0.6656
LNTEC does not cause LNPX		0.06896	0.7948
Lags: 2			
LNCX does not cause LNTEC	30	1.09122	0.3513
LNTEC does not cause LNCX		5.25588	0.0124
LNPX does not cause LNTEC	30	0.18961	0.8285
LNTEC does not cause LNPX		3.43678	0.0480
Lags: 3			
LNCX does not cause LNTEC	29	1.04349	0.3930
LNTEC does not cause LNCX		5.84641	0.0043
LNPX does not cause LNTEC	29	1.04893	0.3907
LNTEC does not cause LNPX		2.13182	0.1252
Lags: 4			
LNCX does not cause LNTEC	28	1.88264	0.1550
LNTEC does not cause LNCX		3.81603	0.0193
LNPX does not cause LNTEC	28	1.21362	0.3378
LNTEC does not cause LNPX		2.03465	0.1301
Lags: 5			
LNCX does not cause LNTEC	27	1.95788	0.1404
LNTEC does not cause LNCX		4.10484	0.0137
LNPX does not cause LNTEC	27	1.22070	0.3443
LNTEC does not cause LNPX		7.04657	0.0012

Table **E3** **Pairwise Granger causality tests (series: LNCEC, LNCM, and LNPM)**

Sample: 1981−2012			
Null hypothesis	Observations	F-Statistic	Probability
Lags: 1			
LNCM does not cause LNCEC	31	7.32735	0.0114
LNCEC does not cause LNCM		0.55522	0.4624
LNPM does not cause LNCEC	31	0.00139	0.9705
LNCEC does not cause LNPM		0.00059	0.9808
Lags: 2			
LNCM does not cause LNCEC	30	1.71571	0.2003
LNCEC does not cause LNCM		0.08807	0.9160
LNPM does not cause LNCEC	30	1.37556	0.2712
LNCEC does not cause LNPM		3.08016	0.0637
Lags: 3			
LNCM does not cause LNCEC	29	1.46837	0.2505
LNCEC does not cause LNCM		1.74652	0.1868
LNPM does not cause LNCEC	29	2.54021	0.0826
LNCEC does not cause LNPM		3.94688	0.0215
Lags: 4			
LNCM does not cause LNCEC	28	3.44191	0.0282
LNCEC does not cause LNCM		1.27396	0.3149
LNPM does not cause LNCEC	28	2.90313	0.0496
LNCEC does not cause LNPM		3.25910	0.0340
Lags: 5			
LNCM does not cause LNCEC	27	2.67897	0.0607
LNCEC does not cause LNCM		2.97003	0.0439
LNPM does not cause LNCEC	27	2.93027	0.0459
LNCEC does not cause LNPM		15.5610	1.E-05
Lags: 6			
LNCM does not cause LNCEC	26	1.53023	0.2441
LNCEC does not cause LNCM		2.00840	0.1374
LNPM does not cause LNCEC	26	1.05748	0.4344
LNCEC does not cause LNPM		14.0708	5.E-05

Table E4 Pairwise Granger causality tests (series: LNCEC, LNCX, and LNPX)

Sample: 1981–2012

Null hypothesis	Observations	F-Statistic	Probability
Lags: 1			
LNCX does not cause LNCEC	31	4.40005	0.0451
LNCEC does not cause LNCX		1.89912	0.1791
LNPX does not cause LNCEC	31	0.05884	0.8101
LNCEC does not cause LNPX		0.11411	0.7380
Lags: 2			
LNCX does not cause LNCEC	30	3.05503	0.0650
LNCEC does not cause LNCX		3.02641	0.0665
LNPX does not cause LNCEC	30	0.79129	0.4643
LNCEC does not cause LNPX		3.08358	0.0635
Lags: 3			
LNCX does not cause LNCEC	29	2.86864	0.0596
LNCEC does not cause LNCX		4.17744	0.0175
LNPX does not cause LNCEC	29	2.51068	0.0851
LNCEC does not cause LNPX		2.01937	0.1406
Lags: 4			
LNCX does not cause LNCEC	28	3.15787	0.0378
LNCEC does not cause LNCX		3.10925	0.0398
LNPX does not cause LNCEC	28	2.11414	0.1188
LNCEC does not cause LNPX		1.48786	0.2453
Lags: 5			
LNCX does not cause LNCEC	27	2.38435	0.0849
LNCEC does not cause LNCX		3.38554	0.0282
LNPX does not cause LNCEC	27	1.42837	0.2672
LNCEC does not cause LNPX		5.51295	0.0039

Table E5 Pairwise Granger causality tests (series: LNPC, LNCM, and LNPM)

Sample: 1981–2012			
Null hypothesis	**Observations**	**F-Statistic**	**Probability**
Lags: 1			
LNCM does not cause LNPEC	31	0.75109	0.3935
LNPEC does not cause LNCM		3.21123	0.0839
LNPM does not cause LNPEC	31	4.01264	0.0549
LNPEC does not cause LNPM		0.04516	0.8333
Lags: 2			
LNCM does not cause LNPEC	30	0.31607	0.7319
LNPEC does not cause LNCM		2.01953	0.1538
LNPM does not cause LNPEC	30	0.81961	0.4521
LNPEC does not cause LNPM		0.33594	0.7178
Lags: 3			
LNCM does not cause LNPEC	29	0.40208	0.7529
LNPEC does not cáuse LNCM		1.95533	0.1502
LNPM does not cause LNPEC	29	0.58571	0.6307
LNPEC does not cause LNPM		0.43476	0.7303
Lags: 4			
LNCM does not cause LNPEC	28	0.73267	0.5809
LNPEC does not cause LNCM		1.84214	0.1624
LNPM does not cause LNPEC	28	0.70606	0.5976
LNPEC does not cause LNPM		0.63880	0.6412
Lags: 5			
LNCM does not cause LNPEC	27	1.42483	0.2684
LNPEC does not cause LNCM		2.18825	0.1067
LNPM does not cause LNPEC	27	0.65970	0.6590
LNPEC does not cause LNPM		0.59809	0.7021
Lags: 6			
LNCM does not cause LNPEC	26	1.23111	0.3519
LNPEC does not cause LNCM		3.51726	0.0272
LNPM does not cause LNPEC	26	1.07847	0.4236
LNPEC does not cause LNPM		1.81244	0.1734

Table E6 Pairwise Granger causality tests (series: LNPEC, LNCX, and LNPX)

Sample: 1981–2012			
Null hypothesis	Observations	F-Statistic	Probability
Lags: 1			
LNCX does not cause LNPEC	31	0.94803	0.3386
LNPEC does not cause LNCX		7.29516	0.0116
LNPX does not cause LNPEC	31	3.80469	0.0612
LNPEC does not cause LNPX		0.04192	0.8393
Lags: 2			
LNCX does not cause LNPEC	30	0.37395	0.6918
LNPEC does not cause LNCX		3.48259	0.0463
LNPX does not cause LNPEC	30	0.99417	0.3842
LNPEC does not cause LNPX		0.99153	0.3851
Lags: 3			
LNCX does not cause LNPEC	29	0.40434	0.7513
LNPEC does not cause LNCX		1.77250	0.1818
LNPX does not cause LNPEC	29	0.40952	0.7477
LNPEC does not cause LNPX		0.79091	0.5119
Lags: 4			
LNCX does not cause LNPEC	28	0.56134	0.6935
LNPEC does not cause LNCX		1.19350	0.3457
LNPX does not cause LNPEC	28	0.61501	0.6571
LNPEC does not cause LNPX		1.08019	0.3940
Lags: 7			
LNCX does not cause LNPEC	25	1.77578	0.1978
LNPEC does not cause LNCX		1.60566	0.2397
LNPX does not cause LNPEC	25	2.52299	0.0896
LNPEC does not cause LNPX		2.89809	0.0623
Lags: 8			
LNCX does not cause LNPEC	24	1.16578	0.4263
LNPEC does not cause LNCX		1.02191	0.4952
LNPX does not cause LNPEC	24	5.46084	0.0187
LNPEC does not cause LNPX		1.58134	0.2797

Table E7 Pairwise Granger causality tests (series: LNNEC, LNCM, and LNPM)

Sample: 1981−2012			
Null hypothesis	**Observations**	**F-Statistic**	**Probability**
Lags: 1			
LNCM does not cause LNNEC	31	12.1504	0.0016
LNNEC does not cause LNCM		0.12997	0.7212
LNPM does not cause LNNEC	31	3.08735	0.0898
LNNEC does not cause LNPM		0.01148	0.9154
Lags: 2			
LNCM does not cause LNNEC	30	5.74091	0.0089
LNNEC does not cause LNCM		0.42906	0.6558
LNPM does not cause LNNEC	30	0.49524	0.6153
LNNEC does not cause LNPM		0.66516	0.5231
Lags: 3			
LNCM does not cause LNNEC	29	6.73781	0.0022
LNNEC does not cause LNCM		0.12390	0.9450
LNPM does not cause LNNEC	29	0.38030	0.7682
LNNEC does not cause LNPM		0.19879	0.8961
Lags: 4			
LNCM does not cause LNNEC	28	4.95732	0.0066
LNNEC does not cause LNCM		0.30780	0.8692
LNPM does not cause LNNEC	28	0.79696	0.5419
LNNEC does not cause LNPM		0.60010	0.6671

Table E8 Pairwise Granger causality tests (series: LNNEC, LNCX, and LNPX)

Sample: 1981−2012			
Null hypothesis	Observations	F-Statistic	Probability
Lags: 1			
LNCX does not cause LNNEC	31	4.83048	0.0364
LNNEC does not cause LNCX		0.00783	0.9301
LNPX does not cause LNNEC	31	2.67153	0.1134
LNNEC does not cause LNPX		7.6E-05	0.9931
Lags: 2			
LNCX does not cause LNNEC	30	1.57386	0.2271
LNNEC does not cause LNCX		3.15495	0.0600
LNPX does not cause LNNEC	30	0.61946	0.5463
LNNEC does not cause LNPX		0.46517	0.6334
Lags: 3			
LNCX does not cause LNNEC	29	1.04471	0.3924
LNNEC does not cause LNCX		1.98203	0.1461
LNPX does not cause LNNEC	29	0.45447	0.7168
LNNEC does not cause LNPX		0.20480	0.8920

Table E9 Pairwise Granger causality tests (series: LNHEC, LNCM, and LNPM)

Sample: 1981–2012			
Null hypothesis	**Observations**	**F-Statistic**	**Probability**
Lags: 1			
LNCM does not cause LNHEC	31	4.45155	0.0439
LNHEC does not cause LNCM		2.99631	0.0945
LNPM does not cause LNHEC	31	0.15521	0.6966
LNHEC does not cause LNPM		0.01420	0.9060
Lags: 2			
LNCM does not cause LNHEC	30	1.63579	0.2150
LNHEC does not cause LNCM		1.74587	0.1951
LNPM does not cause LNHEC	30	0.68388	0.5138
LNHEC does not cause LNPM		0.50983	0.6067
Lags: 3			
LNCM does not cause LNHEC	29	2.08786	0.1310
LNHEC does not cause LNCM		0.91476	0.4500
LNPM does not cause LNHEC	29	1.33586	0.2883
LNHEC does not cause LNPM		0.44011	0.7266
Lags: 4			
LNCM does not cause LNHEC	28	1.68759	0.1944
LNHEC does not cause LNCM		1.30672	0.3031
LNPM does not cause LNHEC	28	0.80709	0.5359
LNHEC does not cause LNPM		0.34657	0.8431
Lags: 5			
LNCM does not cause LNHEC	27	1.25493	0.3303
LNHEC does not cause LNCM		3.81720	0.0182
LNPM does not cause LNHEC	27	1.10108	0.3979
LNHEC does not cause LNPM		0.68132	0.6441
Lags: 6			
LNCM does not cause LNHEC	26	1.54787	0.2389
LNHEC does not cause LNCM		3.78851	0.0210
LNPM does not cause LNHEC	26	0.64411	0.6943
LNHEC does not cause LNPM		0.49847	0.7987

Table E10 Pairwise Granger causality tests (series: LNHEC, LNCX, and LNPX)

Sample: 1981–2012			
Null hypothesis	Observations	F-Statistic	Probability
Lags: 1			
LNCX does not cause LNHEC	31	7.17195	0.0122
LNHEC does not cause LNCX		2.50339	0.1248
LNPX does not cause LNHEC	31	0.04906	0.8263
LNHEC does not cause LNPX		0.03561	0.8517
Lags: 2			
LNCX does not cause LNHEC	30	2.74132	0.0839
LNHEC does not cause LNCX		1.13859	0.3363
LNPX does not cause LNHEC	30	0.24901	0.7815
LNHEC does not cause LNPX		0.04816	0.9531
Lags: 3			
LNCX does not cause LNHEC	29	1.51756	0.2378
LNHEC does not cause LNCX		0.41423	0.7445
LNPX does not cause LNHEC	29	0.33085	0.8031
LNHEC does not cause LNPX		0.09650	0.9612

Appendix F Impulse responses function

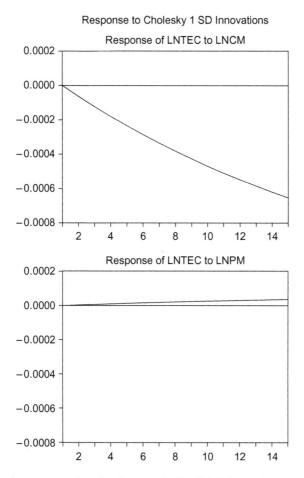

Figure F1 Impulse responses function (between LNTEC, LNCM, and LNPM).

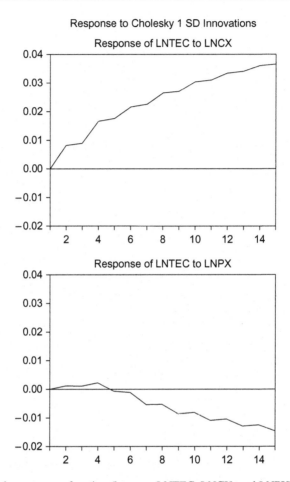

Figure F2 Impulse responses function (between LNTEC, LNCX, and LNPX).

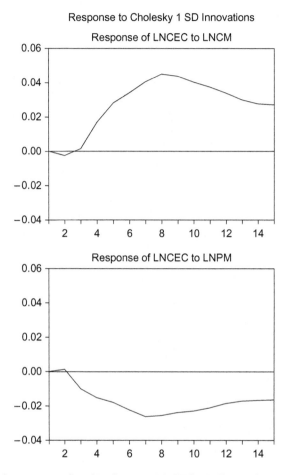

Figure F3 Impulse responses function (between LNCEC, LNCM, and LNPM).

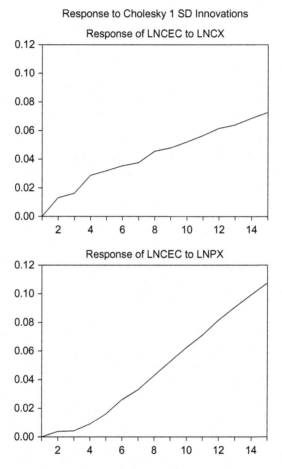

Figure F4 Impulse responses function (between LNCEC, LNCX, and LNPX).

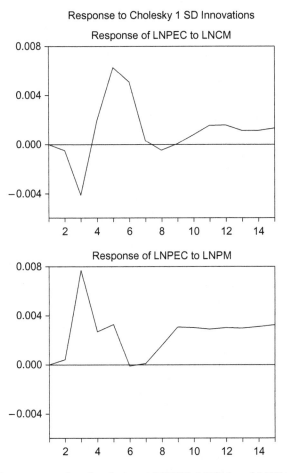

Figure F5 Impulse responses function (between LNPEC, LNCM, and LNPM).

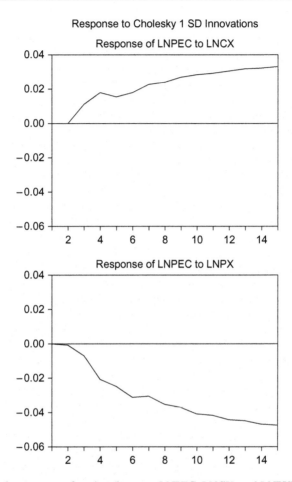

Figure F6 Impulse responses function (between LNPEC, LNCX, and LNPX).

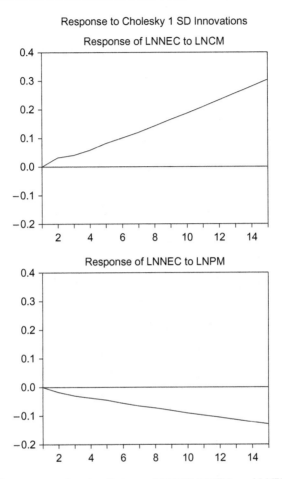

Figure F7 Impulse responses function (between LNNEC, LNCM, and LNPM).

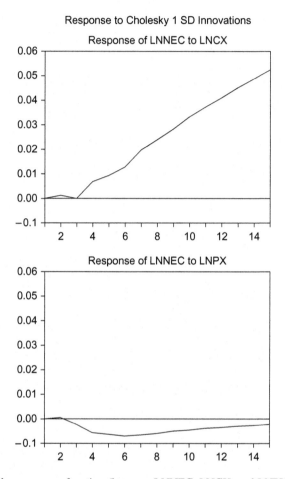

Figure F8 Impulse responses function (between LNNEC, LNCX, and LNPX).

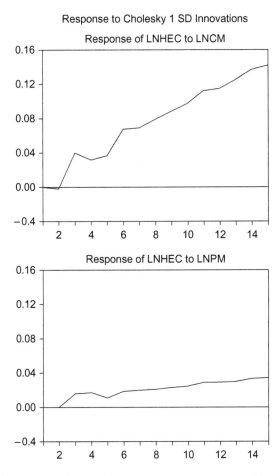

Figure F9 Impulse responses function (between LNHEC, LNCM, and LNPM).

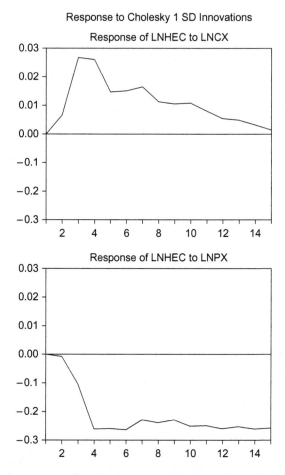

Figure F10 Impulse responses function (between LNHEC, LNCX, and LNPX).

Appendix G   Results of variance decomposition

Table G1 **Decomposition of LNTEC (Cholesky Ordering: LNTEC, LNCM, and LNPM)**

Period	SE	LNTEC	LNCM	LNPM
1	0.033019	100.0000	0.000000	0.000000
2	0.046716	99.99982	0.000182	5.55E-07
3	0.057240	99.99941	0.000584	1.78E-06
4	0.066123	99.99882	0.001181	3.59E-06
5	0.073957	99.99804	0.001952	5.94E-06
6	0.081048	99.99712	0.002876	8.75E-06
7	0.087575	99.99605	0.003936	1.20E-05
8	0.093656	99.99487	0.005114	1.56E-05
9	0.099372	99.99358	0.006397	1.95E-05
10	0.104784	99.99221	0.007770	2.36E-05
11	0.109936	99.99075	0.009221	2.81E-05
12	0.114862	99.98923	0.010738	3.27E-05
13	0.119590	99.98765	0.012313	3.75E-05
14	0.124142	99.98602	0.013935	4.24E-05
15	0.128538	99.98436	0.015597	4.75E-05

Table G2 **Decomposition of LNTEC (Cholesky Ordering: LNTEC, LNCX, and LNPX)**

Period	SE	LNTEC	LNCX	LNPX
1	0.034739	100.0000	0.000000	0.000000
2	0.049547	97.16050	2.780546	0.058957
3	0.069399	96.84953	3.095283	0.055183
4	0.080822	93.38880	6.492471	0.118725
5	0.093895	91.60270	8.304369	0.092932
6	0.102858	88.59482	11.31608	0.089099
7	0.113266	86.41515	13.28607	0.298787
8	0.121788	83.33494	16.21990	0.445165
9	0.131132	80.95202	18.23664	0.811343
10	0.139378	78.04738	20.89771	1.054912
11	0.148171	75.65430	22.87288	1.472818
12	0.156187	73.06440	25.16408	1.771528
13	0.164569	70.84006	26.95139	2.208541
14	0.172432	68.54837	28.91859	2.533042
15	0.180477	66.55020	30.49639	2.953405

Table G3 **Decomposition of LNCEC (Cholesky Ordering: LNCEC, LNCM, and LNPM)**

Period	SE	LNCEC	LNCM	LNPM
1	0.025398	100.0000	0.000000	0.000000
2	0.046918	99.62932	0.290349	0.080335
3	0.067288	97.55947	0.202707	2.237825
4	0.081167	90.41980	4.578198	5.002004
5	0.094360	80.32238	12.38762	7.289999
6	0.106608	69.88682	20.02746	10.08573
7	0.118485	58.97119	27.98200	13.04681
8	0.129708	49.77773	35.46638	14.75589
9	0.139150	43.46998	40.78057	15.74944
10	0.146788	39.18219	44.23576	16.58205
11	0.153047	36.13311	46.71534	17.15155
12	0.158031	34.07034	48.46640	17.46326
13	0.162121	32.78335	49.50868	17.70798
14	0.165874	31.96641	50.10386	17.92973
15	0.169603	31.42700	50.49018	18.08282

Table G4 **Decomposition of LNCEC (Cholesky Ordering: LNCEC, LNCX, and LNPX)**

Period	SE	LNCEC	LNCX	LNPX
1	0.032922	100.0000	0.000000	0.000000
2	0.074327	96.62171	3.116968	0.261321
3	0.117639	96.59787	3.171701	0.230425
4	0.155841	94.29274	5.242952	0.464306
5	0.192692	92.82680	6.190440	0.982759
6	0.228654	91.21103	6.796210	1.992763
7	0.264963	89.88022	7.081420	3.038363
8	0.302258	87.93096	7.720676	4.348362
9	0.340603	86.12229	8.068418	5.809289
10	0.379245	84.20000	8.399984	7.400015
11	0.418551	82.30624	8.722667	8.971093
12	0.458937	80.32633	9.056735	10.61694
13	0.500088	78.51287	9.263545	12.22359
14	0.541857	76.74025	9.493062	13.76669
15	0.584433	75.06687	9.709244	15.22389

Table G5 **Decomposition of LNPEC (Cholesky Ordering: LNPEC, LNCM, and LNPM)**

Period	SE	LNPEC	LNCM	LNPM
1	0.037390	100.0000	0.000000	0.000000
2	0.053056	99.98470	0.008861	0.006436
3	0.061167	97.92065	0.464392	1.614959
4	0.064445	97.85291	0.512977	1.634116
5	0.069057	97.06281	1.283548	1.653646
6	0.074767	97.02534	1.563772	1.410889
7	0.079817	97.38812	1.373692	1.238184
8	0.084205	97.61418	1.237394	1.148428
9	0.088035	97.69247	1.132098	1.175431
10	0.091747	97.75693	1.049693	1.193379
11	0.095635	97.81469	0.992677	1.192638
12	0.099590	97.86520	0.941081	1.193717
13	0.103297	97.91839	0.887227	1.194378
14	0.106793	97.95492	0.841458	1.203624
15	0.110200	97.97638	0.804866	1.218753

Table G6 **Decomposition of LNPEC (Cholesky Ordering: LNPEC, LNCX, and LNPX)**

Period	SE	LNPEC	LNCX	LNPX
1	0.038731	100.0000	0.000000	0.000000
2	0.053608	99.98168	0.000139	0.018183
3	0.065119	95.94401	2.904853	1.151141
4	0.078675	85.05548	7.169998	7.774517
5	0.091735	78.79541	8.088224	13.11636
6	0.107696	73.40877	8.630141	17.96109
7	0.122760	69.90190	10.05610	20.04200
8	0.137707	66.45739	11.02447	22.51814
9	0.152178	63.46761	12.15310	24.37929
10	0.167010	60.76335	12.98203	26.25462
11	0.181051	58.68291	13.65275	27.66434
12	0.195110	56.81103	14.20739	28.98158
13	0.208537	55.21553	14.76747	30.01700
14	0.221677	53.76994	15.18859	31.04146
15	0.234304	52.51289	15.58597	31.90113

Table **G7** **Decomposition of LNNEC (Cholesky Ordering: LNNEC, LNCM, and LNPM)**

Period	SE	LNNEC	LNCM	LNPM
1	0.039763	100.0000	0.000000	0.000000
2	0.067083	70.81952	22.38430	6.796186
3	0.092610	55.23329	30.68694	14.07976
4	0.127033	46.50032	37.19169	16.30799
5	0.170560	40.25862	43.76222	15.97916
6	0.216951	34.69095	48.74326	16.56579
7	0.266769	30.44023	52.52334	17.03643
8	0.322063	27.60160	55.63734	16.76106
9	0.381902	25.24474	58.34256	16.41270
10	0.444939	23.14394	60.64586	16.21020
11	0.511706	21.47085	62.60124	15.92792
12	0.582596	20.11346	64.32030	15.56625
13	0.656976	18.90596	65.84946	15.24458
14	0.734589	17.84671	67.20048	14.95282
15	0.815697	16.94617	68.40364	14.65019

Table **G8** **Decomposition of LNNEC (Cholesky Ordering: LNNEC, LNCX, and LNPX)**

Period	SE	LNNEC	LNCX	LNPX
1	0.057234	100.0000	0.000000	0.000000
2	0.081521	99.97108	0.024471	0.004447
3	0.105125	99.93829	0.014727	0.046988
4	0.131955	99.50836	0.280241	0.211398
5	0.155947	99.12371	0.561645	0.314647
6	0.177349	98.64215	0.957923	0.399925
7	0.197674	97.79118	1.776732	0.432084
8	0.216915	96.86564	2.700209	0.434147
9	0.235036	95.82975	3.755444	0.414803
10	0.252965	94.63195	4.977251	0.390795
11	0.270665	93.38754	6.251143	0.361315
12	0.288183	92.11983	7.546796	0.333379
13	0.305702	90.80009	8.894248	0.305665
14	0.323262	89.47947	10.24042	0.280114
15	0.340798	88.15409	11.58991	0.256001

Table G9 **Decomposition of LNHEC (Cholesky Ordering: LNHEC, LNCM, and LNPM)**

Period	SE	LNHEC	LNCM	LNPM
1	0.064817	100.0000	0.000000	0.000000
2	0.093099	99.96219	0.037805	8.32E-06
3	0.132471	89.42580	9.154228	1.419973
4	0.170551	89.12610	9.008241	1.865664
5	0.209564	89.43639	9.054191	1.509417
6	0.265342	86.37938	12.19084	1.429784
7	0.313223	84.90163	13.66984	1.428533
8	0.364227	83.75003	14.86136	1.388609
9	0.421528	83.14921	15.51806	1.332733
10	0.476965	82.37174	16.32365	1.304603
11	0.536149	81.35436	17.32310	1.322540
12	0.595225	80.88968	17.79913	1.311199
13	0.655739	80.38762	18.32347	1.288916
14	0.718951	79.80999	18.90287	1.287145
15	0.781089	79.38175	19.33539	1.282853

Table G10 **Decomposition of LNHEC (Cholesky Ordering: LNHEC, LNCX, and LNPX)**

Period	SE	LNHEC	LNCX	LNPX
1	0.068932	100.0000	0.000000	0.000000
2	0.094444	99.50263	0.490568	0.006801
3	0.113784	93.25917	5.898236	0.842591
4	0.136167	87.91170	7.799239	4.289057
5	0.156320	87.16398	6.803026	6.032992
6	0.174577	86.66015	6.205424	7.134430
7	0.191305	86.70498	5.914241	7.380778
8	0.207517	87.06976	5.324499	7.605741
9	0.222803	87.49489	4.843473	7.661636
10	0.237513	87.66113	4.471218	7.867650
11	0.251857	87.94030	4.078454	7.981244
12	0.265978	88.18391	3.698733	8.117355
13	0.279572	88.45025	3.378543	8.171209
14	0.292937	88.66773	3.089628	8.242644
15	0.306041	88.90173	2.833110	8.265164

Vertical specialization and strengthening indigenous innovation: comparing impacts of conventional trade and processing trade patterns on innovation in China

7

7.1 Introduction

Vertical specialization has become a dominant feature of Chinese trade and economy, reflecting the increasing fragmentation and sophistication of production. An implication of vertical specialization is that imports and exports by processing trade in China have been steadily growing over the past three decades.

It is recognized that productivity is a major source of increasing income and that technology innovation is a driver of inclusive growth. Therefore, indigenous innovation is a key element of achieving inclusive growth in China. China has increased its outlays on research and development (R&D) with the deliberate aim of narrowing the gap in productivity and income in relation to leading countries. China's intramural expenditure on R&D increased from 0.5% of the GDP in 1994 to 1.98% in 2012. Therefore, what are the drivers of technology innovation and inclusive growth in China? To what extent can China successfully build its own national innovation system through technology acquisition via vertically specialized trade? What are the roles of imports and exports by processing trade? What is the relationship between vertical specialization and indigenous innovation in an increasingly integrated global value chain, and how does this interaction change to respond to the specific characteristics of China?

Impressively rapid vertically specialized trade growth in China has important implications for developing countries, not only in terms of its economic impact but also in terms of its experiences in guiding and promoting the inclusive growth process. China has opened up to international trade and investment with inclusive growth strategies, and at the same time it has put an increasing emphasis on indigenous knowledge creation and innovation. Experiences in China may provide valuable lessons for other developing countries with regard to industrial, technology, and trade policies.

Globalization and vertical specialization in the global production value chain require examination of innovation input factors in an international context, especially when foreign-invested enterprises already have built a strong existence, often in the form of international joint ventures in China. Policymakers need to explore success factors for innovation input to remain competitive. A better understanding of the relationship between environmental constraints and indigenous innovation in various local contexts becomes one of the most important sources of productivity and inclusive growth. Identifying factors that influence product innovation in the international context thus becomes crucially important to researchers and managers.

Section 7.2 provides institutional background and Section 7.3 discusses the interactions between vertical specialization and indigenous innovation in the context of the exchange of intermediate goods and services. Section 7.4 concludes with an evaluation of the evidence and discusses policy implications.

7.2 Institutional background

Technological innovation is an important driving force for inclusive growth in China. Innovation depends largely on industrial firms' technological capabilities through strengthening their internal R&D expenditures. China's efforts to strengthen its innovation capacity are part of inclusive growth in which an implication is a focus on "indigenous innovation" to increase wages and living standards so that it can utilize science and technology to support inclusive growth. Governments can actively encourage innovation through providing seed grants, start-up money, and direct support payments that enhance the capability of a firm through the increase in knowledge that can be a basis for innovation (Peerasit, 2014). In general, China is the largest contributor to R&D expenditure in non-OECD countries (Martin, 2009).

Before turning to empirical evidence, this section describes the institutional environment in China that is relevant to our analysis—the innovation policies and trends. The institution school focuses on the institution environment that shapes innovation capabilities. The unique Chinese institution and processing trade systems also necessitate the study on what impact the institutional constraints have on innovation input and the resulting indigenous innovation performance of inclusive growth in the Chinese context. As a kind of institutional arrangement covering R&D-related activities, innovation policies play a critical role in remedying market failures and creating a fertile innovation environment. In transition economies such as China, the government plays an important role in developing innovation capabilities through science and technology (S&T) policies. Since 1978, China has implemented a package of institutional changes to adopt an open policy toward facilitating technological progress of domestic firms. The strategic National S&T Conferences (NSTC, 1978, 1985, 1995, 1999, 2006) have marked the different phases of the country's S&T policy reform during the period of China's economic transition (OECD, 2008; Jian, 2015). A major objective of China's FDI-related policy is to "exchange markets for technology." China also needs indigenous innovation to upgrade its economy while still integrating into vertical specialization and keeping markets open. Initiated in 2006, China's national medium and long-term science and technology development plan (2006−20) signaled its emphasis on the indigenous innovation system.

Among different institutional factors, trade liberalization and innovation policies are particularly relevant to innovation activities due to the potential significant implications for international managers and Chinese policymakers. Tang and Hussler (2011) found that the Chinese national innovation system is composed of two complementary building blocks: an FDI-based innovation system and an indigenous innovation system. China has established Economic and Technological Development Zones (ETDZs), Export Processing Zones (EPZs), and High Tech Development Zones (HTDZs) to attract FDI. China's processing trade growth has relied on its international openness and ability to attract inward FDI. Foreign-invested enterprises in these areas were mostly engaged in processing trade. The indigenous innovation system, however, does not seem as influential as the FDI-based one if both systems are shown to have a positive influence on China's catching-up process. The factors that explain the accelerating trend of utilizing external sources of knowledge include declining transaction costs of acquiring external R&D inputs and shortening product cycle times (Narula, 2003; Fu et al., 2011). For China, with a huge market size very attractive to FDI and a powerful government controlling R&D resources, financial input from the government might signal its attitude of sustainable support to indigenous innovation (Georghiou et al., 2014). The setup of the institutional environment can be an enabler to the enhancement of indigenous innovation capabilities, depending on how the innovation input influences output through policies aimed at greatly improving intramural expenditures on R&D, through strong links with government expenditure for science and technology.

7.3 Empirical evidence of the impact of vertically specialized trade on indigenous innovation in China

7.3.1 Data and methodology

The Vector Autoregression is an ad hoc dynamic multivariate model treating simultaneous sets of variables equally; each endogenous variable is regressed on its own lags and the lags of all other variables in a finite-order system (Sims, 1980; Sun et al., 2010). If all variables are integrated with order 1, and if the cointegration relationships among them are in existence, then they can be simulated by the Vector error correction model (VECM) to estimate the variance decomposition functions and impulse response.

Although China hardly figured as a patenting player at all in China Science and Technology Statistics Year Report (up to the year 2000), the size of its R&D expenditure has made China a global R&D player. R&D efforts are recognized as the engine of sustained economic growth in endogenous growth literatures (Romer, 1990; Yuan, 2014). In empirical studies, R&D efforts can be measured by input indicators (R&D expenditure, government expenditure for science and technology) or output indicators (patents, citations). The objective of this section is to determine to what extent China's innovative capacity has been enhanced by vertical specialization. R&D expenditures are widely used as a proxy for innovation input. The more incentive in terms of appropriation for science and technology that the government provides, the more it increases the willingness of firms to change, resulting in higher numbers of innovations. To assess the efficiency of the two complementary parts of the Chinese foreign trade (conventional trade and processing trade), we use the analytical indicators presented in the China Statistics Yearbook on innovation, namely, appropriation for science and technology and total intramural expenditure on R&D.

All data have been obtained from the database of China Statistical Yearbook and China Trade and External Economics Statistical Yearbook published by National Bureau of Statistics of China; the sample covers the annual observations from 1981 to 2012. All variables are used and transformed into a natural logarithm. This study used the variables groups in Table A1 to find the relationship.

LNCM = natural logarithm of imports by conventional trade (CM);
LNPM = natural logarithm of imports by processing trade (PM);
LNPX = natural logarithm of exports by processing trade (PX);
LNCX = natural logarithm of exports by conventional trade (CX);
LNICM = natural logarithm of index of imports by conventional trade (ICM);
LNIPM = natural logarithm of index of imports by processing trade (IPM);
LNICX = natural logarithm of index of exports by conventional trade (ICX);
LNIPX = natural logarithm of index of exports by conventional trade (IPX);
LNASTS = natural logarithm of the ratio of appropriation for science and technology to total government budgetary expenditure;
LNRDG = natural logarithm of the ratio of total intramural expenditure on R&D to gross domestic products (GDP).

7.3.2 Unit root test

To test if all the time series used for the study are stable and to explore the existence cointegration equations, the augmented Dickey Fuller (ADF) test for unit roots was conducted to determine the order of integration of all variables. The results of the ADF unit roots tests (see Table B1) show that all the variables are found to be integrated with I(1); therefore, there may exist some cointegration between the employed variables. Thus, we use Johansen's technique to conduct the cointegration test.

7.3.3 Cointegration test

Cointegration means economic variables share the same stochastic trend, so they are combined together in the long-term. Even if they deviate from each other in the short-term, they tend to come back to the trend in the long-term. A necessary condition for the cointegration test is that all the variables should be integrated at the same order or should contain a deterministic trend (Engle and Granger, 1991). The unit root test results in Table B1 show that all the time series are integrated at the first difference but are not integrated at the level form during 1981 through 2012. Therefore, the time series during this period are valid in the cointegration test. Once the variables are cointegrated, the short-term changes can be explained through the VECM (Engle and Granger, 1987). Following the cointegration test, the VECM was used to analyze the causality within the four variable groups.

The results of trace statistics and the results of maximum eigen statistics are shown in Tables C1−C4. Trace statistics and maximum eigen statistics values help to find the rank(s), which shows the number of vectors containing long-term relations. It is evident that the null hypothesis of no rank is rejected. Therefore, the results of both trace and max-eigen statistics confirm that cointegration vectors exist in the model. It means the long-term relationship prevails among the variables. In summary, the Johansen cointegration test results show that the four variable groups in Table A1 are cointegrated during the periods and had a long-term equilibrium relationship during 1981 and 2012.

Following Johansen's technique, the normalized long-term cointegration relationships and the comparison coefficients are shown in Tables C1−C4. The normalized long-term cointegration relationships are very revealing. The observed signs are as anticipated. Moreover, the long-term relationships are also as expected, given the intrinsic interdependence between the variables.

From Tables C1−C4, we can obtain the following equations for the long-term:

1. The ratio of appropriation for science and technology to total government budgetary expenditure, index of imports and exports by conventional trade, and index of imports and exports by processing trade:

$$\text{LNASTS} = \underset{(0.22909)}{-1.287732\text{LNICM}} + \underset{(0.24258)}{0.047339\text{LNIPM}} \tag{7.1}$$

$$\text{LNASTS} = \underset{(0.33047)}{-1.666101\text{LNICX}} + \underset{(0.21810)}{0.539178\text{LNIPX}} \tag{7.2}$$

According to the results from Eqs. (7.1) and (7.2), the 1% increase in the index of imports by conventional trade (LNICM) will have a negative impact of 1.287732% on the ratio of appropriation for science and technology to total government budgetary expenditure (LNASTS), the 1% increase in the index of imports by processing trade (LNIPM) will have a positive impact of 0.047339% on the ratio of appropriation for science and technology to total government budgetary expenditure (LNASTS), the 1% increase in the index of exports by conventional trade (LNICX) will have a negative impact of 1.666101%, and the 1% increase in the index of exports by processing trade (LNIPX) will have a positive impact of 0.539178% on the ratio of appropriation for science and technology to total government budgetary (LNASTS).

Eqs. (7.1) and (7.2) show that the increase in the index of imports and exports by processing trade could increase the ratio of appropriation for science and technology to total government budgetary expenditure, and the index of imports and exports by conventional trade decreases the ratio of appropriation for science and technology to total government budgetary expenditure in the long-term. This provides support for evidence of the foreign trade and vertically specialized trade channels.

2. The ratio of total intramural expenditure on R&D to gross domestic products, imports and exports by conventional trade, and imports and exports by processing trade:

$$\underset{(0.10717)}{\text{LNRDG}} = -0.291413\text{LNCM} + \underset{(0.13721)}{0.873825\text{LNPM}} \tag{7.3}$$

$$\underset{(0.14312)}{\text{LNRDG}} = -0.089710\text{LNCX} + \underset{(0.15731)}{0.476452\text{LNPX}} \tag{7.4}$$

From Eqs. (7.3) and (7.4), we observe that the 1% increase in imports by conventional trade (LNCM) will have a negative impact of 0.291413% on the ratio of total intramural expenditure on R&D to gross domestic products (LNRDG), the 1% increase in imports by processing trade will have a positive impact of 0.873825% on the ratio of total intramural expenditure on R&D to gross domestic products (LNRDG), the 1% increase in exports by conventional trade (LNCX) will have a negative impact of 0.089710% on the ratio of total intramural expenditure on R&D to gross domestic products (LNRDG), and the 1% increase in exports by processing trade (LNPX) will have a positive impact of 0.476452% on the ratio of total intramural expenditure on R&D to gross domestic products (LNRDG).

Eqs. (7.3) and (7.4) demonstrate that the increase in imports and exports by processing trade can cause the increase in the ratio of total intramural expenditure on R&D to gross domestic products (LNRDG) in the long-term. This confirms the existence of the vertical specialization channel.

The above mentioned equations show that the vertical specialization variables (LNIPM, LNPM, LNIPX, LNPX) have important effects on the indigenous innovation, which connects the vertically specialized trade policy variables with the indigenous innovation variables (LNASTS and LNRDG). These long-term equations support the existence of the vertical specialization channel in the trade policy transmission process in China.

Proposition 1. The contribution and importance of imports and exports by conventional trade to the increasing the ratio of appropriation for science and technology to total government budgetary expenditure are lower than that by processing trade.

Proposition 2. The contribution and importance of imports and exports by conventional trade to increasing the ratio of total intramural expenditure on R&D to gross domestic products are lower than that by processing trade.

7.3.4 Vector error correction model

The VECM is used to estimate the short-term and long-term impacts across a variety of variables, and the error correction model (ECM) coefficients show the speed with which the system converges to equilibrium. When the first difference variables are confirmed to have stationarity, ECM can be regressed in which vecm-1 is one difference error correction item whose coefficient represents the impact of the last period's error correction on this period's variable. The results of VECM are reported in Tables D1−D4.

In Table D1, for D(LNICM), the coefficient of error correction term is −0.835786. It shows that if a deviation from the long-term happens as a shock, then the adjustment speed toward long-term equilibrium will be 83.5786% and there will be full adjustment of deviation.

In Table D2, for D(LNICX), the coefficient of error correction term is −0.790859. It shows that if a deviation from the long-term happens as a shock, then the adjustment speed toward the long-term equilibrium will be 79.0859% and there will be full adjustment of deviation. For D(LNIPX), the coefficient of error correction term is −0.095428. It shows that if a deviation from the long-term happens as a shock, then the adjustment speed toward long-term equilibrium will be 9.5428%.

In Table D3, for D(LNRDG), the coefficient of error correction term is −0.404207. It shows that if a deviation from the long-term happens as a shock, then the adjustment speed toward long-term equilibrium will be 40.4207% and there will be full adjustment of deviation. For D(LNCM), the coefficient of error correction term is −0.102958. It shows that if a deviation from the long-term happens as a shock, then the adjustment speed toward long-run equilibrium will be 10.2958%.

In Table E4, for D(LNRDG), the coefficient of error correction term is −0.770029. It shows that if a deviation from the long-term happens as a shock, then the adjustment speed toward long-term equilibrium will be 77.0029% and there will be full adjustment of deviation.

7.3.5   Granger causality tests

The structures of the causal relationships between variables were analyzed through the Granger causality approach. If probability value is less than any α level, then the hypothesis would be rejected at that level.

The results in Table E1 indicate the existence of unidirectional causality running from LNICM to LNASTS when one lag is applied at the 5% level of significance. They also reveal unidirectional causality running from LNASTS to LNCM when two lags are applied at the 10% level of significance. The results in Table E2 indicate the existence of unidirectional causality running from LNIPX to LNASTS when two lags are applied at the 10% level of significance. They also reveal unidirectional causality running from LNICX to LNASTS when two and four lags are applied at the 5% and 10% level of significance. When one lag is applied, we found unidirectional causality running from LNASTS to LNICX at the 10% level of significance.

The results in Table E3 indicate the existence of bidirectional causality running from LNPM to LNRDG when one lag is applied at the 5% and 10% level of significance. They also reveal unidirectional causality running from LNPM to LNRDG when two lags and three lags are applied at the 10% level of significance. We found unidirectional causality running from LNCM to LNRDG when one lag, two lags, and three lags were applied at the 10% or 5% level of significance. The results in Table E4 indicate the existence of unidirectional causality running from LNPX to LNRDG when one lag, two lags, and three lags are applied at the 5% level of significance. They also reveal unidirectional causality running from LNCX to LNRDG when one lag and three lags are applied at the 10% level of significance.

7.3.6   Impulse response function

To scrutinize the behavior of each variable once confronted with an increase in a single specific variable, as well as the duration of its effect, the impulse response functions (IRFs) are exhibited. The IRF curves simulated by the analytic method are reported in Figs. F1–F4. The curves indicate how a one-time positive shock of 1 standard deviation (SD) (±2 SE innovations) to the conventional trade and processing trade endures on the innovation in China. We consider the response of four variable groups to 1 SD in innovation of conventional trade and processing trade.

In Fig. F1, following an index of imports by conventional trade shock (an innovation in LNICM), the ratio of appropriation for science and technology to total government budgetary expenditure (LNASTS) declines immediately (negative change rate). By contrast, following an index of imports by processing trade shock (an innovation in LNIPM), the ratio of appropriation for science and technology to total government budgetary expenditure (LNASTS) increases immediately (positive change rate). By observing Fig. F2, we find that the LNASDS declines quickly at the time of the LNICX and the LNIPX shocks. The decline of the LNASTS after the LNICM and LNIPM shocks indicate possible evidence of a vertical specialization channel in China's trade policy transmission.

In Figs. F3 and F4, following an imports and exports by processing trade shock (an innovation in LNPM and LNPX), the ratio of total intramural expenditure on R&D to gross domestic products increases immediately (positive change rate). This suggests the existence of the vertical specialization channel in China's trade policy transmission: increasing total intramural expenditure on R&D is caused by the increase in the processing trade.

7.3.7 Variance decomposition

The variance decomposition functions are reported in Tables G1–G4.

In Table G1, LNASTS, LNICM, and LNIPM are the contributions of the innovation to forecasting variance, respectively, which sum to 100. It can be seen from Table G1 that, at the end of the forecast period, LNIPM explains approximately 0.796936% of the forecast error variance, supporting the evidence for the vertical specialization channel. In Table G2, at the end of the forecast period, LNIPX contributes 1.111208% to the forecasted variance decomposition of LNASTS, which supports the effects on the indigenous innovation of trade through the vertical specialization channel in China.

The variance decompositions in Tables G3 and G4 show that imports and exports by processing trade contribute to the forecasted variance of LNRDG (14.08126% and 17.60934%, respectively, at the end of the period), thus supporting the effects on the indigenous innovation of trade through the vertical specialization channel in China.

In summary, the results of variance decompositions in Tables G1–G4 also support the existence of strengthening indigenous innovation effects of vertical specialization trade policy because imports and exports by processing trade provide diverse contributions to the variance decomposition of LNASTS and LNRDG.

7.4   Concluding remarks and policy implications

This chapter discusses the characteristics of the institutional environment built in China and assesses the effect of the vertically specialized trade on indigenous innovation. The Chinese foreign trade is mainly composed of two complementary patterns, namely, imports and exports by conventional trade and imports and exports by processing trade. The former type comprises final goods and the latter comprises intermediate inputs. The database of China Statistical Yearbook and China Trade and External Economics Statistical Yearbook deconstruct China's trade in the actual pattern of flows of final versus intermediate goods by linking processing trade to production sharing or vertical specialization. The imports and exports by conventional trade have a negative effect on China's innovation, whereas the imports and exports by processing trade play a key role in fostering government expenditure for science and technology and intramural expenditure on R&D. Finally, this vertically specialized trade pattern has led to inclusive growth: all the figures indicate progress of innovation capability in China and a significant increase of innovative inputs over time.

These findings have important implications for the trade policy in China. First, the vertical specialization efforts drive indigenous technological upgrading in China. Imports and exports by processing trade will be more efficient than imports and exports by conventional trade. China specializes in the production of intermediate inputs, and China's trade in intermediates can be seen as a means of strengthening indigenous innovation. Therefore, China's trade liberalization policies among goods at different stages of processing have an important role in encouraging indigenous innovation for technological upgrading and inclusive growth. Second, there is evidence that higher processing trade flows lead to China's higher outlays on R&D with the deliberate aim of narrowing the gap in productivity and income in relation to leading countries. This should be taken into account in strategies for inclusive growth.

China's technological development from technology transfer to indigenous innovation should be part of a policy focusing on investment and intermediate trade liberalization.

Appendix A Variables grouping

Table A1 Variables grouping

Group number	Variables	Sample range
1	LNASTS, LNICM, and LNIPM	1981−2012
2	LNASTS, LNICX, and LNIPX	1981−2012
3	LNRDG, LNCM, and LNPM	1990−2012
4	LNRDG, LNCX, and LNPX	1990−2012

Note: ASTS indicates the ratio of appropriation for science and technology to total government budgetary expenditure; RDG stands for the ratio of total intramural expenditure on R&D to gross domestic products (GDP); PM is imports by processing trade; CM is imports by conventional trade; PX is exports by processing trade; CX is exports by conventional trade; IPM is index of imports by processing trade, preceding year = 100; ICM is index of imports by conventional trade, preceding year = 100; IPX is index of exports by processing trade, preceding year = 100; ICX is index of exports by conventional trade, preceding year = 100.

Appendix B   The results of unit root tests

Table B1 **Augmented Dickey Fuller test on unit roots for all variables**

S.No.	Variables	Test type (C,T,P)	ADF test statistic	Order of integration
1	LNASTS	(0,0,0)	−0.770150	I(1)
2	D(LNASTS)	(0,0,0)	−5.498861*	I(0)
3	LNRDG	(C,0,0)	0.731570	I(1)
4	D(LNRDG)	(C,0,0)	−3.410453**	I(0)
5	LNICM	(0,0,0)	0.192686	I(1)
6	D(LNICM)	(0,0,0)	−6.190714*	I(0)
7	LNIPM	(0,0,0)	−0.233714	I(1)
8	D(LNIPM)	(0,0,0)	−5.684092*	I(0)
9	LNICX	(0,0,0)	0.586035	I(1)
10	D(LNICX)	(0,0,0)	−8.757645*	I(0)
11	LNIPX	(0,0,0)	−0.047070	I(1)
12	D(LNIPX)	(0,0,0)	−9.234865*	I(0)
13	LNCM	(C,0,0)	1.011811	I(1)
14	D(LNCM)	(C,0,0)	−4.501031*	I(0)
15	LNCM	(0,0,0)	4.219038	I(1)
16	D(LNCM)	(0,0,0)	−3.282345*	I(0)
17	LNPM	(0,0,0)	5.500450	I(1)
18	D(LNPM)	(0,0,0)	−1.800021***	I(0)
19	LNPX	(0,0,1)	1.264734	I(1)
20	D(LNPX)	(0,0,0)	−1.676241***	I(0)
21	LNCX	(C,0,0)	1.335614	I(1)
22	D(LNCX)	(C,0,0)	−5.742582*	I(0)

Note: C, T, and P in test type stand for constant, trend, and lag orders, respectively. At three remarkable levels, when the ADF value is greater than the critical value, the corresponding series has the unit root. D stands for the first differential of the variables.
***, **, and * denote the rejection of the null hypothesis of unit root at the 10%, 5%, and 1% significance levels, respectively.

Appendix C   Results of cointegration tests

Table C1 **The series cointegration test result (between LNASTS, LNICM, and LNIPM)**

Sample (adjusted): 1985−2012
Included observations: 28 after adjustments
Trend assumption: Linear deterministic trend
Lags interval (in first differences): 1−2

Unrestricted cointegration rank test (trace)

Hypothesized number of CE(s)	Eigenvalue	Trace statistic	0.05 Critical value	Probability[a]
None[b]	0.559014	34.40720	29.79707	0.0137
At most 1	0.217158	11.48240	15.49471	0.1835
At most 2[b]	0.152327	4.627303	3.841466	0.0315

Trace test indicates 1 cointegrating equation at the 0.05 level

Unrestricted cointegration rank test (maximum eigenvalue)

Hypothesized number of CE(s)	Eigenvalue	Max-eigen statistic	0.05 Critical value	Probability[a]
None[b]	0.559014	22.92479	21.13162	0.0277
At most 1	0.217158	6.855100	14.26460	0.5064
At most 2[b]	0.152327	4.627303	3.841466	0.0315

Max-eigenvalue test indicates 1 cointegrating equation at the 0.05 level

1 Cointegrating equation		Log likelihood	92.82482

Normalized cointegrating coefficients (standard error in parentheses)

LNASTS	LNICM	LNIPM
1.000000	1.287732	−0.047339
	(0.22909)	(0.24258)

[a]MacKinnon−Haug−Michelis (1999) P values.
[b]Rejection of the hypothesis at the 0.05 level.

Table C2 **The series cointegration test result (between LNASTS, LNICX, and LNIPX)**

Sample (adjusted): 1985−2012
Included observations: 28 after adjustments
Trend assumption: Linear deterministic trend
Lags interval (in first differences): 1−2

Unrestricted cointegration rank test (trace)

Hypothesized number of CE(s)	Eigenvalue	Trace statistic	0.05 Critical value	Probability[a]
None[b]	0.424513	30.30712	29.79707	0.0437
At most 1	0.324387	14.83605	15.49471	0.0627
At most 2[b]	0.128660	3.856254	3.841466	0.0496

Trace test indicates 1 cointegrating equation at the 0.05 level

Unrestricted cointegration rank test (maximum eigenvalue)

Hypothesized number of CE(s)	Eigenvalue	Max-eigen statistic	0.05 Critical value	Probability[a]
None	0.424513	15.47108	21.13162	0.2573
At most 1	0.324387	10.97979	14.26460	0.1552
At most 2[b]	0.128660	3.856254	3.841466	0.0496

Max-eigenvalue test indicates no cointegration at the 0.05 level

1 Cointegrating equation		Log likelihood	103.3107

Normalized cointegrating coefficients (standard error in parentheses)

LNASTS	LNICX	LNIPX
1.000000	1.666101	−0.539178
	(0.33047)	(0.21810)

[a]MacKinnon−Haug−Michelis (1999) *P* values.
[b]Rejection of the hypothesis at the 0.05 level.

Table C3 The series cointegration test result (between LNRDG, LNCM, and LNPM)

Sample (adjusted): 1994−2012
Included observations: 19 after adjustments
Trend assumption: Linear deterministic trend
Lags interval (in first differences): 2−3

Unrestricted cointegration rank test (trace)

Hypothesized number of CE(s)	Eigenvalue	Trace statistic	0.05 Critical value	Probability[a]
None[b]	0.829924	43.98621	29.79707	0.0006
At most 1	0.379001	10.32757	15.49471	0.2564
At most 2	0.064926	1.275472	3.841466	0.2587

Trace test indicates 1 cointegrating equation at the 0.05 level

Unrestricted cointegration rank test (maximum eigenvalue)

Hypothesized number of CE(s)	Eigenvalue	Max-eigen statistic	0.05 Critical value	Probability[a]
None[b]	0.829924	33.65864	21.13162	0.0005
At most 1	0.379001	9.052102	14.26460	0.2818
At most 2	0.064926	1.275472	3.841466	0.2587

Max-eigenvalue test indicates 1 cointegrating equation at the 0.05 level

1 Cointegrating equation		Log likelihood	72.70622

Normalized cointegrating coefficients (standard error in parentheses)

LNRDG	LNCM	LNPM
1.000000	0.291413	−0.873825
	(0.10717)	(0.13721)

[a]MacKinnon−Haug−Michelis (1999) P values.
[b]Rejection of the hypothesis at the 0.05 level.

Table C4 **The series cointegration test result (between LNRDG, LNCX, and LNPX)**

Sample (adjusted): 1994−2012
Included observations: 19 after adjustments
Trend assumption: Linear deterministic trend
Lags interval (in first differences): 2−3

Unrestricted cointegration rank test (trace)

Hypothesized number of CE(s)	Eigenvalue	Trace statistic	0.05 Critical value	Probability[a]
None[b]	0.801528	43.89595	29.79707	0.0007
At most 1	0.500028	13.17091	15.49471	0.1087
At most 2	2.04E-06	3.87E-05	3.841466	0.9969

Trace test indicates 1 cointegrating equation at the 0.05 level

Unrestricted cointegration rank test (maximum eigenvalue)

Hypothesized number of CE(s)	Eigenvalue	Max-eigen statistic	0.05 Critical value	Probability[a]
None[b]	0.801528	30.72504	21.13162	0.0017
At most 1	0.500028	13.17087	14.26460	0.0739
At most 2	2.04E-06	3.87E-05	3.841466	0.9969

Max-eigenvalue test indicates 1 cointegrating equation at the 0.05 level

1 Cointegrating equation		**Log likelihood**	**81.76398**

Normalized cointegrating coefficients (standard error in parentheses)

LNRDG	LNCX	LNPX
1.000000	0.089710	−0.476452
	(0.14312)	(0.15731)

[a]MacKinnon−Haug−Michelis (1999) P values.
[b]Rejection of the hypothesis at the 0.05 level.

Appendix D   Results of vector error correction model

Table D1 **Vector error correction estimates (series: LNASTS, LNICM, and LNIPM)**

Sample (adjusted): 1985–2012 Included observations: 28 after adjustments Standard errors in parentheses ( ) and t-statistics in brackets [ ]			
Cointegrating equation			**CointEq1**
LNASTS(−1) LNICM(−1) LNIPM(−1) C			1.000000 1.287732 (0.22909) [5.62105] −0.047339 (0.24258) [−0.19515] −7.369311
Error correction	**D(LNASTS)**	**D(LNICM)**	**D(LNIPM)**
CointEq1	−0.083109 (0.08397) [−0.98978]	− 0.835786 (0.30530) [−2.73762]	0.227589 (0.22346) [1.01846]

Table D2 **Vector error correction estimates (series: LNASTS, LNICX, and LNIPX)**

Sample (adjusted): 1985–2012 Included observations: 28 after adjustments Standard errors in parentheses ( ) and t-statistics in brackets [ ]			
Cointegrating equation			**CointEq1**
LNASTS(−1) LNICX(−1) LNIPX(−1) C			1.000000 1.666101 (0.33047) [5.04168] −0.539178 (0.21810) [−2.47217] −6.783502
Error correction	**D(LNASTS)**	**D(LNICX)**	**D(LNIPX)**
CointEq1	−0.040995 (0.11010) [−0.37234]	−0.790859 (0.30463) [−2.59611]	−0.095428 (0.28040) [−0.34033]

Table D3 Vector error correction estimates (series: LNRDG, LNCM, and LNPM)

Sample (adjusted): 1994−2012			
Included observations: 19 after adjustments			
Standard errors in parentheses ( ) and t-statistics in brackets [ ]			

Cointegrating equation			CointEq1
LNRDG(−1)			1.000000
LNCM(−1)			0.291413
			(0.10717)
			[2.71928]
LNPM(−1)			−0.873825
			(0.13721)
			[−6.36845]
C			4.216957

Error correction	D(LNRDG)	D(LNCM)	D(LNPM)
CointEq1	−0.404207	−0.102958	0.590305
	(0.13029)	(0.29035)	(0.21275)
	[−3.10242]	[−0.35460]	[2.77469]

Table D4 Vector error correction estimates (series: LNRDG, LNCX, and LNPX)

Sample (adjusted): 1994−2012			
Included observations: 19 after adjustments			
Standard errors in parentheses ( ) and t-statistics in brackets [ ]			

Cointegrating equation			CointEq1
LNRDG(−1)			1.000000
LNCX(−1)			0.089710
			(0.14312)
			[0.62680]
LNPX(−1)			−0.476452
			(0.15731)
			[−3.02876]
C			2.987862

Error correction	D(LNRDG)	D(LNCX)	D(LNPX)
CointEq1	−0.770029	1.007972	0.661448
	(0.15047)	(0.40417)	(0.33764)
	[−5.11757]	[2.49391]	[1.95902]

Appendix E   Results of Granger causality tests

Table E1 **Pairwise Granger causality tests (series: LNASTS, LNICM, and LNIPM)**

Sample: 1982–2012			
Null hypothesis	**Observations**	**F-statistic**	**Probability**
Lags: 1			
LNICM does not cause LNASTS	30	4.96047	0.0345
LNASTS does not cause LNICM		0.68550	0.4150
LNIPM does not cause LNASTS	30	0.09761	0.7571
LNASTS does not cause LNIPM		1.16523	0.2899
Lags: 2			
LNICM does not cause LNASTS	29	1.87848	0.1746
LNASTS does not cause LNICM		2.89582	0.0747
LNIPM does not cause LNASTS	29	1.39429	0.2674
LNASTS does not cause LNIPM		1.05292	0.3645
Lags: 3			
LNICM does not cause LNASTS	28	1.92474	0.1565
LNASTS does not cause LNICM		1.71019	0.1955
LNIPM does not cause LNASTS	28	0.69270	0.5667
LNASTS does not cause LNIPM		1.82344	0.1738
Lags: 4			
LNICM does not cause LNASTS	27	1.27134	0.3177
LNASTS does not cause LNICM		1.91441	0.1517
LNIPM does not cause LNASTS	27	1.08968	0.3913
LNASTS does not cause LNIPM		1.35282	0.2892

Table E2 **Pairwise Granger causality tests (series: LNASTS, LNICX, and LNIPX)**

Sample: 1982–2012			
Null hypothesis	**Observations**	**F-statistic**	**Probability**
Lags: 1			
LNICX does not cause LNASTS	30	2.48421	0.1266
LNASTS does not cause LNICX		3.62502	0.0676
LNIPX does not cause LNASTS	30	0.20162	0.6570
LNASTS does not cause LNIPX		1.32069	0.2605
Lags: 2			
LNICX does not cause LNASTS	29	3.45545	0.0480
LNASTS does not cause LNICX		4.84012	0.0171
LNIPX does not cause LNASTS	29	2.63040	0.0927
LNASTS does not cause LNIPX		0.54119	0.5890
Lags: 3			
LNICX does not cause LNASTS	28	2.02855	0.1407
LNASTS does not cause LNICX		1.84451	0.1700
LNIPX does not cause LNASTS	28	1.72999	0.1915
LNASTS does not cause LNIPX		1.66575	0.2048
Lags: 4			
LNICX does not cause LNASTS	27	2.37349	0.0908
LNASTS does not cause LNICX		1.72337	0.1887
LNIPX does not cause LNASTS	27	1.46624	0.2537
LNASTS does not cause LNIPX		1.21105	0.3405

Table E3 **Pairwise Granger causality tests (series: LNRDG, LNCM, and LNPM)**

Sample: 1990–2012			
Null hypothesis	Observations	F-statistic	Probability
Lags: 1			
LNCM does not cause LNRDG	22	3.52529	0.0759
LNRDG does not cause LNCM		1.69110	0.2090
LNPM does not cause LNRDG	22	4.85983	0.0400
LNRDG does not cause LNPM		3.49749	0.0769
Lags: 2			
LNCM does not cause LNRDG	21	2.76586	0.0930
LNRDG does not cause LNCM		1.04926	0.3731
LNPM does not cause LNRDG	21	3.44538	0.0570
LNRDG does not cause LNPM		1.35620	0.2857
Lags: 3			
LNCM does not cause LNRDG	20	3.52542	0.0458
LNRDG does not cause LNCM		1.66066	0.2242
LNPM does not cause LNRDG	20	3.33639	0.0530
LNRDG does not cause LNPM		1.03090	0.4112

Table E4 **Pairwise Granger causality tests (series: LNRDG, LNCX, and LNPX)**

Sample: 1990–2012			
Null hypothesis	Observations	F-statistic	Probability
Lags: 1			
LNCX does not cause LNRDG	22	3.84743	0.0646
LNRDG does not cause LNCX		2.79204	0.1111
LNPX does not cause LNRDG	22	6.74498	0.0177
LNRDG does not cause LNPX		1.08551	0.3105
Lags: 2			
LNCX does not cause LNRDG	21	2.52561	0.1114
LNRDG does not cause LNCX		2.58206	0.1067
LNPX does not cause LNRDG	21	4.35031	0.0310
LNRDG does not cause LNPX		0.47059	0.6330
Lags: 3			
LNCX does not cause LNRDG	20	3.02717	0.0678
LNRDG does not cause LNCX		2.03062	0.1593
LNPX does not cause LNRDG	20	4.01314	0.0318
LNRDG does not cause LNPX		0.43065	0.7345

Appendix F Impulse response function

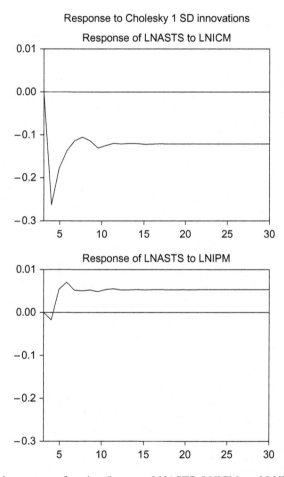

Figure F1 Impulse response function (between LNASTS, LNICM, and LNIPM).

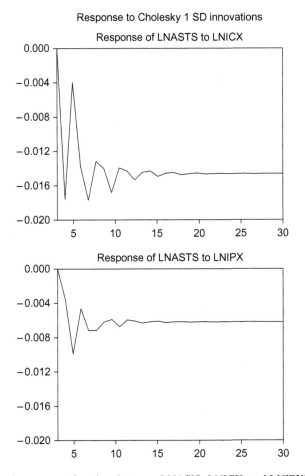

Figure F2 Impulse response function (between LNASIS, LNICX, and LNIPX).

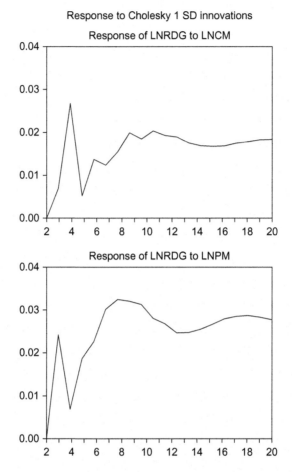

Figure F3 Impulse response function (between LNRDG, LNCM, and LNPM).

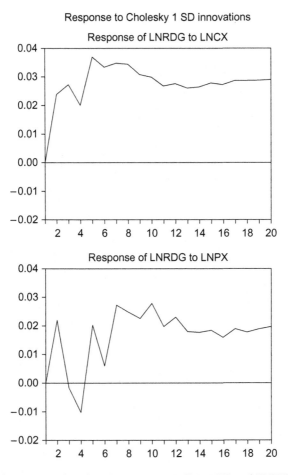

Figure F4 Impulse response function (between LNRDG, LNCX, and LNPX).

Appendix G   Results of variance decomposition

Table G1 **Decomposition of LNASTS (Cholesky ordering: LNASTS, LNICM, and LNIPM)**

Period	SE	LNASTS	LNICM	LNIPM
1	0.048919	100.0000	0.000000	0.000000
2	0.074595	87.47370	12.47040	0.055893
3	0.095908	88.63507	11.01223	0.352701
4	0.112024	89.76712	9.576744	0.656139
5	0.125730	90.87851	8.427672	0.693818
6	0.137976	91.70377	7.583626	0.712600
7	0.150043	92.28117	6.992330	0.726500
8	0.161337	92.57217	6.707135	0.720698
9	0.171809	92.82151	6.444894	0.733594
10	0.181677	93.04934	6.200923	0.749734
11	0.190995	93.23036	6.014481	0.755158
12	0.199866	93.38445	5.855164	0.760385
13	0.208404	93.51383	5.720425	0.765742
14	0.216610	93.61751	5.613608	0.768884
15	0.224503	93.70832	5.519247	0.772432
16	0.232132	93.78949	5.434511	0.776002
17	0.239516	93.85989	5.361572	0.778540
18	0.246677	93.92243	5.296705	0.780867
19	0.253639	93.97843	5.238489	0.783086
20	0.260416	94.02820	5.186863	0.784936
21	0.267019	94.07321	5.140144	0.786651
22	0.273463	94.11420	5.097542	0.788258
23	0.279759	94.15144	5.058892	0.789669
24	0.285916	94.18551	5.023525	0.790965
25	0.291943	94.21684	4.990991	0.792173
26	0.297849	94.24566	4.961066	0.793272
27	0.303639	94.27231	4.933397	0.794289
28	0.309321	94.29704	4.907717	0.795239
29	0.314901	94.32003	4.883857	0.796118
30	0.320384	94.34145	4.861617	0.796936

Table G2 **Decomposition of LNASTS (Cholesky ordering: LNASTS, LNICX, and LNIPX)**

Period	SE	LNASTS	LNICX	LNIPX
1	0.051236	100.0000	0.000000	0.000000
2	0.078294	94.69541	5.091200	0.213392
3	0.097422	95.35835	3.459106	1.182544
4	0.115342	95.09129	3.900822	1.007885
5	0.132588	94.19196	4.748355	1.059686
6	0.144991	94.06026	4.806491	1.133253
7	0.156926	93.96655	4.908545	1.124900
8	0.168278	93.62094	5.276571	1.102489
9	0.178216	93.54941	5.322945	1.127642
10	0.187646	93.49368	5.387379	1.118942
11	0.196930	93.38386	5.503434	1.112708
12	0.205543	93.33130	5.551655	1.117042
13	0.213837	93.30239	5.581291	1.116320
14	0.221937	93.24851	5.638722	1.112769
15	0.229683	93.21428	5.671219	1.114497
16	0.237160	93.19002	5.695847	1.114136
17	0.244462	93.15943	5.727688	1.112885
18	0.251526	93.13444	5.752428	1.113130
19	0.258387	93.11553	5.771379	1.113094
20	0.265089	93.09498	5.792564	1.112452
21	0.271620	93.07691	5.810663	1.112427
22	0.277990	93.06189	5.825775	1.112337
23	0.284226	93.04706	5.840911	1.112026
24	0.290326	93.03341	5.854687	1.111907
25	0.296297	93.02148	5.866699	1.111821
26	0.302153	93.01009	5.878277	1.111634
27	0.307898	92.99945	5.889027	1.111520
28	0.313536	92.98983	5.898742	1.111431
29	0.319075	92.98075	5.907939	1.111308
30	0.324520	92.97222	5.916574	1.111208

Table G3 **Decomposition of LNRDG (Cholesky ordering: LNRDG, LNCM, and LNPM)**

Period	SE	LNRDG	LNCM	LNPM
1	0.070875	100.0000	0.000000	0.000000
2	0.094473	92.85684	0.543372	6.599792
3	0.115192	89.43261	5.767845	4.799548
4	0.125839	88.76606	5.007264	6.226676
5	0.137280	86.82356	5.205777	7.970668
6	0.152533	84.73487	4.875588	10.38954
7	0.166323	82.46428	4.969484	12.56623
8	0.182699	81.18044	5.312921	13.50663
9	0.197728	80.54071	5.413086	14.04620
10	0.212461	80.46682	5.609611	13.92356
11	0.225778	80.55137	5.700930	13.74770
12	0.237325	80.66929	5.799020	13.53169
13	0.247722	80.74852	5.826087	13.42539
14	0.257166	80.71277	5.839078	13.44815
15	0.266293	80.60636	5.843057	13.55059
16	0.275252	80.43681	5.845141	13.71805
17	0.284277	80.26791	5.859529	13.87256
18	0.293319	80.13034	5.875269	13.99439
19	0.302280	80.04071	5.898881	14.06041
20	0.311038	79.99701	5.921731	14.08126

Table G4 **Decomposition of LNRDG (Cholesky ordering: LNRDG, LNCX, and LNPX)**

Period	SE	LNRDG	LNCX	LNPX
1	0.052664	100.0000	0.000000	0.000000
2	0.067346	76.72590	12.61356	10.66054
3	0.078633	70.80483	21.32832	7.866842
4	0.084855	67.83586	23.95108	8.213056
5	0.097424	56.79549	32.64686	10.55765
6	0.108097	54.97649	36.13549	8.888022
7	0.119638	49.51450	38.02101	12.46448
8	0.130844	47.20548	38.76385	14.03067
9	0.139335	45.88489	39.09995	15.01516
10	0.147996	44.38800	38.74871	16.86329
11	0.154772	44.50221	38.44109	17.05670
12	0.161282	43.89015	38.34789	17.76197
13	0.167021	44.05812	38.21155	17.73033
14	0.172329	44.01937	38.26318	17.71745
15	0.177783	43.85823	38.41486	17.72691
16	0.182844	43.91768	38.55441	17.52791
17	0.188121	43.66295	38.75636	17.58069
18	0.193295	43.56937	38.92588	17.50475
19	0.198366	43.39032	39.07481	17.53486
20	0.203470	43.20546	39.18520	17.60934

Vertical specialization and upgrading utilization of foreign capital: comparing impacts of conventional trade and processing trade patterns on foreign investment in China

8

8.1 Introduction

Policymakers, particularly in China, have a propensity to regard utilization of foreign capital as a useful springboard that helps to achieve inclusive growth. The expected positive effects of upgrading utilization of foreign capital on inclusive growth include the following: the inflow of new technological and managerial knowledge; capital inputs; and employment opportunities (Inkpen, 1998; Kobrin, 2005; Adams, 2009; Jeon, 2013). Due to the significant positive effects of utilization of foreign capital on inclusive growth, the volume of foreign direct investment (FDI) in China has increased dramatically in the past 35 years.

Does vertical specialization play a role in the utilization of foreign capital in China? The answer to this question is of interest for at least two reasons. First, it has implications for China's inclusive growth. If vertical specialization influences the inclusive growth in China, then the impact of imports and exports by processing trade on inclusive growth goes beyond the direct role of vertical specialization in the utilization of foreign capital. Moreover, with the attitude of the developing world toward inclusive growth turning increasingly positive, many policymakers are interested in how to formulate a strategy to promote upgrading the utilization of foreign capital. Does the Chinese experience tell us that vertical specialization is important for upgrading the utilization of foreign capital? China has been one of the most successful countries integrating into global vertical specialization in recent years. The lessons learned from China's experience can contribute to a better understanding of the determinants of upgrading utilization of foreign capital.

This chapter is organized as follows. Section 8.2 provides an overview of the institutional background of utilization of foreign capital in China and takes a preliminary look at the relationship between upgrading the utilization of foreign capital in China and vertical specialization. Section 8.3 describes the data and methodology used in this study, specifies the empirical model, and shows the findings. Concluding remarks are presented in Section 8.4.

Achieving Inclusive Growth in China Through Vertical Specialization.

8.2   Institutional background

China started opening up to the utilization of foreign capital under the "open-door" policy in 1978. Starting with its accession into the World Trade Organization (WTO) in 2001, China has made substantial changes to improve its institutional environment and has implemented uniform, transparent, and simplified licensing procedures for foreign-invested enterprises. There exists a large disparity between coastal and inland provinces in the amount of the utilization of foreign capital received. In the southeast coastal areas, Guangdong, which is geographically close to Hong Kong, has received the dominant share. The utilization of foreign capital plays an important role in the inclusive growth of China. A high percentage of FDI to net private capital flows during the past 35 years is almost the norm for China.

In view of China's impressive record opening to foreign capital, attention has been shifted toward the roles played by utilization of foreign capital in China's inclusive growth. China's Ministry of Commerce issued the Catalogue for the Guidance of Foreign Investment Industries—lists of industries in which FDI was categorized as "encouraged," "restricted," or "prohibited." The neoclassical theory suggests that FDI is likely to be an engine of growth (Baharumshah and Thanoon, 2006; Balasubramanyam et al., 1996; Grossman and Helpman, 1991; Markusen and Venables, 1999). Lardy (1995) and Pomfret (1997) concluded that no other transitional economy has played such a significant and dynamic role as China has (Baharumshah and Thanoon, 2006). In China, foreign trade has expanded the absorption of FDI. The role of upgrading utilization of foreign capital as an engine of inclusive growth has long been recognized in China. Vertical specialization also has been the source of utilization of foreign capital. Compared to imports and exports by conventional trade, Chinese imports and exports by processing trade is distinctive to the degree at which it has relied on utilization of foreign capital and FDI.

8.3   Empirical evidence of the impact of vertical specialization trade policy on utilization of foreign capital in China

8.3.1   Data and methodology

The Vector Autoregression (VAR) is an ad hoc dynamic multivariate model treating simultaneous sets of variables equally, and each endogenous variable is regressed on its own lags and the lags of all other variables in a finite-order system (Sims, 1980; Lixin Sun et al., 2010). If all variables are integrated with order 1, and if the cointegration relationships among them exist, then the Vector Error Correction Model (VECM) can be used to estimate the variance decomposition functions and impulse response (Johansen, 1995; Juselius, 2006; Sun et al., 2010).

All data were obtained from the database of China Statistical Yearbook and China Trade and External Economics Statistical Yearbook published by National

Bureau of Statistics of China; the sample covers annual observations from 1981 to 2012. All variables are used and transformed into a natural logarithm. This study used the variable groups in Table A1 to find the relationship.

LNRRCM = natural logarithm of the ratio of imports by conventional trade to gross domestic products (GDP);

LNRPM = natural logarithm of the ratio of imports by processing trade to GDP;

LNRPM = natural logarithm of the ratio of exports by conventional trade to GDP;

LNRPX = natural logarithm of the ratio of exports by processing trade to GDP;

LNNE = natural logarithm of the number of enterprises with foreign capital (Unit);

LNNCE = natural logarithm of the number of corporation enterprises with foreign capital (Unit);

LNRTIG = natural logarithm of the ratio of total investment of enterprises with foreign capital to GDP;

LNRSRCG = natural logarithm of the ratio of subtotal registered capital of enterprises with foreign capital to GDP;

LNRFPG = natural logarithm of the ratio of foreign partner−registered capital of enterprises with foreign capital to GDP;

LNRFUG = natural logarithm of the ratio of total amount of foreign capital used to GDP;

LNRFG = natural logarithm of the ratio of FDI to GDP;

LNRFDINIG = natural logarithm of the ratio of FDI net inflow to GDP.

8.3.2   Unit root test

The augmented Dickey Fuller (ADF) test for unit roots was conducted for all the time series used for the study. Table B1 shows the result of unit root tests using the ADF unit root test at the first difference level. The null hypothesis of nonstationarity was performed at the 1%, 5%, and 10% significance levels. In Table B1, the result of the ADF test illustrates that all the data series are nonstationary at level. However, the result of the ADF test on the first difference strongly supports that all data series are stationary after the first difference at the 10%, 5%, or 1% significance levels, respectively. The ADF results show that all the variable series were integrated series of order I (1).

8.3.3   Cointegration test

Cointegration means economic variables share the same stochastic trend so that they are combined together in the long term. Even if they deviate from each other in the short term, they tend to come back to the trend in the long term. A necessary condition for the cointegration test is that all the variables should be integrated at the same order or should contain a deterministic trend (Engle and Granger, 1991). The unit root test results in Table B1 show that all the time series are integrated at first difference but are not integrated at level form during 1981 to 2012. Therefore, the time series during the period are valid in the cointegration test.

The results of trace statistics and the results of maximum Eigen statistics are shown in Tables C1−C16. Trace statistics and maximum Eigen statistics values help to find the rank(s), which shows the number of vector(s) containing long-term relations. It is evident that the null hypothesis of no rank is rejected. Therefore, the results of both trace and/or max-Eigen statistics confirm that cointegration vectors exist in the model. This means the long-term relationship prevails among the variables. In summary, the Johansen cointegration test results show the 16 variables groups in Table B1 are cointegrated in the periods and have a long-term equilibrium relationship during 1981 to 2012.

Following Johansen's technique, the normalized long-term cointegration relationships and the comparison coefficients are shown in Tables C1−C16. The normalized long-term cointegration relationships are very revealing. The observed signs are as anticipated. Moreover, the long-term relationships are also as expected given the intrinsic interdependence between the variables.

From Tables C1−C16, we can obtain the following equations for the long term:

1. The number of enterprises with foreign capital, the ratio of conventional trade to GDP, and the ratio of processing trade to GDP:

$$\text{LNNE} = -0.095567\text{LNRCM} + 1.498461\text{LNRPM} \qquad (8.1)$$
$$\phantom{\text{LNNE} = -0.09}{\scriptstyle(0.23351)}\phantom{\text{LNRCM} + 1.49846}{\scriptstyle(0.21562)}$$

$$\text{LNNE} = -1.044547\text{LNRCX} + 0.316111\text{LNRPX} \qquad (8.2)$$
$$\phantom{\text{LNNE} = -1.04}{\scriptstyle(0.39912)}\phantom{\text{LNRCX} + 0.31611}{\scriptstyle(0.21173)}$$

From Eqs. (8.1) and (8.2), we observe that the 1% increase in the ratio of imports by conventional trade to GDP (LNRCM) will have a negative impact of 0.095567% on the number of enterprises with foreign capital (LNNE), the 1% increase in the ratio of imports by processing trade to GDP (LNRPM) will have a positive impact of 1.498461% on the number of enterprises with foreign capital (LNNE), the 1% increase in the ratio of exports by conventional trade to GDP (LNRCX) will have a negative impact of 1.044547% on the number of enterprises with foreign capital (LNNE), the 1% increase in the ratio of exports by processing trade to GDP (LNRPX) will have a positive impact of 0.316111% on the number of enterprises with foreign capital (LNNE).

Eqs. (8.1) and (8.2) demonstrate that the increase in imports and exports by processing trade can cause the increase in the number of enterprises with foreign capital in the long term. This confirms the existence of the vertical specialization channel.

2. The number of corporation enterprises with foreign capital, the ratio of conventional trade to GDP, and the ratio of processing trade to GDP:

$$\text{LNNCE} = -0.416645\text{LNRCM} + 1.660624\text{LNRPM} \qquad (8.3)$$
$$\phantom{\text{LNNCE} = -0.4}{\scriptstyle(0.21698)}\phantom{\text{LNRCM} + 1.6606}{\scriptstyle(0.19123)}$$

$$\text{LNNCE} = -0.707155\text{LNRCX} + 1.212416\text{LNRPX} \qquad (8.4)$$
$$\phantom{\text{LNNCE} = -0.7}{\scriptstyle(0.35373)}\phantom{\text{LNRCX} + 1.2124}{\scriptstyle(0.13200)}$$

From Eqs. (8.3) and (8.4), we observe that the 1% increase in the ratio of imports by conventional trade to GDP (LNRCM) will have a negative impact of 0.416645% on the number of corporation enterprises with foreign capital (LNNCE), the 1% increase in the ratio of imports by processing trade to GDP (LNRPM) will have a positive impact of 1.660624% on the number of corporation enterprises with foreign capital (LNNCE), the 1% increase in the ratio of exports by conventional trade to GDP (LNRCX) will have a negative impact of 0.707155% on the number of corporation enterprises with foreign capital (LNNCE), and the 1% increase in the ratio of exports by processing trade to GDP (LNRPX) will have a positive impact of 1.212416% on the number of corporation enterprises with foreign capital (LNNCE).

Eqs. (8.3) and (8.4) demonstrate that the increase in imports and exports by processing trade can cause the increase in the number of corporation enterprises with foreign capital in the long term. This confirms the existence of the vertical specialization channel.

3. The ratio of total investment of enterprises with foreign capital to GDP, the ratio of conventional trade to GDP, and the ratio of processing trade to GDP:

$$\underset{(0.16198)}{LNRTIG} = -0.901404 \underset{}{LNRCM} + 1.319898 \underset{(0.13101)}{LNRPM} \tag{8.5}$$

$$\underset{(0.22027)}{LNRTIG} = -1.774602 \underset{}{LNRCX} + 1.649882 \underset{(0.10378)}{LNRPX} \tag{8.6}$$

From Eqs. (8.5) and (8.6), we observe that the 1% increase in LNRCM will have a negative impact of 0.901404% on LNRTIG, the 1% increase in LNRPM will have a positive impact of 1.319898% on LNRTIG, the 1% increase in LNRCX will have a negative impact of 1.774602% on LNRTIG, and the 1% increase in LNRPX will have a positive impact of 1.649882% on LNRTIG.

4. The ratio of subtotal registered capital of enterprises with foreign capital to GDP, the ratio of conventional trade to GDP, and the ratio of processing trade to GDP:

$$\underset{(0.12641)}{LNRSRCG} = -1.033363 \underset{}{LNRCM} + 1.429172 \underset{(0.11699)}{LNRPM} \tag{8.7}$$

$$\underset{(0.23718)}{LNRSRCG} = -1.941086 \underset{}{LNRCX} + 1.752782 \underset{(0.10007)}{LNRPX} \tag{8.8}$$

From Eqs. (8.7) and (8.8), we observe that the 1% increase in LNRCM will have a negative impact of 1.033363% on LNRSRCG, the 1% increase in LNRPM will have a positive impact of 1.429172% on LNRSRCG, the 1% increase in LNRCX will have a negative impact of 1.941086% on LNRSRCG, and the 1% increase in LNRPX will have a positive impact of 1.752782% on LNRSRCG.

5. The ratio of foreign partner–registered capital of enterprises with foreign capital to GDP, the ratio of conventional trade to GDP, and the ratio of processing trade to GDP:

$$\underset{(0.12867)}{LNRFPG} = -0.810078 \underset{}{LNRCM} + 1.321366 \underset{(0.12164)}{LNRPM} \tag{8.9}$$

$$\underset{(0.23206)}{LNRFPG} = -1.678505 \underset{}{LNRCX} + 1.5997 \underset{(0.09259)}{LNRPX} \tag{8.10}$$

Eq. (8.9) reveals that the 1% increase in LNRCM will have a negative impact of 0.810078% on LNRFPG and the 1% increase in LNRPM will have a positive impact of 1.321366% on LNRFPG. Eq. (8.10) reveals that the 1% increase in LNRCX will have a negative impact of 1.678505% on LNRFPG and the 1% increase in LNRPX will have a positive impact of 1.5997% on LNRFPG.

6. The ratio of total amount of foreign capital used to GDP, the ratio of conventional trade to GDP, and the ratio of processing trade to GDP:

$$\text{LNRFUG} = -1.393272\text{LNRCM} + 0.470871\text{LNRPM} \tag{8.11}$$
$$\phantom{\text{LNRFUG} = -1.}(0.12921)\phantom{\text{LNRCM} + 0.4}(0.07467)$$

$$\text{LNRFUG} = -1.857243\text{LNRCX} + 3.535869\text{NRPX} \tag{8.12}$$
$$\phantom{\text{LNRFUG} = -1.}(0.58075)\phantom{\text{LNRCX} + 3.5}(0.58352)$$

Eq. (8.11) reveals that the 1% increase in LNRCM will have a negative impact of 1.393272% on LNRFUG and the 1% increase in LNRPM will have a positive impact of 0.470871% on LNRFUG. Eq. (8.12) reveals that 1% increase in LNRCX will have a negative impact of 1.857243% on LNRFUG and the 1% increase in LNRPX will have a positive impact of 3.535869% on LNRFUG.

7. The ratio of FDI to GDP, the ratio of conventional trade to GDP, and the ratio of processing trade to GDP:

$$\text{LNRFG} = -0.634709\text{LNRCM} + 4.650694\text{LNRPM} \tag{8.13}$$
$$\phantom{\text{LNRFG} = -0.}(0.94389)\phantom{\text{LNRCM} + 4.6}(0.64162)$$

$$\text{LNRFG} = -1.871948\text{LNRCX} + 3.622666\text{LNRPX} \tag{8.14}$$
$$\phantom{\text{LNRFG} = -1.}(0.26062)\phantom{\text{LNRCX} + 3.6}(0.26550)$$

From Eq. (8.13), we observe that the 1% increase in LNRCM will have a negative impact of 0.634709% on LNRFG and the 1% increase in LNRPM will have a positive impact of 4.650694% on LNRFG. Eq. (8.14) reveals that the 1% increase in LNRCX will have a negative impact of 1.871948% on LNRFG and the 1% increase in LNRPX will have a positive impact of 3.622666% on LNRFG.

8. The ratio of FDI net inflow to GDP, the ratio of conventional trade to GDP, and the ratio of processing trade to GDP:

$$\text{LNRFDINIG} = -0.622375\text{LNRCM} + 1.839386\text{LNRPM} \tag{8.15}$$
$$\phantom{\text{LNRFDINIG} = -0.}(0.19238)\phantom{\text{LNRCM} + 1.8}(0.17697)$$

$$\text{LNRFDINIG} = -0.838899\text{LNRCX} + 1.172453\text{LNRPX} \tag{8.16}$$
$$\phantom{\text{LNRFDINIG} = -0.}(0.31752)\phantom{\text{LNRCX} + 1.1}(0.11118)$$

Furthermore, from Eqs. (8.15) and (8.16), we observe that the 1% increase in LNRCM will have a negative impact of 0.622375% on LNRFDINIG, the 1% increase in LNRPM will have a positive impact of 1.839386% on LNRFDINIG, the 1% increase in LNRCX will have a negative impact of 0.838899% on LNRFDINIG, and the 1% increase in LNRPX will have a positive impact of 1.172453% on LNRFDINIG.

These equations show that the vertical specialization variables (LNRPM and LNRPX) have important effects on upgrading utilization of foreign capital, which connects the vertically specialized trade policy variables with the utilization of foreign capital variables (LNNE, LNNCE, LNRTIG, LNRSRCG, LNRFPG, LNRFUG, LNRFG, and LNRFDINIG). These long-term equations support the existence of the vertical specialization channel in the trade policy transmission process in China.

Proposition 1. The contribution and importance of imports and exports by conventional trade to increasing the number of enterprises with foreign capital are lower than that by processing trade.

Proposition 2. The contribution and importance of imports and exports by conventional trade to increasing the number of corporation enterprises with foreign capital are lower than that by processing trade.

Proposition 3. The contribution and importance of imports and exports by conventional trade to raising total investment of enterprises with foreign capital are lower than that by processing trade.

Proposition 4. The contribution and importance of imports and exports by conventional trade to raising subtotal registered capital of enterprises with foreign capital are lower than that by processing trade.

Proposition 5. The contribution and importance of imports and exports by conventional trade to raising foreign partner—registered capital of enterprises with foreign capital are lower than that by processing trade.

Proposition 6. The contribution and importance of imports and exports by conventional trade to raising total amount of foreign capital used are lower than that by processing trade.

Proposition 7. The contribution and importance of imports and exports by conventional trade to raising FDIs are lower than that by processing trade.

Proposition 8. The contribution and importance of imports and exports by conventional trade to raising FDI net inflow are lower than that by processing trade.

8.3.4 Vector error correction model

ECM is used to estimate the short-term and long-term impacts across a variety of variables, and the ECM coefficients show the speed with which the system converges to equilibrium. When the first difference variables are confirmed to have stationarity, ECM can be regressed in which vecm − 1 is one difference error correction item whose coefficient represents the impact of the last period's error correction on this period's variable. The negative sign of the estimated error correction coefficients suggest from low to moderate speed of convergence to equilibrium. The results of VECM are reported in Tables D1−D16.

In Table D1, for D(LNRPM), the coefficient of error correction term is −0.20868. It shows that if a deviation from long term happens as a shock, then the adjustment speed toward long-term equilibrium will be 20.868% and there will be full adjustment of deviation. For D(LNRCM), the coefficient of error correction term is −0.169788. It also reveals that if a deviation from long term happens as a shock, then the adjustment speed toward long-term equilibrium will be 16.9788%.

In Table D2, for D(LNRPM), the coefficient of error correction term is −0.185671; for D(LNRCM), the coefficient of error correction term is −0.117266.

In Table D3, for D(LNRPM), the coefficient of error correction term is −0.235353; for D(LNRCM), the coefficient of error correction term is −0.191826.

In Table D4, for D(LNRPX), the coefficient of error correction term is −0.043699.

In Table D5, for D(LNRPM), the coefficient of error correction term is −0.015304; for D(LNRCM), the coefficient of error correction term is −0.169567.

In Table D6, for D(LNRCX), the coefficient of error correction term is -0.122036. In Table D7, for D(LNRCM), the coefficient of error correction term is -0.155255. In Table D8, for D(LNRCX), the coefficient of error correction term is -0.203433. In Table D9, for D(LNRPM), the coefficient of error correction term is -0.268334; for D(LNRCM), the coefficient of error correction term is -0.184271. In Table D10, for D(LNRCX), the coefficient of error correction term is -0.174273. In Table D11, for D(LNRCM), the coefficient of error correction term is -0.4444906. In Table D12, for D(LNRCX), the coefficient of error correction term is -0.015076. In Table D13, for D(LNRCM), the coefficient of error correction term is -0.006291. In Table D14, for D(LNRFG), the coefficient of error correction term is -0.010308. In Table D15, for D(LNRCM), the coefficient of error correction term is -0.106308. In Table D16, for D(LNRCM), the coefficient of error correction term is -0.224005; for D(LNRPM), the coefficient of error correction term is -0.030705.

8.3.5 Granger causality tests

The structures of the causal relationships between variables were analyzed through the Granger causality approach. The Granger causality test is a statistical hypothesis test for determining whether one time series is useful in forecasting another. If the probability value is less than any α level, then the hypothesis would be rejected at that level.

From Table E1, when three lags, four lags, five lags, and six lags are applied, the hypothesis that LNRPM does not involve Granger causality in LNNE can be rejected at the 10%, 5%, or 1% levels of significance. Thus, we found unidirectional causality running from LNRPM to LNNE.

The results in Table E2 indicate the existence of bidirectional causality running from LNRPX to LNNE when three lags and four lags are applied at the 5% level of significance. Unidirectional causality running from LNRCX to LNNE when one lag is applied at the 10% level of significance and unidirectional causality running from LNNE to LNRCX when four lags and five lags are applied at the 5% level of significance are also revealed.

The results in Table E3 indicate the existence of unidirectional causality running from LNRPM to LNNCE when one lag, two lags, three lags, four lags, five lags, and six lags are applied at the 10% or 5% levels of significance. Unidirectional causality running from LNNCE to LNRCM when three lags, five lags, and six lags at the 10% level of significance is also revealed.

The results in Table E4 indicate the existence of bidirectional causality running from LNRPX to LNNCE when three lags are applied at the 5% level of significance.

The results in Table E5 indicate the existence of unidirectional causality running from LNRPM to LNRTIG when six lags, seven lags, and eight lags are applied at the 10% level or 5% level of significance. Bidirectional causality running from LNRCM to LNRTIG when seven lags are applied at the 10% level of significance is also revealed.

The results in Table E6 indicate the existence of unidirectional causality running from LNRPX to LNRTIG when seven lags and eight lags are applied at the 1% level of significance. The results also reveal unidirectional causality running from LNRTIG to LNRPX when one lag is applied at the 10% level of significance and unidirectional causality running from LNRCX to LNRTIG when seven lags are applied at the 10% level of significance.

The results in Table E7 indicate the existence of unidirectional causality running from LNRPM to LNRSRCG when seven lags and eight lags are applied at the 1% and 5% levels of significance, respectively. The results also reveal bidirectional causality running from LNRCM to LNRSRCG when seven lags are applied at the 5% level of significance.

The results in Table E8 indicate the existence of unidirectional causality running from LNRPX to LNRSRCG when seven lags, eight lags, and nine lags are applied at the 1% and 10% levels of significance, respectively. The results also reveal unidirectional causality running from LNRSRCG to LNRCX when four lags are applied at the 10% level of significance and unidirectional causality running from LNRSRCG to LNRCX when seven lags are applied at the 5% level of significance.

The results in Table E9 indicate the existence of unidirectional causality running from LNRPM to LNRFPG when six lags, seven lags, and eight lags are applied at the 10%, 1%, and 5% levels of significance, respectively. The results also reveal unidirectional causality running from LNRFPG to LNRCM when six lags, seven lags, and eight lags are applied at the 5% level of significance.

The results in Table E10 indicate the existence of unidirectional causality running from LNRCX to LNRFPG when seven lags are applied at the 5% level of significance. The results also reveal unidirectional causality running from LNRPX to LNRFPG when six lags, seven lags, and eight lags are applied at the 10% and 1% levels of significance, respectively.

The results in Table E11 indicate the existence of unidirectional causality running from LNRPM to LNRFUG when two lags are applied at the 5% level of significance. The results also reveal bidirectional causality running from LNRCM to LNRFUG when two lags are applied at the 10% level of significance.

The results in Table E12 indicate the existence of unidirectional causality running from LNRPX to LNRFUG when two lags, seven lags, and eight lags are applied at the 5% level or 1% level of significance, respectively. The results also reveal unidirectional causality running from LNRCX to LNRFUG when two lags are applied at the 10% level of significance and unidirectional causality running from LNRFUG to LNRCX when five lags are applied at the 10% level of significance.

The results in Table E13 indicate the existence of unidirectional causality running from LNRFG to LNRCM when five lags, six lags, seven lags, eight lags, and nine lags are applied at the 10%, 1%, or 5% levels of significance, respectively.

The results in Table E14 indicate the existence of unidirectional causality running from LNRPX to LNRFG when seven lags and eight lags are applied at the 1% level and 5% level of significance, respectively.

The results in Table E15 indicate the existence of bidirectional causality running from LNRPM to LNRFDINIG when one lag is applied at the 10% level of significance. The results also reveal unidirectional causality running from LNRFDINIG to LNRCM when five lags and six lags are applied at the 5% and 10% levels of significance, respectively.

The results in Table E16 indicate the existence of unidirectional causality running from LNRPX to LNRFDINIG when one lag and two lags are applied at the 10% and 5% levels of significance, respectively.

8.3.6 Impulse response function

The impulse-response function curves simulated by analytic method are shown in Figs. F1−F16. The curves indicate how a one-time positive shock of 1 standard deviation (SD) (± 2 standard error (SE) innovations) to the conventional trade and processing trade endures in the utilization of foreign capital of China. We consider the response of eight variables to 1 SD (standard deviation) innovation of conventional trade and processing trade.

Figs. F2, F4, and F14 illustrate that the responses of the LNNE, LNNCE, and LNRFG to a 1 SD shock on LNRCX are negative and powerful, with a persistent effect; however, the responses of the LNNE, LNNCE, and LNRFG to a 1 SD shock on LNRPX are positive and increase abruptly. Figs. F5, F7, and F11 illustrate that the responses of LNRTIG, LNRSRCG, and LNRFUG to a 1 SD shock on LNRCM are negative and powerful, with a persistent effect; however, the responses of the LNRTIG, LNRSRCG, and LNRFUG to a 1 SD shock on LNRPM are positive and increase abruptly.

Figs. F6, F8, and F10 illustrate that the responses of the LNRTIG, LNRSRCG, and LNRFPG to a 1 SD shock on LNRCX and LNRPX are positive and powerful, with a persistent effect. However, the influence of LNRCX is lower than that of LNRPX.

8.3.7 Variance decomposition

The forecast error variance decomposition follows. It aims to capture the intensity of the response of a variable in the face of shocks suffered on the other variables. Tables G1−G16 reveal the percentages of the forecast error variance in all variables generated by a shock on each of the other variables.

In Tables G1−G16, the first columns are the periods that are set to a maximum of 30. The data in the SE column are the forecasting variance of various periods, which are caused by the change of the present or future value.

In Tables G1, G3, G5, G7, G9, G11, and G15, the utilization of foreign capital variables (LNNE, LNNCE, LNRTIG, LNRSRCG, LNRFPG, LNRFUG, and LNRFDINIG), LNRCM and LNRPM, contribute to innovation in forecasting variance, and these sum to 100. It can be seen that the impact of a shock to LNRCM in the utilization of foreign capital variables (LNNE, LNNCE, LNRTIG, LNRSRCG, LNRFPG, LNRFUG, and LNRFDINIG) is relatively low when compared with the impact of a shock to LNRPM in the utilization of foreign capital variables (LNNE,

LNNCE, LNRTIG, LNRSRCG, LNRFPG, LNRFUG, and LNRFDINIG). For example, in Table G1, at period 10 of the forecast period, LNRPM explains approximately 40% of the forecast error variance. This is approximately 20% points higher than in the LNRCM case.

In Tables G4, G6, G8, G10, and G16, the utilization of foreign capital variables (LNNCE, LNRTIG, LNRSRCG, LNRFPG, and LNRFDINIG), LNRCX and LNRPX, contribute to the innovations in forecasting variance, and these sum to 100. It can be seen that the impact of a shock to LNRCX in the utilization of foreign capital variables (LNNCE, LNRTIG, LNRSRCG, LNRFPG, and LNRFDINIG) is relatively low when compared with the impact of a shock to LNRPX in the utilization of foreign capital variables (LNNCE, LNRTIG, LNRSRCG, LNRFPG, and LNRFDINIG). For example, in Table G4, at the end of the forecast period, LNRPX explains approximately 71% of the forecast error variance. This is approximately 70 percentage points higher than in the LNRCX case.

8.4 Concluding remarks and policy implications

This study is concerned with the evidence that vertical specialization is significant in explaining the upgrade in the utilization of foreign capital in China. Data on FDI and imports and exports by conventional trade and processing trade in China during 1981−2012 were used, and more detailed data do reveal a significant and positive role of vertical specialization in upgrading the utilization of foreign capital. Dividing foreign trade into two types, conventional and processing, it was found that the upgrading utilization of foreign capital is more sensitive to processing. The upgrading utilization of foreign capital responds to the vertical specialization policy, as proxied by the imports and exports by processing trade.

It has been shown in this chapter that the development of conventional trade and development of processing trade have occurred at vastly different paces. In many important aspects, the impact on upgrading the utilization of foreign capital of processing trade seems to be superior to the impact on conventional trade. There is some preliminary evidence that this vertically specialized trade has created an institutional environment that is more "friendly" to upgrading the utilization of foreign capital than conventional trade.

The support for vertical specialization upgrading the utilization of foreign capital is reassuring for China's inclusive growth, and the support points to the need for the open-door policy and integration into the global value chain. One policy implication is that China should accelerate liberalizing trade in intermediates. This will not only help China to make the external trade system more efficient but also support upgrading the utilization of foreign capital to a certain extent.

Another policy implication of this analysis is that China will further open its market to processing trade and experience more imports and, therefore, integration into vertical specialization. This study calls for improvements in institutions, including economic transformation and China's policy of opening to the outside world, which would further unleash China's inclusive growth.

Appendix A   Variables grouping

Table A1   Variable grouping

Group number	Variables	Sample range
1	LNNE, LNRCM, and LNRPM	1981−2012
2	LNNE, LNRCX, and LNRPX	1981−2012
3	LNNCE, LNRCM, and LNRPM	1981−2012
4	LNNCE, LNRCX, and LNRPX	1981−2012
5	LNRTIG, LNRCM, and LNRPM	1981−2012
6	LNRTIG, LNRCX, and LNRPX	1981−2012
7	LNRSRCG, LNRCM, and LNRPM	1981−2012
8	LNRSRCG, LNRCX, and LNRPX	1981−2012
9	LNRFPG, LNRCM, and LNRPM	1981−2012
10	LNRFPG, LNRCM, and LNRPM	1981−2012
11	LNRFUG, LNRCM, and LNRPM	1981−2012
12	LNRFUG, LNRCX, and LNRPX	1981−2012
13	LNRFG, LNRCM, and LNRPM	1981−2012
14	LNRFG, LNRCM, and LNRPM	1981−2012
15	LNRFDINIG, LNRCM, and LNRPM	1981−2012
16	LNRFDINIG, LNRCX, and LNRPX	1981−2012

Note: RCM is the ratio of imports by conventional trade to GDP; RPM is the ratio of imports by processing trade to GDP; RCX is the ratio of exports by conventional trade to GDP; RPX is the ratio of exports by processing trade to GDP; NE indicates number of enterprises with foreign capital (Unit); NCE indicates number of corporation enterprises with foreign capital (Unit); RTIG indicates the ratio of total investment of enterprises with foreign capital to GDP; RSRCG stands for the ratio of subtotal registered capital of enterprises with foreign capital to GDP; RFPG indicates the ratio of foreign partner−registered capital of enterprises with foreign capital to GDP; RFUG indicates the ratio of total amount of foreign capital used to GDP; RFG indicates the ratio of FDI to GDP; RFDINIG indicates the ratio of FDI net inflow to GDP.

Appendix B   The results of unit root tests

Table B1 ADF test on unit roots for all variables

S. No.	Variables	Test type (C, T, P)	ADF test statistic	Order of integration
1	LNRCM	(0,0,0)	−0.588764	I(1)
2	D(LNRCM)	(0,0,0)	−4.062425*	I(0)
3	LNRPM	(0,0,1)	−1.435178	I(1)
4	D(LNRPM)	(0,0,0)	−2.372501**	I(0)
5	LNRCX	(0,0,0)	−0.371061	I(1)
6	D(LNRCX)	(0,0,0)	−5.549134*	I(0)
7	LNRPX	(C,T,1)	−1.639388	I(1)
8	D(LNRPX)	(C,T,0)	−3.825039**	I(0)
9	LNNE	(0,0,1)	0.543851	I(1)
10	D(LNNE)	(0,0,0)	−2.068225**	I(0)
11	LNNCE	(0,0,1)	0.368145	I(1)
12	D(LNNCE)	(0,0,6)	−1.886466***	I(0)
13	LNRTIG	(0,0,1)	−2.901886*	I(1)
14	D(LNRTIG)	(0,0,0)	−2.797042*	I(0)
15	LNRSRCG	(C,T,2)	−2.265940	I(1)
16	D(LNRSRCG)	(C,T,1)	−3.568088***	I(0)
17	LNRFPG	(C,T,1)	−2.103037	I(1)
18	D(LNRFPG)	(C,T,1)	−3.565024***	I(0)
19	LNRFUG	(C,0,0)	−1.927551	I(1)
20	D(LNRFUG)	(C,0,0)	−9.050763*	I(0)
21	LNRFG	(0,0,2)	−0.399800	I(1)
22	D(LNRFG)	(0,0,1)	−3.205415*	I(0)
23	LNRFDINIG	(C,T,1)	−2.079473	I(1)
24	D(LNRFDINIG)	(C,T,1)	−4.730460*	I(0)

Note: C, T, and P in test type stand for constant, trend, and lag orders, respectively. At three remarkable levels, when the ADF value is greater than the critical value, the corresponding series has unit root. D stands for the first differential of the variables.
***, **, and *denote the rejection of the null hypothesis of the unit root at the 10%, 5%, and 1% significance levels, respectively.

Appendix C   Results of cointegration tests

Table C1 **The series cointegration test results (between LNNE, LNRCM, and LNRPM)**

Sample (adjusted): 1986–2012
Included observations: 27 after adjustments
Trend assumption: Linear deterministic trend
Lags interval (in first differences): 2–3

Unrestricted cointegration rank test (trace)

Hypothesized number of CE(s)	Eigenvalue	Trace statistic	0.05 Critical value	Probability[a]
None[b]	0.625701	43.73931	29.79707	0.0007
At most 1[b]	0.435970	17.20638	15.49471	0.0274
At most 2	0.062582	1.744906	3.841466	0.1865

Trace test indicates 2 cointegrating equations at the 0.05 level

Unrestricted cointegration rank test (maximum eigenvalue)

Hypothesized number of CE(s)	Eigenvalue	Max-eigen statistic	0.05 Critical value	Probability[a]
None[b]	0.625701	26.53292	21.13162	0.0079
At most 1[b]	0.435970	15.46148	14.26460	0.0322
At most 2	0.062582	1.744906	3.841466	0.1865

Max-eigenvalue test indicates 2 cointegrating equations at the 0.05 level

1 Cointegrating equation	Log likelihood	61.89732

Normalized cointegrating coefficients (standard error in parentheses)

LNNE	LNRCM	LNRPM
1.000000	0.095567	−1.498461
	(0.23351)	(0.21562)

[a]MacKinnon–Haug–Michelis (1999) *P* values.
[b]Rejection of the hypothesis at the 0.05 level.

Table C2 The series cointegration test results (between LNNE, LNRCX, and LNRPX)

Sample (adjusted): 1986–2012
Included observations: 27 after adjustments
Trend assumption: Linear deterministic trend
Lags interval (in first differences): 2–3

Unrestricted cointegration rank test (trace)

Hypothesized number of CE(s)	Eigenvalue	Trace statistic	0.05 Critical value	Probability[a]
None[b]	0.802775	69.35336	29.79707	0.0000
At most 1[b]	0.551071	25.52125	15.49471	0.0011
At most 2[b]	0.134408	3.897208	3.841466	0.0484

Trace test indicates 3 cointegrating equations at the 0.05 level

Unrestricted cointegration rank test (maximum eigenvalue)

Hypothesized number of CE(s)	Eigenvalue	Max-eigen statistic	0.05 Critical value	Probability[a]
None[b]	0.802775	43.83211	21.13162	0.0000
At most 1[b]	0.551071	21.62404	14.26460	0.0029
At most 2[b]	0.134408	3.897208	3.841466	0.0484

Max-eigenvalue test indicates 3 cointegrating equations at the 0.05 level

1 Cointegrating equation	Log likelihood	83.20692

Normalized cointegrating coefficients (standard error in parentheses)

LNNE	LNRCX	LNRPX
1.000000	1.044547	−0.316111
	(0.39912)	(0.21173)

[a]MacKinnon–Haug–Michelis (1999) *P* values.
[b]Rejection of the hypothesis at the 0.05 level.

Table C3 The series cointegration test results (between LNNCE, LNRCM, and LNRPM)

Sample (adjusted): 1986−2012
Included observations: 27 after adjustments
Trend assumption: Linear deterministic trend
Lags interval (in first differences): 2−3

Unrestricted cointegration rank test (trace)

Hypothesized number of CE(s)	Eigenvalue	Trace statistic	0.05 Critical value	Probability[a]
None[b]	0.589783	42.78765	29.79707	0.0010
At most 1[b]	0.462125	18.72878	15.49471	0.0157
At most 2	0.070892	1.985312	3.841466	0.1588

Trace test indicates 2 cointegrating equations at the 0.05 level

Unrestricted cointegration rank test (maximum eigenvalue)

Hypothesized number of CE(s)	Eigenvalue	Max-eigen statistic	0.05 Critical value	Probability[a]
None[b]	0.589783	24.05887	21.13162	0.0188
At most 1[b]	0.462125	16.74346	14.26460	0.0199
At most 2	0.070892	1.985312	3.841466	0.1588

Max-eigenvalue test indicates 2 cointegrating equations at the 0.05 level

1 Cointegrating equation	Log likelihood	63.88150

Normalized cointegrating coefficients (standard error in parentheses)

LNNCE	LNRCM	LNRPM
1.000000	0.416645	−1.660624
	(0.21698)	(0.19123)

[a]MacKinnon−Haug−Michelis (1999) *P* values.
[b]Rejection of the hypothesis at the 0.05 level.

Table C4 The series cointegration test results (between LNNCE, LNRCX, and LNRPX)

Sample (adjusted): 1984−2012
Included observations: 29 after adjustments
Trend assumption: Linear deterministic trend
Lags interval (in first differences): 1−1

Unrestricted cointegration rank test (trace)

Hypothesized number of CE(s)	Eigenvalue	Trace statistic	0.05 Critical value	Probability[a]
None[b]	0.653042	42.99738	29.79707	0.0009
At most 1	0.292251	12.29942	15.49471	0.1431
At most 2	0.075454	2.275115	3.841466	0.1315

Trace test indicates 1 cointegrating equation at the 0.05 level

Unrestricted cointegration rank test (maximum eigenvalue)

Hypothesized number of CE(s)	Eigenvalue	Max-eigen statistic	0.05 Critical value	Probability[a]
None[b]	0.653042	30.69796	21.13162	0.0017
At most 1	0.292251	10.02430	14.26460	0.2103
At most 2	0.075454	2.275115	3.841466	0.1315

Max-eigenvalue test indicates 1 cointegrating equation at the 0.05 level

1 Cointegrating equation	Log likelihood	69.14989

Normalized cointegrating coefficients (standard error in parentheses)

LNNCE	LNRCX	LNRPX
1.000000	0.707155	−1.212416
	(0.35373)	(0.13200)

[a]MacKinnon−Haug−Michelis (1999) P values.
[b]Rejection of the hypothesis at the 0.05 level.

Table C5 The series cointegration test results (between LNRTIG, LNRCM, and LNRPM)

Sample (adjusted): 1985−2012
Included observations: 28 after adjustments
Trend assumption: Linear deterministic trend
Lags interval (in first differences): 1−2

Unrestricted cointegration rank test (trace)

Hypothesized number of CE(s)	Eigenvalue	Trace statistic	0.05 Critical value	Probability[a]
None[b]	0.611642	37.52770	29.79707	0.0053
At most 1	0.287250	11.04450	15.49471	0.2088
At most 2	0.054292	1.562989	3.841466	0.2112

Trace test indicates 1 cointegrating equation at the 0.05 level

Unrestricted cointegration rank test (maximum eigenvalue)

Hypothesized number of CE(s)	Eigenvalue	Max-eigen statistic	0.05 Critical value	Probability[a]
None[b]	0.611642	26.48320	21.13162	0.0080
At most 1	0.287250	9.481507	14.26460	0.2483
At most 2	0.054292	1.562989	3.841466	0.2112

Max-eigenvalue test indicates 1 cointegrating equation at the 0.05 level

1 Cointegrating equation		Log likelihood	57.10079

Normalized cointegrating coefficients (standard error in parentheses)

LNRTIG	LNRCM	LNRPM
1.000000	0.901404	−1.319898
	(0.16198)	(0.13101)

[a]MacKinnon−Haug−Michelis (1999) P values.
[b]Rejection of the hypothesis at the 0.05 level.

Table C6 The series cointegration test results (between LNRTIG, LNRCX, and LNRPX)

Sample (adjusted): 1985−2012
Included observations: 28 after adjustments
Trend assumption: Linear deterministic trend
Lags interval (in first differences): 1−2

Unrestricted cointegration rank test (trace)

Hypothesized number of CE(s)	Eigenvalue	Trace statistic	0.05 Critical value	Probability[a]
None[b]	0.714534	51.57564	29.79707	0.0000
At most 1[b]	0.370080	16.47390	15.49471	0.0355
At most 2	0.118554	3.533349	3.841466	0.0601

Trace test indicates 2 cointegrating equations at the 0.05 level

Unrestricted cointegration rank test (maximum eigenvalue)

Hypothesized number of CE(s)	Eigenvalue	Max-eigen statistic	0.05 Critical value	Probability[a]
None[b]	0.714534	35.10173	21.13162	0.0003
At most 1	0.370080	12.94056	14.26460	0.0801
At most 2	0.118554	3.533349	3.841466	0.0601

Max-eigenvalue test indicates 1 cointegrating equation at the 0.05 level

1 Cointegrating equation		Log likelihood	72.17959

Normalized cointegrating coefficients (standard error in parentheses)

LNRTIG	LNRCX	LNRPX	
1.000000	1.774602	−1.649882	
	(0.22027)	(0.10378)	

[a]MacKinnon−Haug−Michelis (1999) P values.
[b]Rejection of the hypothesis at the 0.05 level.

Table   C7 The   series   cointegration   test   results   (between LNRSCG, LNRCM, and LNRPM)

Sample (adjusted): 1984−2012
Included observations: 29 after adjustments
Trend assumption: No deterministic trend
Lags interval (in first differences): 1−1

Unrestricted cointegration rank test (trace)

Hypothesized number of CE(s)	Eigenvalue	Trace statistic	0.05 Critical value	Probability[a]
None[b]	0.503681	25.36862	24.27596	0.0363
At most 1	0.151526	5.053045	12.32090	0.5602
At most 2	0.009878	0.287882	4.129906	0.6526

Trace test indicates 1 cointegrating equation at the 0.05 level

Unrestricted cointegration rank test (maximum eigenvalue)

Hypothesized number of CE(s)	Eigenvalue	Max-eigen statistic	0.05 Critical value	Probability[a]
None[b]	0.503681	20.31557	17.79730	0.0205
At most 1	0.151526	4.765163	11.22480	0.5110
At most 2	0.009878	0.287882	4.129906	0.6526

Max-eigenvalue test indicates 1 cointegrating equation at the 0.05 level

1 Cointegrating equation		Log likelihood	53.90613

Normalized cointegrating coefficients (standard error in parentheses)

LNRSCG	LNRCM	LNRPM
1.000000	1.033363	−1.429172
	(0.12641)	(0.11699)

[a]MacKinnon−Haug−Michelis (1999) P values.
[b]Rejection of the hypothesis at the 0.05 level.

Table C8 The series cointegration test results (between LNRSRCG, LNRCX, and LNRPX)

Sample (adjusted): 1985−2012
Included observations: 28 after adjustments
Trend assumption: Linear deterministic trend
Lags interval (in first differences): 1−2

Unrestricted cointegration rank test (trace)

Hypothesized number of CE(s)	Eigenvalue	Trace statistic	0.05 Critical value	Probability[a]
None[b]	0.666878	45.51429	29.79707	0.0004
At most 1	0.336237	14.73542	15.49471	0.0648
At most 2	0.109913	3.260195	3.841466	0.0710

Trace test indicates 1 cointegrating equation at the 0.05 level

Unrestricted cointegration rank test (maximum eigenvalue)

Hypothesized number of CE(s)	Eigenvalue	Max-eigen statistic	0.05 Critical value	Probability[a]
None[b]	0.666878	30.77887	21.13162	0.0016
At most 1	0.336237	11.47522	14.26460	0.1320
At most 2	0.109913	3.260195	3.841466	0.0710

Max-eigenvalue test indicates 1 cointegrating equation at the 0.05 level

1 Cointegrating equation		Log likelihood	73.36702

Normalized cointegrating coefficients (standard error in parentheses)

LNRSRCG	LNRCX	LNRPX
1.000000	1.941086	−1.752782
	(0.23718)	(0.10007)

[a]MacKinnon−Haug−Michelis (1999) *P* values.
[b]Rejection of the hypothesis at the 0.05 level.

Table C9 The series cointegration test results (between LNRFPG, LNRCM, and LNRPM)

| Sample (adjusted): 1986−2012 |
| Included observations: 27 after adjustments |
| Trend assumption: No deterministic trend |
| Lags interval (in first differences): 2−3 |

Unrestricted cointegration rank test (trace)

Hypothesized number of CE(s)	Eigenvalue	Trace statistic	0.05 Critical value	Probability[a]
None[b]	0.510806	29.91922	24.27596	0.0088
At most 1	0.304275	10.61432	12.32090	0.0950
At most 2	0.029868	0.818715	4.129906	0.4215

Trace test indicates 1 cointegrating equation at the 0.05 level

Unrestricted cointegration rank test (maximum eigenvalue)

Hypothesized number of CE(s)	Eigenvalue	Max-eigen statistic	0.05 Critical value	Probability[a]
None[b]	0.510806	19.30489	17.79730	0.0295
At most 1	0.304275	9.795608	11.22480	0.0882
At most 2	0.029868	0.818715	4.129906	0.4215

Max-eigenvalue test indicates 1 cointegrating equation at the 0.05 level

1 Cointegrating equation		**Log likelihood**	**50.23088**
Normalized cointegrating coefficients (standard error in parentheses)			
LNRFPG	LNRCM	LNRPM	
1.000000	0.810078	−1.321366	
	(0.12867)	(0.12164)	

[a]MacKinnon−Haug−Michelis (1999) P values.
[b]Rejection of the hypothesis at the 0.05 level.

Table C10 The series cointegration test results (between LNRFPG, LNRCX, and LNRPX)

Sample (adjusted): 1985−2012
Included observations: 28 after adjustments
Trend assumption: Linear deterministic trend
Lags interval (in first differences): 1−2

Unrestricted cointegration rank test (trace)

Hypothesized number of CE(s)	Eigenvalue	Trace statistic	0.05 Critical value	Probability[a]
None[b]	0.663349	44.89671	29.79707	0.0005
At most 1	0.333686	14.41290	15.49471	0.0723
At most 2	0.103048	3.045082	3.841466	0.0810

Trace test indicates 1 cointegrating equation at the 0.05 level

Unrestricted cointegration rank test (maximum eigenvalue)

Hypothesized number of CE(s)	Eigenvalue	Max-eigen statistic	0.05 Critical value	Probability[a]
None[b]	0.663349	30.48381	21.13162	0.0018
At most 1	0.333686	11.36782	14.26460	0.1367
At most 2	0.103048	3.045082	3.841466	0.0810

Max-eigenvalue test indicates 1 cointegrating equation at the 0.05 level

1 Cointegrating equation		Log likelihood	70.86138

Normalized cointegrating coefficients (standard error in parentheses)

LNRFPG	LNRCX	LNRPX
1.000000	1.678505	−1.599700
	(0.23206)	(0.09259)

[a]MacKinnon−Haug−Michelis (1999) *P* values.
[b]Rejection of the hypothesis at the 0.05 level.

Table C11 **The series cointegration test results (between LNRFUG, LNRCM, and LNRPM)**

Sample (adjusted): 1984−2012
Included observations: 29 after adjustments
Trend assumption: Linear deterministic trend
Lags interval (in first differences): 1−1

Unrestricted cointegration rank test (trace)

Hypothesized number of CE(s)	Eigenvalue	Trace statistic	0.05 Critical value	Probability[a]
None[b] At most 1[b] At most 2	0.587735 0.417449 0.016492	41.84862 16.15205 0.482242	29.79707 15.49471 3.841466	0.0013 0.0398 0.4874

Trace test indicates 2 cointegrating equations at the 0.05 level

Unrestricted cointegration rank test (maximum eigenvalue)

Hypothesized number of CE(s)	Eigenvalue	Max-eigen statistic	0.05 Critical value	Probability[a]
None[b] At most 1[b] At most 2	0.587735 0.417449 0.016492	25.69657 15.66981 0.482242	21.13162 14.26460 3.841466	0.0106 0.0298 0.4874

Max-eigenvalue test indicates 2 cointegrating equations at the 0.05 level

1 Cointegrating equation	Log likelihood	53.69342

Normalized cointegrating coefficients (standard error in parentheses)

LNRFUG	LNRCM	LNRPM
1.000000	1.393272 (0.12921)	−0.470871 (0.07467)

[a]MacKinnon−Haug−Michelis (1999) P values.
[b]Rejection of the hypothesis at the 0.05 level.

Table C12 The series cointegration test results (between LNRFUG, LNRCX, and LNRPX)

Sample (adjusted): 1985−2012
Included observations: 28 after adjustments
Trend assumption: No deterministic trend
Lags interval (in first differences): 1−2

Unrestricted cointegration rank test (trace)

Hypothesized number of CE(s)	Eigenvalue	Trace statistic	0.05 Critical value	Probability[a]
None[b]	0.575467	27.13564	24.27596	0.0212
At most 1	0.100671	3.146210	12.32090	0.8291
At most 2	0.006238	0.175223	4.129906	0.7288

Trace test indicates 1 cointegrating equation at the 0.05 level

Unrestricted cointegration rank test (maximum eigenvalue)

Hypothesized number of CE(s)	Eigenvalue	Max-eigen statistic	0.05 Critical value	Probability[a]
None[b]	0.575467	23.98943	17.79730	0.0052
At most 1	0.100671	2.970988	11.22480	0.7922
At most 2	0.006238	0.175223	4.129906	0.7288

Max-eigenvalue test indicates 1 cointegrating equation at the 0.05 level

1 Cointegrating equation	Log likelihood	**72.16598**

Normalized cointegrating coefficients (standard error in parentheses)

LNRFUG	LNRCX	LNRPX
1.000000	1.857243	−3.535869
	(0.58075)	(0.58352)

[a]MacKinnon−Haug−Michelis (1999) P values.
[b]Rejection of the hypothesis at the 0.05 level.

Table C13 **The series cointegration test results (between LNRFG, LNRCM, and LNRPM)**

Sample (adjusted): 1986−2012
Included observations: 27 after adjustments
Trend assumption: Linear deterministic trend
Lags interval (in first differences): 2−3

Unrestricted cointegration rank test (trace)

Hypothesized number of CE(s)	Eigenvalue	Trace statistic	0.05 Critical value	Probability[a]
None[b]	0.641221	38.51958	29.79707	0.0039
At most 1	0.268899	10.84326	15.49471	0.2213
At most 2	0.084604	2.386773	3.841466	0.1224

Trace test indicates 1 cointegrating equation at the 0.05 level

Unrestricted cointegration rank test (maximum eigenvalue)

Hypothesized number of CE(s)	Eigenvalue	Max-eigen statistic	0.05 Critical value	Probability[a]
None[b]	0.641221	27.67632	21.13162	0.0052
At most 1	0.268899	8.456488	14.26460	0.3342
At most 2	0.084604	2.386773	3.841466	0.1224

Max-eigenvalue test indicates 1 cointegrating equation at the 0.05 level

1 Cointegrating equation	Log likelihood	47.90214

Normalized cointegrating coefficients (standard error in parentheses)

LNRFG	LNRCM	LNRPM
1.000000	0.634709 (0.94389)	−4.650694 (0.64162)

[a]MacKinn−Haug−Michelis (1999) P values.
[b]Rejection of the hypothesis at the 0.05 level.

Table C14 The series cointegration test results (between LNRFG, LNRCX, and LNRPX)

Sample (adjusted): 1986–2012
Included observations: 27 after adjustments
Trend assumption: No deterministic trend
Lags interval (in first differences): 2–3

Unrestricted cointegration rank test (trace)

Hypothesized number of CE(s)	Eigenvalue	Trace statistic	0.05 Critical value	Probability[a]
None[b]	0.863480	56.30029	24.27596	0.0000
At most 1	0.086489	2.535535	12.32090	0.9015
At most 2	0.003443	0.093112	4.129906	0.8020

Trace test indicates 1 cointegrating equation at the 0.05 level

Unrestricted cointegration rank test (maximum eigenvalue)

Hypothesized number of CE(s)	Eigenvalue	Max-eigen statistic	0.05 Critical value	Probability[a]
None[b]	0.863480	53.76476	17.79730	0.0000
At most 1	0.086489	2.442423	11.22480	0.8688
At most 2	0.003443	0.093112	4.129906	0.8020

Max-eigenvalue test indicates 1 cointegrating equation at the 0.05 level

1 Cointegrating equation		Log likelihood	72.00202

Normalized cointegrating coefficients (standard error in parentheses)

LNRFG	LNRCX	LNRPX
1.000000	1.871948 (0.26062)	−3.622666 (0.26550)

[a]MacKinnon–Haug–Michelis (1999) P values.
[b]Rejection of the hypothesis at the 0.05 level.

298 Achieving Inclusive Growth in China Through Vertical Specialization

Table C15 The series cointegration test results (between LNRFDINIG, LNRCM, and LNRPM)

Sample (adjusted): 1986−2012
Included observations: 27 after adjustments
Trend assumption: No deterministic trend
Lags interval (in first differences): 2−3

Unrestricted cointegration rank test (trace)

Hypothesized number of CE(s)	Eigenvalue	Trace statistic	0.05 Critical value	Probability[a]
None[b]	0.439941	27.07479	24.27596	0.0216
At most 1	0.308784	11.42254	12.32090	0.0704
At most 2	0.052335	1.451354	4.129906	0.2675

Trace test indicates 1 cointegrating equation at the 0.05 level

Unrestricted cointegration rank test (maximum eigenvalue)

Hypothesized number of CE(s)	Eigenvalue	Max-eigen statistic	0.05 Critical value	Probability[a]
None	0.439941	15.65225	17.79730	0.1021
At most 1	0.308784	9.971188	11.22480	0.0824
At most 2	0.052335	1.451354	4.129906	0.2675

Max-eigenvalue test indicates no cointegration at the 0.05 level

1 Cointegrating equation		Log likelihood	38.35069

Normalized cointegrating coefficients (standard error in parentheses)

LNRFDINIG	LNRCM	LNRPM
1.000000	0.622375	−1.839386
	(0.19238)	(0.17697)

[a]MacKinnon−Haug−Michelis (1999) P values.
[b]Rejection of the hypothesis at the 0.05 level.

Table   C16 The   series   cointegration   test   results   (between LNRFDINIG, LNRCX, and LNRPX)

Sample (adjusted): 1985−2012
Included observations: 28 after adjustments
Trend assumption: Linear deterministic trend
Lags interval (in first differences): 1−2

Unrestricted cointegration rank test (trace)

Hypothesized number of CE(s)	Eigenvalue	Trace statistic	0.05 Critical value	Probability[a]
None[b]	0.557931	37.33627	29.79707	0.0056
At most 1	0.330818	14.48020	15.49471	0.0707
At most 2	0.109035	3.232603	3.841466	0.0722

Trace test indicates 1 cointegrating equation at the 0.05 level

Unrestricted cointegration rank test (maximum eigenvalue)

Hypothesized number of CE(s)	Eigenvalue	Max-eigen statistic	0.05 Critical value	Probability[a]
None[b]	0.557931	22.85607	21.13162	0.0283
At most 1	0.330818	11.24760	14.26460	0.1422
At most 2	0.109035	3.232603	3.841466	0.0722

Max-eigenvalue test indicates 1 cointegrating equation at the 0.05 level

1 Cointegrating equation	Log likelihood	64.09726

Normalized cointegrating coefficients (standard error in parentheses)

LNRFDINIG	LNRCX	LNRPX
1.000000	0.838899	−1.172453
	(0.31752)	(0.11118)

[a]MacKinnon−Haug−Michelis (1999) P values.
[b]Rejection of the hypothesis at the 0.05 level.

Appendix D   Results of vector error correction model

Table D1 Vector error correction estimates (series: LNNE, LNRCM, and LNRPM)

Sample (adjusted): 1986—2012 Included observations: 27 after adjustments Standard errors in parentheses (·) and t-statistics in brackets [·]			
Cointegrating equation	**CointEq1**		
LNNE(−1)	1.000000		
LNRCM(−1)	0.095567		
	(0.23351)		
	[0.40926]		
LNRPM(−1)	−1.498461		
	(0.21562)		
	[−6.94941]		
C	−15.49174		
Error correction	**D(LNNE)**	**D(LNRCM)**	**D(LNRPM)**
CointEq1	−0.249413	−0.169788	−0.208680
	(0.08052)	(0.07228)	(0.05874)
	[−3.09769]	[−2.34912]	[−3.55264]
R-squared	0.633381	0.437411	0.662207
Adj. R-squared	0.498311	0.230141	0.537757

Table D2 Vector error correction estimates (series: LNNE, LNRCX, and LNRPX)

Sample (adjusted): 1986–2012
Included observations: 27 after adjustments
Standard errors in parentheses (·) and t-statistics in brackets [·]

Cointegrating equation	CointEq1
LNNE(−1)	1.000000
LNRCX(−1)	1.044547
	(0.39912)
	[2.61710]
LNRPX(−1)	−0.316111
	(0.21173)
	[−1.49298]
C	−10.03556

Error correction	D(LNNE)	D(LNRCX)	D(LNRPX)
CointEq1	0.010673	− 0.117266	− 0.185671
	(0.06627)	(0.04109)	(0.02459)
	[0.16106]	[− 2.85406]	[− 7.55027]
R-squared	0.486954	0.429580	0.883082
Adj. R-squared	0.297937	0.219426	0.840007

Table D3 Vector error correction estimates (series: LNNCE, LNRCM, and LNRPM)

Sample (adjusted): 1986–2012
Included observations: 27 after adjustments
Standard errors in parentheses (·) and t-statistics in brackets [·]

Cointegrating equation	CointEq1
LNNCE(−1)	1.000000
LNRCM(−1)	0.416645
	(0.21698)
	[1.92018]
LNRPM(−1)	−1.660624
	(0.19123)
	[−8.68398]
C	−15.09516

Error correction	D(LNNCE)	D(LNRCM)	D(LNRPM)
CointEq1	−0.315128	−0.191826	−0.235353
	(0.08131)	(0.08624)	(0.07403)
	[−3.87555]	[−2.22439]	[−3.17931]
R-squared	0.726331	0.432795	0.620049
Adj. R-squared	0.625506	0.223825	0.480067

Table D4 **Vector error correction estimates (series: LNNCE, LNRCX, and LNRPX)**

Sample (adjusted): 1984—2012
Included observations: 29 after adjustments
Standard errors in parentheses (·) and t-statistics in brackets [·]

Cointegrating equation	CointEq1		
LNNCE(−1)	1.000000		
LNRCX(−1)	0.707155		
	(0.35373)		
	[1.99915]		
LNRPX(−1)	−1.212416		
	(0.13200)		
	[−9.18512]		
C	− 12.76613		

Error correction	D(LNNCE)	D(LNRCX)	D(LNRPX)
CointEq1	−0.335073	0.009113	−0.043699
	(0.05943)	(0.06210)	(0.05903)
	[−5.63802]	[0.14675]	[−0.74030]
R-squared	0.852475	0.090520	0.531110
Adj. R-squared	0.827887	−0.061060	0.452961

Table D5 **Vector error correction estimates (series: LNRTIG, LNRCM, and LNRPM)**

Sample (adjusted): 1985—2012
Included observations: 28 after adjustments
Standard errors in parentheses (·) and t-statistics in brackets [·]

Cointegrating equation	CointEq1		
LNRTIG(−1)	1.000000		
LNRCM(−1)	0.901404		
	(0.16198)		
	[5.56496]		
LNRPM(−1)	− 1.319898		
	(0.13101)		
	[− 10.0749]		
C	− 0.482042		

Error correction	D(LNRTIG)	D(LNRCM)	D(LNRPM)
CointEq1	−0.588958	−0.169567	−0.015304
	(0.10660)	(0.10821)	(0.09037)
	[−5.52518]	[−1.56701]	[−0.16935]
R-squared	0.809453	0.377317	0.569649
Adj. R-squared	0.742762	0.159378	0.419026

Table D6 Vector error correction estimates (series: LNRTIG, LNRCX, and LNRPX)

Sample (adjusted): 1985–2012
Included observations: 28 after adjustments
Standard errors in parentheses (·) and t-statistics in brackets [·]

Cointegrating equation	CointEq1
LNRTIG(−1)	1.000000
LNRCX(−1)	1.774602
	(0.22027)
	[8.05665]
LNRPX(−1)	−1.649882
	(0.10378)
	[−15.8977]
C	0.960163

Error correction	D(LNRTIG)	D(LNRCX)	D(LNRPX)
CointEq1	−0.474994	−0.122036	0.115939
	(0.13995)	(0.10199)	(0.09641)
	[−3.39405]	[−1.19654]	[1.20251]
R-squared	0.701926	0.207659	0.580763
Adj. R-squared	0.597601	−0.069661	0.434030

Table D7 Vector error correction estimates (series: LNRSRCG, LNRCM, and LNRPM)

Sample (adjusted): 1984–2012
Included observations: 29 after adjustments
Standard errors in parentheses (·) and t-statistics in brackets [·]

Cointegrating equation	CointEq1
LNRSRCG(−1)	1.000000
LNRCM(−1)	1.033363
	(0.12641)
	[8.17473]
LNRPM(−1)	− 1.429172
	(0.11699)
	[−12.2160]

Error correction	D(LNRSRCG)	D(LNRCM)	D(LNRPM)
CointEq1	−0.344161	−0.155255	0.042337
	(0.07594)	(0.09037)	(0.07141)
	[−4.53194]	[−1.71799]	[0.59285]
R-squared	0.793859	0.156158	0.475914
Adj. R-squared	0.769123	0.054897	0.413024

Table D8 Vector error correction estimates (series: LNRSRCG, LNRCX, and LNRPX)

Sample (adjusted): 1985−2012
Included observations: 28 after adjustments
Standard errors in parentheses (·) and t-statistics in brackets [·]

Cointegrating equation	CointEq1
LNRSRCG(−1)	1.000000
LNRCX(−1)	1.941086
	(0.23718)
	[8.18395]
LNRPX(−1)	−1.752782
	(0.10007)
	[−17.5164]
C	1.616294

Error correction	D(LNRSRCG)	D(LNRCX)	D(LNRPX)
CointEq1	−0.228441	−0.203433	0.078490
	(0.13437)	(0.10051)	(0.10475)
	[−1.70007]	[−2.02399]	[0.74928]
R-squared	0.676067	0.285820	0.540684
Adj. R-squared	0.562690	0.035857	0.379923

Table D9 Vector error correction estimates (series: LNRFPG, LNRCM, and LNRPM)

Sample (adjusted): 1986−2012
Included observations: 27 after adjustments
Standard errors in parentheses (·) and t-statistics in brackets [·]

Cointegrating equation	CointEq1
LNRFPG(−1)	1.000000
LNRCM(−1)	0.810078
	(0.12867)
	[6.29577]
LNRPM(−1)	−1.321366
	(0.12164)
	[−10.8631]

Error correction	D(LNRFPG)	D(LNRCM)	D(LNRPM)
CointEq1	−0.465056	−0.184271	−0.268334
	(0.11789)	(0.10522)	(0.09499)
	[−3.94479]	[−1.75125]	[−2.82492]
R-squared	0.607084	0.327091	0.501476
Adj. R-squared	0.489209	0.125218	0.351918

Table D10 Vector error correction estimates (series: LNRFPG, LNRCX, and LNRPX)

Sample (adjusted): 1985–2012
Included observations: 28 after adjustments
Standard errors in parentheses (·) and t-statistics in brackets [·]

Cointegrating equation	CointEq1
LNRFPG(−1)	1.000000
LNRCX(−1)	1.678505
	(0.23206)
	[7.23310]
LNRPX(−1)	−1.599700
	(0.09259)
	[−17.2773]
C	1.799725

Error correction	D(LNRFPG)	D(LNRCX)	D(LNRPX)
CointEq1	−0.412884	−0.174273	0.038962
	(0.13123)	(0.10624)	(0.10700)
	[−3.14621]	[−1.64030]	[0.36412]
R-squared	0.698417	0.235612	0.540920
Adj. R-squared	0.592864	−0.031924	0.380242

Table D11 Vector error correction estimates (series: LNRFUG, LNRCM, and LNRPM)

Sample (adjusted): 1984–2012
Included observations: 29 after adjustments
Standard errors in parentheses (·) and t-statistics in brackets [·]

Cointegrating equation	CointEq1
LNRFUG(−1)	1.000000
LNRCM(−1)	1.393272
	(0.12921)
	[10.7832]
LNRPM(−1)	−0.470871
	(0.07467)
	[−6.30633]
C	5.468697

Error correction	D(LNRFUG)	D(LNRCM)	D(LNRPM)
CointEq1	−0.227382	−0.444906	0.013665
	(0.16595)	(0.09421)	(0.11043)
	[−1.37018]	[−4.72253]	[0.12374]
R-squared	0.159107	0.546555	0.380352
Adj. R-squared	0.018958	0.470981	0.277078

Achieving Inclusive Growth in China Through Vertical Specialization

Table D12 Vector error correction estimates (series: LNRFUG, LNRCX, and LNRPX)

Sample (adjusted): 1985–2012
Included observations: 28 after adjustments
Standard errors in parentheses (·) and t-statistics in brackets [·]

Cointegrating equation	CointEq1
LNRFUG(−1)	1.000000
LNRCX(−1)	1.857243
	(0.58075)
	[3.19801]
LNRPX(−1)	−3.535869
	(0.58352)
	[−6.05950]

Error correction	D(LNRFUG)	D(LNRCX)	D(LNRPX)
CointEq1	0.021091	−0.015076	0.037853
	(0.02610)	(0.01877)	(0.01503)
	[0.80808]	[−0.80328]	[2.51814]
R-squared	0.420476	0.203944	0.697655
Adj. R-squared	0.254898	−0.023500	0.611270

Table D13 Vector error correction estimates (series: LNRFG, LNRCM, and LNRPM)

Sample (adjusted): 1986–2012
Included observations: 27 after adjustments
Standard errors in parentheses (·) and t-statistics in brackets [·]

Cointegrating equation	CointEq1
LNRFG(−1)	1.000000
LNRCM(−1)	0.634709
	(0.94389)
	[0.67244]
LNRPM(−1)	−4.650694
	(0.64162)
	[−7.24835]
C	−7.322337

Error correction	D(LNRFG)	D(LNRCM)	D(LNRPM)
CointEq1	0.011834	−0.006291	0.066502
	(0.03175)	(0.02025)	(0.01522)
	[0.37274]	[−0.31069]	[4.36894]
R-squared	0.244452	0.267375	0.623584
Adj. R-squared	−0.033908	−0.002540	0.484904

Table D14 Vector error correction estimates (series: LNRFG, LNRCX, and LNRPX)

Sample (adjusted): 1986–2012
Included observations: 27 after adjustments
Standard errors in parentheses (·) and t-statistics in brackets [·]

Cointegrating equation	CointEq1
LNRFG(−1)	1.000000
LNRCX(−1)	1.871948
	(0.26062)
	[7.18256]
LNRPX(−1)	−3.622666
	(0.26550)
	[−13.6444]

Error correction	D(LNRFG)	D(LNRCX)	D(LNRPX)
CointEq1	−0.010308	0.012627	0.079455
	(0.03655)	(0.01982)	(0.01452)
	[−0.28200]	[0.63721]	[5.47089]
R-squared	0.247812	0.199432	0.753946
Adj. R-squared	0.022156	−0.040738	0.680130

Table D15 Vector error correction estimates (series: LNRFDINIG, LNRCM, and LNRPM)

Sample (adjusted): 1986–2012
Included observations: 27 after adjustments
Standard errors in parentheses (·) and t-statistics in brackets [·]

Cointegrating equation	CointEq1
LNRFDINIG(−1)	1.000000
LNRCM(−1)	0.622375
	(0.19238)
	[3.23510]
LNRPM(−1)	−1.839386
	(0.17697)
	[−10.3941]

Error correction	D(LNRFDINIG)	D(LNRCM)	D(LNRPM)
CointEq1	−0.143668	−0.106308	0.118496
	(0.13979)	(0.07796)	(0.08501)
	[−1.02777]	[−1.36366]	[1.39388]
R-squared	0.200871	0.308435	0.252383
Adj. R-squared	−0.038868	0.100966	0.028098

Table D16 Vector error correction estimates (series: LNRFDINIG, LNRCX, and LNRPX)

Sample (adjusted): 1985−2012
Included observations: 28 after adjustments
Standard errors in parentheses (·) and t-statistics in brackets [·]

Cointegrating equation	CointEq1
LNRFDINIG(−1)	1.000000
LNRCX(−1)	0.838899
	(0.31752)
	[2.64204]
LNRPX(−1)	−1.172453
	(0.11118)
	[−10.5451]
C	2.659231

Error correction	D(LNRFDINIG)	D(LNRCX)	D(LNRPX)
CointEq1	−0.357110	−0.224005	−0.030705
	(0.16460)	(0.09265)	(0.09814)
	[−2.16956]	[−2.41768]	[−0.31286]
R-squared	0.471585	0.330052	0.554928
Adj. R-squared	0.286639	0.095570	0.399152

Appendix E   Results of Granger causality tests

Table   E1 Pairwise   Granger   causality   tests   (series: LNNE, LNRCM, and LNRPM)

Sample: 1982–2012			
Null hypothesis	Observations	F-statistic	Probability
LNRCM does not cause LNNE	30	0.06361	0.8028
LNNE does not cause LNRCM		0.03765	0.8476
LNRPM does not cause LNNE	30	2.50583	0.1251
LNNE does not cause LNRPM		0.44348	0.5111
LNRCM does not cause LNNE	29	0.28775	0.7525
LNNE does not cause LNRCM		0.71977	0.4971
LNRPM does not cause LNNE	29	3.47675	0.0472
LNNE does not cause LNRPM		0.42589	0.6580
LNRCM does not cause LNNE	28	1.12742	0.3606
LNNE does not cause LNRCM		1.01257	0.4069
LNRPM does not cause LNNE	28	2.58723	0.0801
LNNE does not cause LNRPM		1.90668	0.1595
LNRCM does not cause LNNE	27	0.70936	0.5961
LNNE does not cause LNRCM		1.04911	0.4097
LNRPM does not cause LNNE	27	4.43181	0.0114
LNNE does not cause LNRPM		1.82394	0.1682
LNRCM does not cause LNNE	26	0.57171	0.7208
LNNE does not cause LNRCM		1.23427	0.3415
LNRPM does not cause LNNE	26	5.04339	0.0066
LNNE does not cause LNRPM		1.48695	0.2521
LNRCM does not cause LNNE	25	0.87444	0.5411
LNNE does not cause LNRCM		1.65180	0.2162
LNRPM does not cause LNNE	25	3.70078	0.0256
LNNE does not cause LNRPM		1.32994	0.3167

Table E2 **Pairwise Granger causality tests (series: LNNE, LNRCX, and LNRPX)**

Sample: 1982–2012			
Null hypothesis	**Observations**	**F-statistic**	**Probability**
LNRCX does not cause LNNE	30	2.95631	0.0970
LNNE does not cause LNRCX		0.86941	0.3594
LNRPX does not cause LNNE	30	5.16832	0.0312
LNNE does not cause LNRPX		0.17606	0.6781
LNRCX does not cause LNNE	29	1.78133	0.1900
LNNE does not cause LNRCX		1.26588	0.3002
LNRPX does not cause LNNE	29	7.87966	0.0023
LNNE does not cause LNRPX		1.78685	0.1891
LNRCX does not cause LNNE	28	0.78797	0.5141
LNNE does not cause LNRCX		2.05190	0.1373
LNRPX does not cause LNNE	28	3.91828	0.0229
LNNE does not cause LNRPX		5.99338	0.0041
LNRCX does not cause LNNE	27	0.42326	0.7898
LNNE does not cause LNRCX		3.30651	0.0338
LNRPX does not cause LNNE	27	4.50473	0.0107
LNNE does not cause LNRPX		3.34090	0.0327
LNRCX does not cause LNNE	26	0.39574	0.8441
LNNE does not cause LNRCX		3.09445	0.0408
LNRPX does not cause LNNE	26	4.70809	0.0087
LNNE does not cause LNRPX		1.96480	0.1428
LNRCX does not cause LNNE	25	0.72431	0.6387
LNNE does not cause LNRCX		3.48636	0.0312
LNRPX does not cause LNNE	25	3.11012	0.0447
LNNE does not cause LNRPX		1.40057	0.2911

Table E3 Pairwise Granger causality tests (series: LNNCE, LNRCM, and LNRPM)

Sample: 1982–2012			
Null hypothesis	Observations	F-statistic	Probability
LNRCM does not cause LNNCE	30	0.10703	0.7461
LNNCE does not cause LNRCM		0.04689	0.8302
LNRPM does not cause LNNCE	30	3.29437	0.0806
LNNCE does not cause LNRPM		0.13699	0.7142
LNRCM does not cause LNNCE	29	0.41063	0.6678
LNNCE does not cause LNRCM		0.59408	0.5600
LNRPM does not cause LNNCE	29	3.93409	0.0333
LNNCE does not cause LNRPM		0.34843	0.7093
LNRCM does not cause LNNCE	28	1.15388	0.3507
LNNCE does not cause LNRCM		2.44605	0.0922
LNRPM does not cause LNNCE	28	3.80837	0.0252
LNNCE does not cause LNRPM		0.74706	0.5361
LNRCM does not cause LNNCE	27	0.22887	0.9186
LNNCE does not cause LNRCM		1.31383	0.3025
LNRPM does not cause LNNCE	27	4.25748	0.0134
LNNCE does not cause LNRPM		0.31335	0.8653
LNRCM does not cause LNNCE	26	0.53678	0.7455
LNNCE does not cause LNRCM		2.95973	0.0470
LNRPM does not cause LNNCE	26	2.96925	0.0465
LNNCE does not cause LNRPM		0.72066	0.6181
LNRCM does not cause LNNCE	25	0.99249	0.4723
LNNCE does not cause LNRCM		2.64577	0.0715
LNRPM does not cause LNNCE	25	2.38083	0.0947
LNNCE does not cause LNRPM		1.30591	0.3259

Table E4 **Pairwise Granger causality tests (series: LNNCE, LNRCX, and LNRPX)**

Sample: 1982–2012			
Null hypothesis	**Observations**	**F-statistic**	**Probability**
LNRCX does not cause LNNCE	30	0.70570	0.4083
LNNCE does not cause LNRCX		0.93899	0.3411
LNRPX does not cause LNNCE	30	5.02472	0.0334
LNNCE does not cause LNRPX		7.8E-05	0.9930
LNRCX does not cause LNNCE	29	0.71221	0.5006
LNNCE does not cause LNRCX		0.42196	0.6605
LNRPX does not cause LNNCE	29	8.18813	0.0019
LNNCE does not cause LNRPX		1.18436	0.3232
LNRCX does not cause LNNCE	28	0.59943	0.6225
LNNCE does not cause LNRCX		0.69684	0.5643
LNRPX does not cause LNNCE	28	4.05472	0.0202
LNNCE does not cause LNRPX		3.55916	0.0317
LNRCX does not cause LNNCE	27	0.25036	0.9057
LNNCE does not cause LNRCX		1.26534	0.3199
LNRPX does not cause LNNCE	27	3.33618	0.0328
LNNCE does not cause LNRPX		0.84252	0.5163
LNRCX does not cause LNNCE	26	0.08887	0.9928
LNNCE does not cause LNRCX		1.33650	0.3021
LNRPX does not cause LNNCE	26	1.21654	0.3488
LNNCE does not cause LNRPX		0.57788	0.7164
LNRCX does not cause LNNCE	25	0.85780	0.5514
LNNCE does not cause LNRCX		2.08381	0.1315
LNRPX does not cause LNNCE	25	0.91176	0.5185
LNNCE does not cause LNRPX		0.61725	0.7134

Table E5 Pairwise Granger causality tests (series: LRTIG, LNRCM, and LNRPM)

Sample: 1982–2012			
Null hypothesis	**Observations**	**F-statistic**	**Probability**
LNRCM does not cause LNRTIG	26	1.20357	0.3543
LNRTIG does not cause LNRCM		1.87493	0.1587
LNRPM does not cause LNRTIG	26	0.45533	0.8031
LNRTIG does not cause LNRPM		0.63480	0.6765
LNRCM does not cause LNRTIG	25	1.09420	0.4192
LNRTIG does not cause LNRCM		2.35141	0.0978
LNRPM does not cause LNRTIG	25	2.34682	0.0983
LNRTIG does not cause LNRPM		1.37558	0.2999
LNRCM does not cause LNRTIG	24	3.04218	0.0617
LNRTIG does not cause LNRCM		3.06059	0.0608
LNRPM does not cause LNRTIG	24	5.60859	0.0100
LNRTIG does not cause LNRPM		1.33226	0.3365
LNRCM does not cause LNRTIG	23	1.90797	0.2234
LNRTIG does not cause LNRCM		2.62997	0.1276
LNRPM does not cause LNRTIG	23	5.20793	0.0297
LNRTIG does not cause LNRPM		0.46525	0.8437

Table E6 Pairwise Granger causality tests (series: LNRTIG, LNRCX, and LNRPX)

Sample: 1982−2012			
Null hypothesis	**Observations**	**F-statistic**	**Probability**
LNRCX does not cause LNRTIG	30	0.40532	0.5297
LNRTIG does not cause LNRCX		1.00057	0.3261
LNRPX does not cause LNRTIG	30	0.02253	0.8818
LNRTIG does not cause LNRPX		3.79700	0.0618
LNRCX does not cause LNRTIG	24	2.96509	0.0660
LNRTIG does not cause LNRCX		1.66190	0.2344
LNRPX does not cause LNRTIG	24	9.43075	0.0016
LNRTIG does not cause LNRPX		0.60583	0.7393
LNRCX does not cause LNRTIG	23	1.49229	0.3219
LNRTIG does not cause LNRCX		0.72526	0.6718
LNRPX does not cause LNRTIG	23	8.66347	0.0084
LNRTIG does not cause LNRPX		0.24389	0.9648
LNRCX does not cause LNRTIG	22	0.67156	0.7177
LNRTIG does not cause LNRCX		0.78539	0.6590
LNRPX does not cause LNRTIG	22	2.91110	0.2053
LNRTIG does not cause LNRPX		0.31469	0.9223

Table E7 Pairwise Granger causality tests (series: LNRSRCG, LNRCM, and LNRPM)

Sample: 1982–2012

Null hypothesis	Observations	F-statistic	Probability
LNRCM does not cause LNRSRCG	30	2.00645	0.1681
LNRSRCG does not cause LNRCM		0.31344	0.5802
LNRPM does not cause LNRSRCG	30	0.11241	0.7400
LNRSRCG does not cause LNRPM		0.99178	0.3281
LNRCM does not cause LNRSRCG	26	1.05347	0.4234
LNRSRCG does not cause LNRCM		3.13673	0.0390
LNRPM does not cause LNRSRCG	26	0.50422	0.7686
LNRSRCG does not cause LNRPM		0.57180	0.7207
LNRCM does not cause LNRSRCG	25	0.86157	0.5490
LNRSRCG does not cause LNRCM		3.01665	0.0490
LNRPM does not cause LNRSRCG	25	2.22128	0.1128
LNRSRCG does not cause LNRPM		1.16621	0.3849
LNRCM does not cause LNRSRCG	24	3.40925	0.0455
LNRSRCG does not cause LNRCM		3.42640	0.0448
LNRPM does not cause LNRSRCG	24	7.67915	0.0034
LNRSRCG does not cause LNRPM		1.25925	0.3651
LNRCM does not cause LNRSRCG	23	1.81452	0.2418
LNRSRCG does not cause LNRCM		3.71515	0.0635
LNRPM does not cause LNRSRCG	23	5.37827	0.0275
LNRSRCG does not cause LNRPM		0.40791	0.8801

Table E8 Pairwise Granger causality tests (series: LNRSRCG, LNRCX, and LNRPX)

Null hypothesis	Observations	F-statistic	Probability
Lags: 4			
LNRCX does not cause LNRSRCG	27	0.15670	0.9574
LNRSRCG does not cause LNRCX		2.30009	0.0984
LNRPX does not cause LNRSRCG	27	0.63588	0.6435
LNRSRCG does not cause LNRPX		0.53350	0.7128
Lags: 6			
LNRCX does not cause LNRSRCG	25	1.13628	0.3988
LNRSRCG does not cause LNRCX		1.38761	0.2956
LNRPX does not cause LNRSRCG	25	1.66690	0.2124
LNRSRCG does not cause LNRPX		0.43941	0.8389
Lags: 7			
LNRCX does not cause LNRSRCG	24	3.94076	0.0301
LNRSRCG does not cause LNRCX		2.00687	0.1631
LNRPX does not cause LNRSRCG	24	14.5491	0.0003
LNRSRCG does not cause LNRPX		0.57837	0.7586
Lags: 8			
LNRCX does not cause LNRSRCG	23	2.30449	0.1624
LNRSRCG does not cause LNRCX		0.88755	0.5746
LNRPX does not cause LNRSRCG	23	9.64775	0.0064
LNRSRCG does not cause LNRPX		0.23485	0.9682
Lags: 9			
LNRCX does not cause LNRSRCG	22	0.63222	0.7392
LNRSRCG does not cause LNRCX		1.25630	0.4736
LNRPX does not cause LNRSRCG	22	5.52304	0.0934
LNRSRCG does not cause LNRPX		1.05100	0.5439

Table E9 Pairwise Granger causality tests (series: LNRFPG, LNRCM, and LNRPM)

Null hypothesis	Observations	F-statistic	Probability
Lags: 4			
LNRCM does not cause LNRFPG	27	0.42213	0.7906
LNRFPG does not cause LNRCM		1.82117	0.1687
LNRPM does not cause LNRFPG	27	1.24017	0.3293
LNRFPG does not cause LNRPM		0.49238	0.7414
Lags: 5			
LNRCM does not cause LNRFPG	26	0.90823	0.5014
LNRFPG does not cause LNRCM		2.16599	0.1130
LNRPM does not cause LNRFPG	26	0.42895	0.8214
LNRFPG does not cause LNRPM		0.52510	0.7538
Lags: 6			
LNRCM does not cause LNRFPG	25	0.84961	0.5565
LNRFPG does not cause LNRCM		3.30655	0.0370
LNRPM does not cause LNRFPG	25	2.72529	0.0658
LNRFPG does not cause LNRPM		1.39774	0.2921
Lags: 7			
LNRCM does not cause LNRFPG	24	2.49689	0.1008
LNRFPG does not cause LNRCM		4.20631	0.0248
LNRPM does not cause LNRFPG	24	5.62463	0.0099
LNRFPG does not cause LNRPM		1.39307	0.3145
Lags: 8			
LNRCM does not cause LNRFPG	23	2.37486	0.1540
LNRFPG does not cause LNRCM		4.53707	0.0409
LNRPM does not cause LNRFPG	23	6.02081	0.0210
LNRFPG does not cause LNRPM		0.49283	0.8255

Table E10 **Pairwise Granger causality tests (series: LNRFPG, LNRCX, and LNRPX)**

Null hypothesis	Observations	F-statistic	Probability
Lags: 5			
LNRCX does not cause LNRFPG	26	0.19514	0.9596
LNRFPG does not cause LNRCX		0.99744	0.4522
LNRPX does not cause LNRFPG	26	0.32705	0.8888
LNRFPG does not cause LNRPX		0.38743	0.8497
Lags: 6			
LNRCX does not cause LNRFPG	25	1.17672	0.3801
LNRFPG does not cause LNRCX		1.07280	0.4299
LNRPX does not cause LNRFPG	25	2.90682	0.0547
LNRFPG does not cause LNRPX		0.47539	0.8142
Lags: 7			
LNRCX does not cause LNRFPG	24	3.50162	0.0422
LNRFPG does not cause LNRCX		1.64271	0.2393
LNRPX does not cause LNRFPG	24	9.48170	0.0016
LNRFPG does not cause LNRPX		0.68438	0.6844
Lags: 8			
LNRCX does not cause LNRFPG	23	2.19543	0.1768
LNRFPG does not cause LNRCX		0.75495	0.6532
LNRPX does not cause LNRFPG	23	9.46640	0.0067
LNRFPG does not cause LNRPX		0.27455	0.9521

Table E11 Pairwise Granger causality tests (series: LNRFUG, LNRCM, and LNRPM)

Sample: 1982−2012

Null hypothesis	Observations	F-statistic	Probability
Lags: 1			
LNRCM does not cause LNRFUG	30	1.79184	0.1919
LNRFUG does not cause LNRCM		6.97199	0.0136
LNRPM does not cause LNRFUG	30	2.63311	0.1163
LNRFUG does not cause LNRPM		0.00375	0.9516
Lags: 2			
LNRCM does not cause LNRFUG	29	3.28041	0.0550
LNRFUG does not cause LNRCM		3.91680	0.0337
LNRPM does not cause LNRFUG	29	3.80227	0.0368
LNRFUG does not cause LNRPM		0.46390	0.6343
Lags: 3			
LNRCM does not cause LNRFUG	28	1.76215	0.1852
LNRFUG does not cause LNRCM		3.10326	0.0486
LNRPM does not cause LNRFUG	28	0.95596	0.4317
LNRFUG does not cause LNRPM		0.87105	0.4717
Lags: 4			
LNRCM does not cause LNRFUG	27	1.01198	0.4273
LNRFUG does not cause LNRCM		1.99305	0.1388
LNRPM does not cause LNRFUG	27	0.73660	0.5791
LNRFUG does not cause LNRPM		0.64097	0.6401
Lags: 5			
LNRCM does not cause LNRFUG	26	0.95245	0.4765
LNRFUG does not cause LNRCM		2.37421	0.0892
LNRPM does not cause LNRFUG	26	0.58610	0.7106
LNRFUG does not cause LNRPM		1.20156	0.3551

Table E12 Pairwise Granger causality tests (series: LNRFUG, LNRCX, and LNRPX)

Sample: 1982–2012			
Null hypothesis	Observations	F-statistic	Probability
Lags: 1			
LNRCX does not cause LNRFUG	30	2.13030	0.1560
LNRFUG does not cause LNRCX		0.64941	0.4274
LNRPX does not cause LNRFUG	30	1.76767	0.1948
LNRFUG does not cause LNRPX		0.24601	0.6239
Lags: 2			
LNRCX does not cause LNRFUG	29	3.32405	0.0532
LNRFUG does not cause LNRCX		0.38524	0.6844
LNRPX does not cause LNRFUG	29	4.63347	0.0199
LNRFUG does not cause LNRPX		0.50311	0.6109
Lags: 3			
LNRCX does not cause LNRFUG	28	1.34393	0.2871
LNRFUG does not cause LNRCX		1.09002	0.3751
LNRPX does not cause LNRFUG	28	1.67728	0.2023
LNRFUG does not cause LNRPX		4.14834	0.0186
Lags: 4			
LNRCX does not cause LNRFUG	27	0.66540	0.6242
LNRFUG does not cause LNRCX		1.40256	0.2731
LNRPX does not cause LNRFUG	27	1.08763	0.3922
LNRFUG does not cause LNRPX		0.95597	0.4552
Lags: 5			
LNRCX does not cause LNRFUG	26	0.58791	0.7093
LNRFUG does not cause LNRCX		2.73642	0.0597
LNRPX does not cause LNRFUG	26	1.30660	0.3131
LNRFUG does not cause LNRPX		0.65494	0.6626
Lags: 6			
LNRCX does not cause LNRFUG	25	0.91930	0.5141
LNRFUG does not cause LNRCX		1.72371	0.1987
LNRPX does not cause LNRFUG	25	1.40337	0.2901
LNRFUG does not cause LNRPX		0.42702	0.8473

(Continued)

Table E12 (Continued)

Sample: 1982–2012			
Null hypothesis	Observations	F-statistic	Probability
Lags: 7			
LNRCX does not cause LNRFUG	24	1.34659	0.3312
LNRFUG does not cause LNRCX		2.01884	0.1611
LNRPX does not cause LNRFUG	24	3.52480	0.0415
LNRFUG does not cause LNRPX		0.31942	0.9267
Lags: 8			
LNRCX does not cause LNRFUG	23	1.30008	0.3851
LNRFUG does not cause LNRCX		0.98913	0.5203
LNRPX does not cause LNRFUG	23	10.1824	0.0055
LNRFUG does not cause LNRPX		0.75381	0.6539

Table E13 Pairwise Granger causality tests (series: LNRFG, LNRCM, and LNRPM)

Sample: 1982–2012			
Null hypothesis	Observations	F-statistic	Probability
Lags: 4			
LNRCM does not cause LNRFG	27	0.94447	0.4611
LNRFG does not cause LNRCM		1.10673	0.3837
LNRPM does not cause LNRFG	27	0.23955	0.9122
LNRFG does not cause LNRPM		0.37010	0.8268
Lags: 5			
LNRCM does not cause LNRFG	26	0.60605	0.6966
LNRFG does not cause LNRCM		2.32452	0.0943
LNRPM does not cause LNRFG	26	1.05943	0.4205
LNRFG does not cause LNRPM		0.36394	0.8653
Lags: 6			
LNRCM does not cause LNRFG	25	0.54334	0.7662
LNRFG does not cause LNRCM		5.89206	0.0046
LNRPM does not cause LNRFG	25	1.53976	0.2467
LNRFG does not cause LNRPM		0.52839	0.7768
Lags: 7			
LNRCM does not cause LNRFG	24	0.33879	0.9162
LNRFG does not cause LNRCM		6.56471	0.0059

(Continued)

Table E13 (**Continued**)

Sample: 1982–2012			
Null hypothesis	**Observations**	**F-statistic**	**Probability**
LNRPM does not cause LNRFG	24	2.33744	0.1174
LNRFG does not cause LNRPM		0.58896	0.7512
Lags: 8			
LNRCM does not cause LNRFG	23	2.24556	0.1700
LNRFG does not cause LNRCM		4.10998	0.0510
LNRPM does not cause LNRFG	23	2.67955	0.1232
LNRFG does not cause LNRPM		0.23198	0.9692
Lags: 9			
LNRCM does not cause LNRFG	22	4.77270	0.1127
LNRFG does not cause LNRCM		19.8243	0.0159
LNRPM does not cause LNRFG	22	0.91493	0.5991
LNRFG does not cause LNRPM		0.78563	0.6588

Table E14 **Pairwise Granger causality tests (series: LNRFG, LNRCX, and LNRPX)**

Sample: 1982–2012			
Null hypothesis	**Observations**	**F-statistic**	**Probability**
Lags: 6			
LNRCX does not cause LNRFG	25	0.42605	0.8479
LNRFG does not cause LNRCX		1.90456	0.1612
LNRPX does not cause LNRFG	25	0.87038	0.5436
LNRFG does not cause LNRPX		0.30521	0.9223
Lags: 7			
LNRCX does not cause LNRFG	24	0.73558	0.6495
LNRFG does not cause LNRCX		1.95880	0.1714
LNRPX does not cause LNRFG	24	6.52799	0.0060
LNRFG does not cause LNRPX		0.24735	0.9605
Lags: 8			
LNRCX does not cause LNRFG	23	0.77381	0.6415
LNRFG does not cause LNRCX		1.11084	0.4620
LNRPX does not cause LNRFG	23	4.80498	0.0358
LNRFG does not cause LNRPX		0.62806	0.7351

Table E15 Pairwise Granger causality tests (series: LNRFDINIG, LNRCM, and LNRPM)

Sample: 1982−2012

Null hypothesis	Observations	F-statistic	Probability
Lags: 1			
LNRCM does not cause LNRFDINIG	30	0.00472	0.9457
LNRFDINIG does not cause LNRCM		0.31303	0.5804
LNRPM does not cause LNRFDINIG	30	4.74299	0.0383
LNRFDINIG does not cause LNRPM		3.10935	0.0892
Lags: 2			
LNRCM does not cause LNRFDINIG	29	0.08083	0.9226
LNRFDINIG does not cause LNRCM		0.40071	0.6742
LNRPM does not cause LNRFDINIG	29	3.76286	0.0379
LNRFDINIG does not cause LNRPM		0.70608	0.5035
Lags: 3			
LNRCM does not cause LNRFDINIG	28	0.07047	0.9751
LNRFDINIG does not cause LNRCM		0.79424	0.5108
LNRPM does not cause LNRFDINIG	28	1.89401	0.1616
LNRFDINIG does not cause LNRPM		0.54057	0.6598
Lags: 4			
LNRCM does not cause LNRFDINIG	27	0.36348	0.8314
LNRFDINIG does not cause LNRCM		1.30663	0.3050
LNRPM does not cause LNRFDINIG	27	2.65603	0.0667
LNRFDINIG does not cause LNRPM		0.32852	0.8551
Lags: 5			
LNRCM does not cause LNRFDINIG	26	0.34544	0.8772
LNRFDINIG does not cause LNRCM		3.04635	0.0429
LNRPM does not cause LNRFDINIG	26	2.60445	0.0690
LNRFDINIG does not cause LNRPM		0.44034	0.8136
Lags: 6			
LNRCM does not cause LNRFDINIG	25	0.20377	0.9690
LNRFDINIG does not cause LNRCM		2.97541	0.0510
LNRPM does not cause LNRFDINIG	25	3.24245	0.0393
LNRFDINIG does not cause LNRPM		0.43402	0.8426

Table E16 **Pairwise Granger causality tests (series: LNRFDINIG, LNRCX, and LNRPX)**

Sample: 1982–2012			
Null hypothesis	**Observations**	**F-statistic**	**Probability**
Lags: 1			
LNRCX does not cause LNRFDINIG	30	0.10376	0.7498
LNRFDINIG does not cause LNRCX		0.28901	0.5953
LNRPX does not cause LNRFDINIG	30	3.82644	0.0609
LNRFDINIG does not cause LNRPX		2.14483	0.1546
Lags: 2			
LNRCX does not cause LNRFDINIG	29	0.11325	0.8934
LNRFDINIG does not cause LNRCX		0.05698	0.9447
LNRPX does not cause LNRFDINIG	29	4.91584	0.0162
LNRFDINIG does not cause LNRPX		1.16963	0.3276
Lags: 3			
LNRCX does not cause LNRFDINIG	28	0.28197	0.8378
LNRFDINIG does not cause LNRCX		0.11905	0.9479
LNRPX does not cause LNRFDINIG	28	1.89806	0.1609
LNRFDINIG does not cause LNRPX		0.72330	0.5493
Lags: 4			
LNRCX does not cause LNRFDINIG	27	0.16624	0.9528
LNRFDINIG does not cause LNRCX		0.76025	0.5646
LNRPX does not cause LNRFDINIG	27	1.78623	0.1756
LNRFDINIG does not cause LNRPX		0.58016	0.6808
Lags: 5			
LNRCX does not cause LNRFDINIG	26	0.14479	0.9786
LNRFDINIG does not cause LNRCX		1.14510	0.3799
LNRPX does not cause LNRFDINIG	26	1.19070	0.3598
LNRFDINIG does not cause LNRPX		0.45534	0.8031

Appendix F Impulse response function

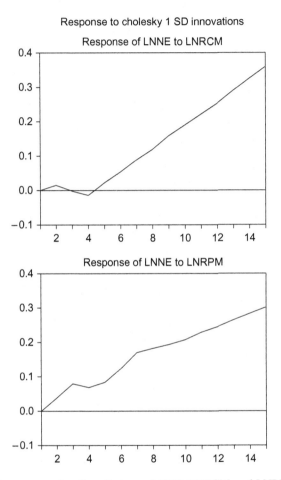

Figure F1 Impulse response functions (between LNNE, LNECM, and LNRPM).

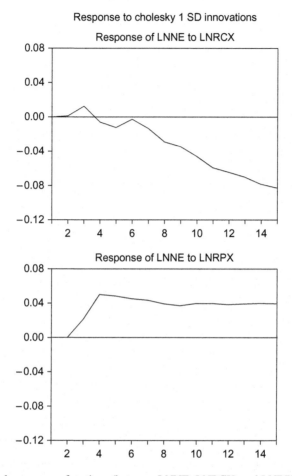

Figure F2 Impulse response functions (between LNNE, LNRCX, and LNRPX).

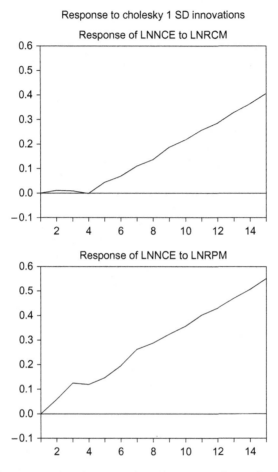

Figure F3 Impulse response functions (between LNNCE, LNRCM, and LNRPM).

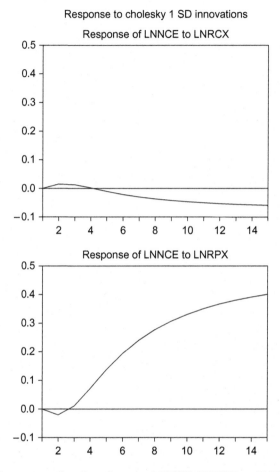

Figure F4 Impulse response functions (between LNNCE, LNRCX, and LNRPX).

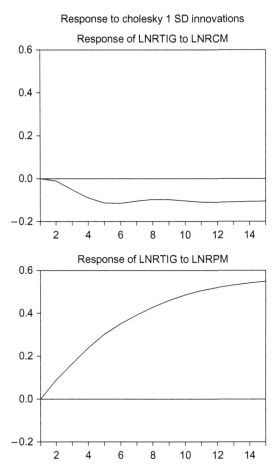

Figure F5 Impulse response functions (between LNRTIG, LNRCM, and LNRPM).

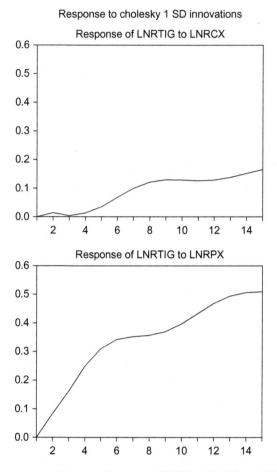

Figure F6 Impulse response functions (between LNRTIG, LNRCX, and LNRPX).

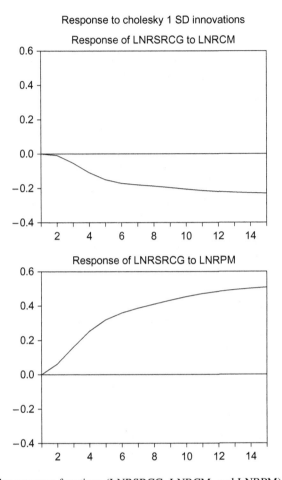

Figure F7 Impulse response functions (LNRSRCG, LNRCM, and LNRPM).

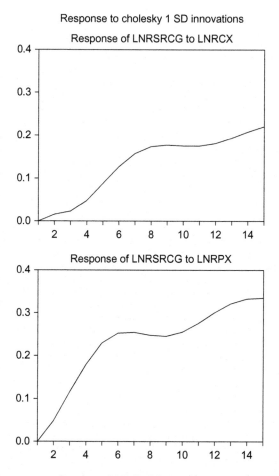

Figure F8 Impulse response functions (LNRSRCG, LNRCX, and LNRPX).

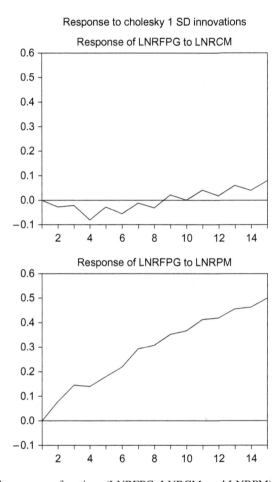

Figure F9 Impulse response functions (LNRFPG, LNRCM, and LNRPM).

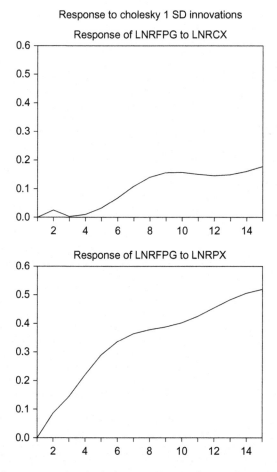

Figure F10 Impulse response functions (between LNRFPG, LNRCX, and LNRPX).

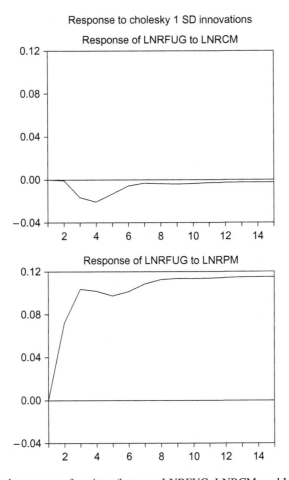

Figure F11 Impulse response functions (between LNRFUG, LNRCM, and LNRPM).

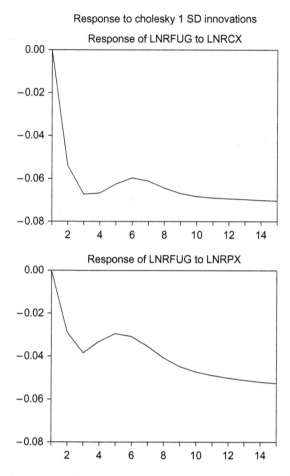

Figure F12 Impulse response functions (between LNRFUG, LNRCX, and LNRPX).

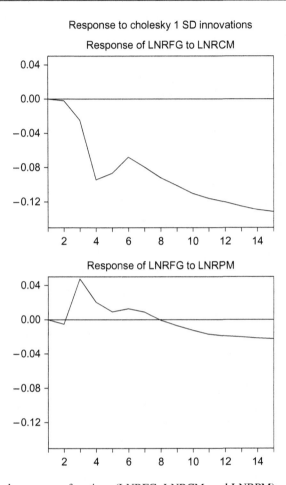

Figure F13 Impulse response functions (LNRFG, LNRCM, and LNRPM).

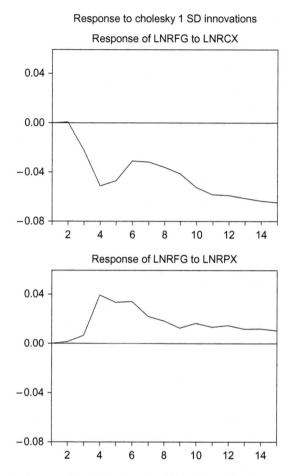

Figure F14 Impulse response functions (between LNRFG, LNRCX, and LNRPX).

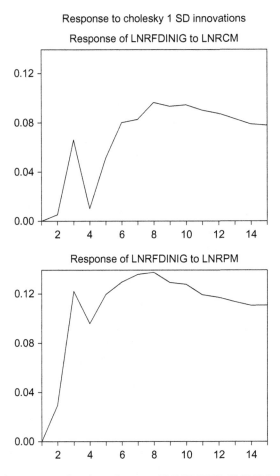

Figure F15 Impulse response functions (between LNRFDINIG, LNRCM, and LNRPM).

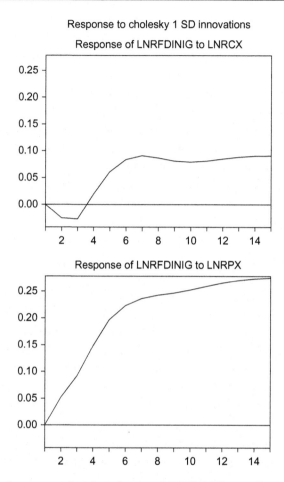

Figure F16 Impulse response functions (between LNRFDINIG, LNRCX, and LNRPX).

Appendix G   Results of variance decomposition

Table G1 **Variance decomposition of LNNE (Cholesky ordering: LNNE, LNRCM, and LNRPM)**

Period	SE	LNNE	LNRCM	LNRPM
1	0.162692	100.0000	0.000000	0.000000
2	0.200234	95.80533	0.552784	3.641882
3	0.229000	84.75521	0.432374	14.81241
4	0.241011	77.73808	0.748204	21.51372
5	0.256374	68.90866	1.378661	29.71268
6	0.292844	54.91721	4.395904	40.68689
7	0.361509	42.11322	8.851322	49.03546
8	0.446427	38.08678	12.90356	49.00967
9	0.545580	37.41946	17.07715	45.50339
10	0.663518	39.68886	19.73165	40.57949
11	0.798320	42.38003	21.30558	36.31439
12	0.946657	45.17209	22.26370	32.56421
13	1.106060	47.18729	23.19515	29.61757
14	1.276738	48.91286	23.90829	27.17884
15	1.456194	50.32824	24.47328	25.19848

Table G2 **Variance decomposition of LNNE (Cholesky ordering: LNNE, LNRCX, and LNRPX)**

Period	SE	LNNE	LNRCX	LNRPX
1	0.192458	100.0000	0.000000	0.000000
2	0.273750	99.99815	0.001819	3.51E-05
3	0.334405	99.45576	0.140111	0.404126
4	0.386085	97.89175	0.129108	1.979141
5	0.423010	96.85932	0.193533	2.947144
6	0.448779	96.19985	0.175581	3.624569
7	0.470176	95.60836	0.241342	4.150299
8	0.486486	94.89370	0.582808	4.523495
9	0.497475	94.08116	1.042453	4.876391
10	0.506744	92.86032	1.831613	5.308064
11	0.515664	91.19463	3.090929	5.714446
12	0.523513	89.40655	4.516366	6.077088
13	0.531289	87.43048	6.128828	6.440691
14	0.539707	85.17145	8.047575	6.780975
15	0.548171	82.82957	10.08252	7.087906

Table G3 Decomposition of LNNCE (Cholesky ordering: LNNCE, LNRCM, and LNRPM)

Period	SE	LNNCE	LNRCM	LNRPM
1	0.138267	100.0000	0.000000	0.000000
2	0.177382	88.78039	0.408822	10.81079
3	0.230956	63.84989	0.409940	35.74017
4	0.260834	50.47433	0.323551	49.20212
5	0.302775	37.59066	2.342798	60.06654
6	0.369669	26.59183	5.079483	68.32869
7	0.472995	18.54123	8.583742	72.87503
8	0.585177	16.86251	11.08163	72.05586
9	0.712809	16.27634	14.35518	69.36848
10	0.855623	17.92807	16.43420	65.63773
11	1.015092	19.49041	18.09205	62.41753
12	1.184124	21.71568	19.12825	59.15607
13	1.364919	23.28665	20.25198	56.46137
14	1.557354	24.94770	21.03706	54.01523
15	1.761155	26.19628	21.76565	52.03807

Table G4 Decomposition of LNNCE (Cholesky ordering: LNNCE, LNRCX, and LNRPX)

Period	SE	LNNCE	LNRCX	LNRPX
1	0.131900	100.0000	0.000000	0.000000
2	0.191293	98.25107	0.613516	1.135414
3	0.207406	97.88285	0.907828	1.209323
4	0.219603	87.54030	0.818555	11.64115
5	0.263275	64.12682	0.725217	35.14796
6	0.340471	45.63762	0.822654	53.53973
7	0.436625	36.13672	0.968343	62.89493
8	0.540934	31.62845	1.090257	67.28129
9	0.647863	29.43602	1.182072	69.38191
10	0.754658	28.33227	1.250873	70.41685
11	0.859865	27.76547	1.303421	70.93110
12	0.962676	27.47576	1.344458	71.17979
13	1.062643	27.33422	1.377154	71.28862
14	1.159543	27.27398	1.403651	71.32237
15	1.253298	27.25894	1.425441	71.31562

Table **G5 Decomposition of LNRTIG (Cholesky ordering: LNRTIG, LNRCM, and LNRPM)**

Period	SE	LNRTIG	LNRCM	LNRPM
1	0.154587	100.0000	0.000000	0.000000
2	0.218479	83.30797	0.224951	16.46708
3	0.286477	53.79650	3.365270	42.83823
4	0.384460	30.09194	7.258676	62.64939
5	0.502968	17.65236	9.314725	73.03291
6	0.625910	11.69286	9.394235	78.91291
7	0.748448	8.671484	8.520848	82.80767
8	0.870049	6.785831	7.545079	85.66909
9	0.990279	5.389584	6.796999	87.81342
10	1.108640	4.343796	6.298404	89.35780
11	1.224074	3.580422	5.962841	90.45674
12	1.335452	3.025264	5.697377	91.27736
13	1.442353	2.616040	5.453860	91.93010
14	1.544994	2.302901	5.227786	92.46931
15	1.643794	2.051311	5.030216	92.91847

Table **G6 Decomposition of LNRTIG (Cholesky ordering: LNRTIG, LNRCX, and LNRPX)**

Period	SE	LNRTIG	LNRCX	LNRPX
1	0.193345	100.0000	0.000000	0.000000
2	0.320013	93.08998	0.184124	6.725895
3	0.459016	84.18399	0.095694	15.72031
4	0.588991	72.43114	0.108696	27.46016
5	0.716883	62.44258	0.305148	37.25227
6	0.842656	55.60195	0.865579	43.53247
7	0.970117	52.18943	1.702914	46.10766
8	1.103416	51.31923	2.524095	46.15668
9	1.243802	51.72333	3.075353	45.20132
10	1.388040	52.18276	3.333656	44.48358
11	1.531542	52.04082	3.420164	44.53901
12	1.671182	51.26488	3.465172	45.26995
13	1.805936	50.19046	3.549794	46.25974
14	1.936347	49.19938	3.700698	47.09993
15	2.063876	48.52478	3.897696	47.57753

Table G7 **Decomposition of LNRSRCG (Cholesky ordering: LNRSRCG, LNRCM, and LNRPM)**

Period	SE	LNRSRCG	LNRCM	LNRPM
1	0.138314	100.0000	0.000000	0.000000
2	0.234458	92.79693	0.126612	7.076460
3	0.336234	70.95218	2.567642	26.48018
4	0.465926	49.50921	6.790805	43.69999
5	0.611729	37.24015	9.948271	52.81158
6	0.758329	31.42397	11.57301	57.00302
7	0.899677	28.65584	12.25667	59.08750
8	1.035416	27.06198	12.53669	60.40133
9	1.166690	25.87205	12.69752	61.43043
10	1.294202	24.87345	12.83835	62.28819
11	1.417899	24.04543	12.97013	62.98444
12	1.537430	23.38628	13.08152	63.53220
13	1.652596	22.87050	13.16732	63.96218
14	1.763473	22.46013	13.23152	64.30835
15	1.870310	22.12228	13.28135	64.59637

Table G8 **Decomposition of LNRSRCG (Cholesky ordering: LNRSRCG, LNRCX, and LNRPX)**

Period	SE	LNRSRCG	LNRCX	LNRPX
1	0.178839	100.0000	0.000000	0.000000
2	0.342606	97.84595	0.201318	1.952734
3	0.506546	93.56610	0.298276	6.135619
4	0.656784	88.15009	0.710441	11.13947
5	0.794718	82.26196	1.704138	16.03390
6	0.926093	77.57169	3.129029	19.29928
7	1.057153	74.72688	4.627496	20.64562
8	1.193506	73.70864	5.755062	20.53630
9	1.337492	73.90979	6.347722	19.74249
10	1.486780	74.52352	6.535363	18.94112
11	1.636076	74.94852	6.549501	18.50198
12	1.780571	74.94193	6.570447	18.48763
13	1.918069	74.56584	6.682352	18.75180
14	2.048965	74.03123	6.889166	19.07960
15	2.175133	73.55022	7.143371	19.30641

Table G9 **Decomposition of LNRFPG (Cholesky ordering: LNRFPG, LNRCM, and LNRPM)**

Period	SE	LNRFPG	LNRCM	LNRPM
1	0.174424	100.0000	0.000000	0.000000
2	0.223018	86.22662	1.460573	12.31280
3	0.291893	66.49410	1.354769	32.15113
4	0.334976	51.15813	6.869103	41.97277
5	0.385089	40.61791	5.709930	53.67216
6	0.446662	30.21476	5.793353	63.99189
7	0.535169	21.17225	4.078723	74.74903
8	0.620626	16.34630	3.282353	80.37134
9	0.714950	12.43656	2.570515	84.99292
10	0.809540	10.97396	2.005034	87.02101
11	0.913650	9.314234	1.785107	88.90066
12	1.015759	9.452900	1.477307	89.06979
13	1.121995	8.874463	1.506509	89.61903
14	1.227487	9.407001	1.367807	89.22519
15	1.336720	9.199276	1.507579	89.29314

Table G10 **Decomposition of LNRFPG (Cholesky ordering: LNRFPG, LNRCX, and LNRPX)**

Period	SE	LNRFPG	LNRCX	LNRPX
1	0.170945	100.0000	0.000000	0.000000
2	0.304276	91.37635	0.675930	7.947719
3	0.424255	83.91480	0.351396	15.73380
4	0.538658	73.25645	0.250759	26.49279
5	0.655464	62.17786	0.407685	37.41445
6	0.778341	53.75856	1.039504	45.20193
7	0.910446	48.69485	2.185272	49.11988
8	1.051380	46.75278	3.416974	49.83025
9	1.198615	46.81687	4.327551	48.85558
10	1.346970	47.56041	4.793876	47.64571
11	1.491203	48.03494	4.937271	47.02779
12	1.628947	47.86246	4.942305	47.19524
13	1.760855	47.13188	4.945864	47.92225
14	1.889024	46.15857	5.022182	48.81925
15	2.015468	45.26875	5.188816	49.54244

Table   G11 Decomposition   of   LNRFUG   (Cholesky   ordering: LNRFUG, LNRCM, and LNRPM)

Period	SE	LNRFUG	LNRCM	LNRPM
1	0.216917	100.0000	0.000000	0.000000
2	0.335330	95.30198	0.000468	4.697557
3	0.426606	91.01491	0.148994	8.836098
4	0.502937	89.25537	0.275365	10.46926
5	0.572348	88.74092	0.266524	10.99255
6	0.637708	88.38250	0.222877	11.39462
7	0.698972	87.91111	0.187628	11.90126
8	0.755976	87.43587	0.162706	12.40142
9	0.809200	87.05585	0.144490	12.79966
10	0.859361	86.77170	0.129859	13.09844
11	0.907001	86.54566	0.117613	13.33672
12	0.952436	86.35196	0.107385	13.54065
13	0.995883	86.18302	0.098852	13.71813
14	1.037546	86.03760	0.091662	13.87074
15	1.077620	85.91317	0.085504	14.00132

Table   G12 Decomposition   of   LNRFUG   (Cholesky   ordering: LNRFUG, LNRCX, and LNRPX)

Period	SE	LNRFUG	LNRCX	LNRPX
1	0.191670	100.0000	0.000000	0.000000
2	0.326766	96.46755	2.748994	0.783453
3	0.433014	94.76460	3.991689	1.243711
4	0.512018	94.12503	4.565121	1.309850
5	0.575236	93.88957	4.808327	1.302099
6	0.632261	93.80727	4.876532	1.316197
7	0.686889	93.68753	4.929640	1.382834
8	0.739538	93.48683	5.014290	1.498878
9	0.789668	93.24206	5.119309	1.638629
10	0.836982	92.99231	5.227256	1.780437
11	0.881680	92.75878	5.326640	1.914577
12	0.924181	92.54672	5.414539	2.038736
13	0.964860	92.35414	5.492588	2.153270
14	1.003970	92.17853	5.562789	2.258676
15	1.041668	92.01852	5.626342	2.355141

Table G13 **Decomposition of LNRFG (Cholesky ordering: LNRFG, LNRCM, and LNRPM)**

Period	SE	LNRFG	LNRCM	LNRPM
1	0.261328	100.0000	0.000000	0.000000
2	0.369604	99.97760	0.002784	0.019617
3	0.470468	98.68282	0.277807	1.039370
4	0.538124	95.77871	3.284403	0.936882
5	0.597576	94.45067	4.766209	0.783121
6	0.660216	94.35850	4.962044	0.679452
7	0.724728	94.10366	5.317678	0.578663
8	0.782881	93.56912	5.934930	0.495953
9	0.836469	92.90141	6.657367	0.441221
10	0.888201	92.14519	7.444248	0.410557
11	0.938570	91.40811	8.191479	0.400413
12	0.987712	90.72770	8.874051	0.398245
13	1.035621	90.07160	9.528827	0.399573
14	1.082069	89.44038	10.15432	0.405297
15	1.127130	88.86627	10.72120	0.412536

Table G14 **Decomposition of LNRFG (Cholesky ordering: LNRFG, LNRCX, and LNRPX)**

Period	SE	LNRFG	LNRCX	LNRPX
1	0.254144	100.0000	0.000000	0.000000
2	0.357609	99.99746	0.000421	0.002120
3	0.431962	99.70283	0.271526	0.025643
4	0.484074	97.96171	1.345731	0.692560
5	0.533054	97.13515	1.895112	0.969740
6	0.572629	96.86018	1.938678	1.201145
7	0.627010	96.99614	1.877042	1.126821
8	0.677644	97.06809	1.892966	1.038946
9	0.728779	97.10958	1.961459	0.928963
10	0.774622	96.93370	2.198257	0.868042
11	0.820295	96.72893	2.469849	0.801217
12	0.861838	96.53604	2.708431	0.755525
13	0.904692	96.37657	2.920444	0.702989
14	0.945430	96.21189	3.127834	0.660274
15	0.985801	96.07128	3.310027	0.618693

Table **G15** **Decomposition of LNRFDINIG (Cholesky ordering: LNRFDINIG, LNRCM, and LNRPM)**

Period	SE	LNRFDINIG	LNRCM	LNRPM
1	0.282993	100.0000	0.000000	0.000000
2	0.390364	99.31233	0.020378	0.667289
3	0.501511	90.68268	2.020109	7.297210
4	0.579171	89.78996	1.550361	8.659681
5	0.660620	87.64843	1.887427	10.46414
6	0.753076	85.73724	2.769277	11.49348
7	0.841238	84.41308	3.343427	12.24350
8	0.923292	83.21214	4.043388	12.74447
9	0.995529	82.57770	4.500854	12.92144
10	1.064043	82.15521	4.856694	12.98810
11	1.125865	82.01042	5.084223	12.90535
12	1.183095	81.92960	5.241804	12.82860
13	1.236620	81.95105	5.324027	12.72492
14	1.286367	82.02272	5.357277	12.62001
15	1.334122	82.08933	5.376106	12.53457

Table **G16** **Decomposition of LNRFDINIG (Cholesky ordering: LNRFDINIG, LNRCX, and LNRPX)**

Period	SE	LNRFDINIG	LNRCX	LNRPX
1	0.230175	100.0000	0.000000	0.000000
2	0.389656	97.78913	0.421789	1.789082
3	0.470634	94.34767	0.619968	5.032366
4	0.523392	87.30461	0.638774	12.05661
5	0.580774	77.11809	1.615766	21.26615
6	0.651757	68.47008	2.931875	28.59805
7	0.739637	63.78745	3.790343	32.42221
8	0.839986	62.51403	4.007916	33.47805
9	0.943838	62.74124	3.911447	33.34731
10	1.044068	63.13506	3.770855	33.09408
11	1.137877	63.27043	3.682447	33.04712
12	1.225935	63.19089	3.652326	33.15678
13	1.309977	63.05036	3.654495	33.29515
14	1.391275	62.95957	3.662075	33.37835
15	1.470320	62.95065	3.661395	33.38795

Concluding remarks

9

An inclusive growth study is an interdisciplinary science that seeks to promote the understanding of sustainable development and responds to some common questions, such as: what is inclusive growth?; what is inclusiveness?; which is the inclusive growth country?; and how do developing countries go upward into the club of inclusive growth countries?

This book deconstructs the inclusive growth effects of China's vertically specialized trade into six components, specifically: (1) GDP growth; (2) employment; (3) income and wage; (4) environment; (5) innovation; and (6) utilization of foreign capital. These provide a comprehensive measure of the inclusive growth effects of external trade in China. Because vertical specialization typically involves the input of labor and few Chinese intermediate inputs, it is important to make a distinction between conventional trade and processing trade. Policies for vertical specialization are an important component of the Chinese government's strategies for inclusive growth. China's policy has transformed to inclusive growth. This transition has been partly driven by having the fastest pace of participation in vertically specialized trade in recorded history by examining whether vertical specialization and processing trade have played a more important role than conventional trade in shifting toward inclusive growth. The focus may need to be specifically on China's policy regime of processing trade that provides incentives for the imports of components and intermediate goods and then transforms them into finished goods for exports.

9.1 Main results of the analysis

First, the book argues that inclusive growth analytics has a distinct character focusing on vertical specialization. Traditionally, vertical specialization and inclusive growth analyses have been performed separately. This book describes the conceptual elements for an analytical methodology aimed at integrating these two strands of analyses and to identify and prioritize China's constraints and sustained and inclusive growth. This book investigates the impact of vertical specialization on the inclusive growth performance of China during the period of 1981−2012 using the vector error correction (VEC) model under the time series framework. The Johansen-Juselius procedure is applied to test the cointegration relationship between variables followed by the VEC regression model. The empirical results trace a long-term equilibrium relationship in the variables.

Second, there are important lessons to learn from the approach in this book, including that China's policy regime of processing trade may involve just a few reforms that can be optimally sequenced to relax binding constraints and may lead to a large positive welfare impact on more inclusive growth in China. The vertical specialization approach uses a longer-term perspective because the focus is on processing trade as a means of transition to inclusive growth in China. Vertical specialization focuses on an *ex ante* analysis of sources of and constraints to sustained and inclusive growth in China. The analysis focuses on ways to raise the pace of growth by more fully utilizing parts of the labor force trapped in low-productivity activities or completely excluded from the growth process.

Third, this book applies the framework to the case of China, focusing on data and qualification studies. Sustained and inclusive growth in China can be realized when vertically specialized trade is expanding, and increasing integration into international production fragmentation is included in the growth process in an efficient way. From an empirical analysis point of view, inclusive growth associated with processing trade will have a greater impact than ordinary trade. Evidence in this book suggests that in a significant number of cases a few reforms can be optimally sequenced to relax binding constraints on trade liberalization, possibly leading to large positive welfare impacts.

Fourth, this book investigates the different impact of conventional trade and processing trade on transition to inclusive growth in China by using the comparative analysis technique. Although vertically specialized trade and China's rapid transition to inclusive growth have been recognized as important economic phenomena, the importance of international production fragmentation in transition to inclusive growth in China has been left unexamined until recently. In this book, we use a new detailed Chinese statistical dataset, from 1981 to 2012, that distinguishes conventional trade and processing trade to explain the transition to inclusive growth in China.

9.2   Policy options

China's inclusive growth is not only a process but also a situation. There are several challenges and issues to be considered by policymakers in a world of inclusive growth strategies to promote reform through opening up. This includes both the advanced level of inclusiveness of six components and the process of catching-up to an advanced level from a policy perspective. China's strength and prosperity require more than inclusive growth, and that inclusive growth must not be "inclusive economic growth" only. The pursuit of inclusive growth must be accompanied by efforts to improve people's well-being and to encourage scientific and technological innovation and technology transfer to boost the development of emerging industries in areas such as clean energy and green production. Inclusive growth cannot gain ground to meet unemployment and poverty reduction goals or to reject trade and investment protectionism in the absence of a global value chain and a free multilateral trading system.

In this book, we reassess the relationship between six components of inclusive growth in China and two types of trade by utilizing the VECM approach. The results of our book support the notation that trade policies aiming at fully benefiting from vertical specialization should reach a higher degree of liberalization and facilitation. Employment policies should take into account removing institutional barriers that affect both rural and urban areas equally, preventing arrears in wages owed to rural migrant workers, and reducing the number of rural population living in poverty. The government should prioritize and emphasize making structural adjustments to initiate improvements in the quality of the ecosystem and environment.

Arguments in favor of trade and investment liberalization are of direct relevance to this study because comparative advantages and trade are enhanced as a whole through vertical specialization. The impacts of conventional trade and processing trade on inclusive growth in China have enormous implications for development policymakers and international agencies to achieve sustainable development, share development resources, and improve systems and mechanisms that boost employment and business startups.

The results of our book support the notion that, in general, the higher level of vertical specialization could help enlarge the size of the economy, increase productive employment, accelerate poverty reduction, lower environmental damage, strengthen indigenous innovation, and upgrade utilization of foreign capital in China. Overall, our empirical evidence indicates that government policy affecting vertical specialization will have an impact on inclusive growth; the government can conduct all the policies and measures for vertical specialization participation and play a fundamental role in driving inclusive growth, stimulating reasonable enlargement of the economy, nurturing and expanding GDP growth, and promoting industrial upgrading.

One obvious policy implication from this study is that opening up, or fostering an equitable and open trading environment, strengthens the case for an active and inclusive growth policy. Another policy implication is that enlarging the size of the economy, increasing productive employment, accelerating poverty reduction, lowering environmental damage, strengthening indigenous innovation, and upgrading utilization of foreign capital should be pursued as six parts of an overall inclusive growth strategy. The evidence in this book shows that various policies that separately address each of these processes—for example, vertically specialized trade strengthening GDP growth, employment, income, environmental protection, innovation, and utilization of foreign capital—need to be coordinated within the broader framework of an overall inclusive growth strategy.

References

Adams, S., 2009. Foreign direct investment, domestic investment, and economic growth in Sub-Saharan Africa. J. Policy Model. 31, 939—949.

Adom, P.K., 2015. Asymmetric impacts of the determinants of energy intensity in Nigeria. Energy Econ. 49, 570—580.

Al-Mulali, U., Ozturk, I., 2015. The effect of energy consumption, urbanization, trade openness, industrial output, and the political stability on the environmental degradation in the MENA (Middle East and North African) region. Energy. 84, 382e389.

Anand, R., et al., 2013a. Inclusive Growth Revisited: Measurement and Evolution. VoxEU. org. Centre for Economic Policy Research. Retrieved 13 January 2015.

Anand, R., et al., 2013b. Inclusive Growth: Measurement and Determinants. IMF Working Paper (WP/13/135). Asia Pacific Department, International Monetary Fund. Retrieved 13 January 2015.

Andersson, R., Quigley, J.M., Wilhelmsson, M., 2009. Urbanization, productivity, and innovation: evidence from investment in higher education. J. Urban Stud. 66, 2—15.

Anwar, S., Sun, S., 2012. Trade liberalization, market competition and wage inequaltilty in China's manufacturing sector. Econ. Model. 29 (4), 1268—1277.

Baharumshah, A.Z., Thanoon, M.A.-M., 2006. Foreign capital flows and economic growth in East Asian countries. China Econ. Rev. 17 (1), 70—83, Elsevier.

Balasubramanyam, V.N., Salisu, M., Sapsford, D., 1996. Foreign direct investment and growth in EP and IS countries. Econ. J. 106, 92—105.

Baldwin, R.E., Robert-Nicoud, F., 2008. Trade and growth with heterogeneous firms. J. Int. Econ. 74, 21—34.

Barrientos, S., Gereffi, G., Rossi, A., 2010. Economic and Social Upgrading in Global Value Chains: Developing a Framework for Analysis. Working Paper, No. 2010/03, Capturing the Gains 2010.

Berg, A., Ostry J., 2011. Inequality and Unsustainable Growth: Two Sides of the Same Coin? IMF Staff Discussion Note No. 11/08. International Monetary Fund, Washington.

Bhagwati, J.N., 1988. Protectionism. The MIT Press, Cambridge, M.A.

Cole, M.A., 2006. Does trade liberalization increase national energy use? Econ. Lett. 92, 108—112.

Dai, M., Maitra, M., Yu, M., Unexceptional Exporter Performance in China? The Role of Processing Trade (November 23, 2011). Available at SSRN: <http://ssrn.com/abstract=1963652> or <http://dx.doi.org/10.2139/ssrn.1963652>, (accessed 23.11.14).

Dallas, M.P., 2014. Manufacturing paradoxes: foreign ownership, governance, and value chains in China's light industries. World Dev. 57, 47—62, http://dx.doi.org/10.1016/j.worlddev.2013.11.015.

Daumal, M., Ozyurt, S., 2011. The impact of international trade flows on economic growth in Brazilian States. Rev. Econ. Inst. 2 (1), 5. ISSN 2038-1379.

Davidson, C., Matusz, S.J., 2004. International Tradeand Labor Markets. Theory, Evidence and Policy Implications. W.E. Upjohn Institute for Employment Research, Kalamazoo, Michigan, Mimeo.

de Souza, E.C., Batista, J.C., 2011. TRIPs, trade and growth: When comparative advantages break down. Struct. Change Econ. Dynamics. 22, 327−341.

Dean, J.M., Lovely, M.E., Mora, J., 2009. Decomposing China−Japan−U.S. trade: vertical specialization, ownership, and organizational form. J. Asian Econ. 20 (6), 596−610. Available at: <http://works.bepress.com/judith_dean/8/>.

Dornbusch, R., Fischer, S., Samuelson, P.A., 1977. Comparative advantage, trade, and payments in a Ricardian model with a continuum of goods. Am. Econ. Rev. 67 (5).

Dutt, P., et al., 2009. International trade and unemployment: theory and cross-national evidence. J. Int. Econ. 78, 32−44.

Engle, R., Granger, C.W., 1987. Cointegration and error correction: representation, estimation and testing. Econometrica. 55 (2), 251−276, Reprinted (1991) In: Engle R., Granger C.W., (Eds.), Long-Run Economic Relationships: Readings in Cointegration. Oxford: Oxford University Press.

Erkan, C., Mucuk, M., Uysal, D., 2010. The impact of energy consumption on exports: the Turkish case. Asian J. Bus. Manage. 2, 17−23.

Fajnzylber, P., Fernandes, A., 2004. International Economic Activities and the Demand for Skilled Labor: Evidence from Brazil and China. Policy Research Working Paper No. 3426. World Bank.

Feenstra, R.C., Hanson, G.H., 1999. The impact of outsourcing and high-technology capital on wages: estimates for the United States, 1979−1990. Quaterly J. Econ. 114 (3), 907−940.

Feenstra, R.C., Hanson G., 2001. Global Production Sharing and Rising Inequality: A Servey of Trade and Wages. NBER Working Paper.

Feenstra, R.C., Hanson, G.H., 1997. Foreign direct investment and relative wages: Evidence from Mexico's maquiladoras. J. Int. Econ. 42, 371−393.

Feenstra, R., Hong, C., 2007. China's exports and employment. NBER Working Paper No. 13552.

Felbermayr, G., et al., 2011. Trade and unemployment: what do the data say? Eur. Econ. Rev. 55, 741−758.

Ferrantino, M., Koopman, R., Wang, Z., Yinug, F., Chen, L., Qu, F., et al., 2007. Classification and Statistical Reconciliation of Trade in Advanced Technology Products: The Cases of China and the United States. Working Paper Series No. WP20070906EN. Brookings-Tsinghua Center For Public Policy.

Fisher-Vanden, K., Jefferson, G.H., Liu, H.M., Tao, Q., 2004. What is driving China's decline in energy intensity? Resour. Energy Econ. 26, 77−97.

Fu, X., Pietrobelli, C., Soete, L., 2011. The role of foreign technology and indigenous innovation in the emerging economies: technological change and catching-up. World Dev. 39 (7), 1204−1212, http://dx.doi:10.1016/j.worlddev.2010.05.009.

Full text of President Hu's speech at the APEC human resources meeting, <http://www.china.org.cn/world/2010-09/16/content_20946540.htm>.

Full text: Report on China's economic, social development plan, 2011−2015. <www.china.org.cn>.

Full text: Report on the Work of the Government, 2011−2015. <www.china.org.cn>.

Fung, K.C., Iizaka, H., Tong, S.Y., 2004. Foreign direct investment in China: policy, recent trend and impact. Glob. Econ. Rev. 33 (2), 99−130.

Gao, T., 2005. Labor quality and the location of foreign direct investment: evidence from China. China Econ. Rev. 16, 274−292.

Gaulier, G., Lemoine, F., Unal-Kesenci, D., 2007. China's emergence and the reorganisation of trade flows in Asia. China Econ. Rev. 18 (3), 209−243.

Georghiou, L., Edler, J., Uyarra, E., Yeow, J., 2014. Policy instruments for public procurement of innovation: choice, design and assessment. Tech. Forecast. Soc. Chang. 86, 1−12.

Grosse, M., Harttgen, K., Klasen, S., 2008. Measuring pro-poor growth in non-income dimensions. World Dev. 36 (6), 1021−1047.

Grossman, G., Helpman, E., 1991. Innovation and Growth in the Global Economy. IMT Press, Cambridge.

Guan, J.C., Yam, R.C.M., 2015. Effects of government financial incentives on firms' innovationperformance in China: evidences from Beijing in the 1990s. Res. Policy. 44, 273−282. Journal home page <www.elsevier.com/locate/respol>.

Habito, C.F., 2009. Patterns of Inclusive Growth in Asia: Insights from an Enhanced Growth-Poverty Elasticity Analysis. ADBI Working Paper Series, No. 145. Asian Development Bank Institute, Tokyo.

Halpern, L., Koren, M., Szeidl, A., 2005. Imports and productivity. CEPR Discussion Papers 5139. CEPR Discussion Papers.

Helpman, E., Krugman, P., 1985. Market Structure and International Trade. MIT Press.

Helpman, E., Itskhoki O., Muendler M.-A., Redding S. 2015. Trade and Inequality: From Theory to Estimation. Working Paper. <http://scholar.harvard.edu/helpman/publications/trade-and-inequality-theory-estimation>, <http://www.princeton.edu/~itskhoki/papers/TradeInequalityEvidence.pdf>, (accessed 15.11.15).

Hijzen, A., 2007. International outsourcing, technological change, and wage inequality. Rev. Int. Econ. 16, 188−205.

HKTDC, 2007. Implications of Mainland Processing Trade Policy on Hong Kong. Research Report. Hong Kong Trade Development Council.

Hopenhayn, H., 1992a. Entry, exit, and firm dynamics in long run equilibrium. Econometrica. 60, 1127−1150.

Hopenhayn, H., 1992b. Exit, selection, and the value of firms. J. Econ. Dyn. Control. 16, 621−653.

Hossain, M.D.S., 2011. Panel estimation for CO_2 emissions, energy consumption, economic growth, trade openness and urbanization of newly industrialized countries. Energy Policy. 39, 6991−6999.

Hu Advocates Inclusive Growth. <http://www.china.org.cn/business/2010-09/29/content_21032034.htm>.

Hye, Q.M.A., Wizarat, S., Lau, W.Y., 2013. Trade-led growth hypothesis: an empirical analysis of South Asian countries. Econ. Model. 35 (2013), 654−660.

Ianchovichina, E., Lundstrom, S., 2009. Inclusive Growth Analytics: Framework and Application. Policy Research Working Paper Series 4851. The World Bank.

Ianchovichina, E., Gable, S.L., 2012. What is inclusive growth? In: Arezki, R., Pattillo, C., Quintyn, M., Zhu, M. (Eds.), Commodity Prices and Inclusive Growth in Low-Income Countries. International Monetary Fund.

Inkpen, A.C., 1998. Learning and knowledge acquisition through international strategic alliances. Acad. Manage. Exec. 12 (4), 69−80.

Jebli, M.B., Youssef, S.B., 2015. Output, renewable and non-renewable energy consumption and international trade: evidence from a panel of 69 countries. Renewable Energy. 83, 799e808.

Jeon, Y., Park, B.I., Ghauri, P.N., 2013. Foreign direct investment spillover effects in China: are they different across industries with different technological levels? China Econ. Rev. 26, 105−117.

Johansen, S., 1995. Likelihood-Based Inference in Cointegrated Vector Autogressive Models. Oxford University Press, Oxford.

Juselius, K., 2006. The Cointegrate VAR Model-Methodology and Applications. Oxford University, Oxford.

Klasen, S., 2010. Measuring and Monitoring Inclusive Growth: Multiple Definitions, Open Questions, and Some Constructive Proposals. ADB Sustainable Development Working Paper Series, No. 12. Manila, Asian Development Bank.

Kobrin, S., 2005. The determinants of liberalization of FDI policy in developing countries: 1991−2001. Transnatl. Corporations. 14 (1), 67−103.

Koopman, R., Wang, Z., Wei, S.-J., 2008. How Much Chinese Exports Is Really Made in China—Assessing Foreign and Domestic Value-added in Gross Exports. NBER Working Paper 14109.

Kraay, A., 2004. When Is Growth Pro-Poor? Cross-Country Evidence. IMF Working Paper No. 04/47, Washington, DC.

Krugman, P., 2000. Technonolgy, trade and factor prices. J. Int. Econ. 50 (1), 51−72.

Kuroda, H., 2006. The role of regional cooperation and integration: Toward an integrated poverty-free and peaceful East Asia. <http://www.adb.org/Documents/ Speeches/2006/ ms2006067.asp>.

Lardy, N.R., 1995. The role of foreign trade and investment in China's economic transformation. China Q. 144, 1065−1082.

Laursen, K., 2015. Revealed comparative advantage and the alternatives as measures of international specialization. Eurasian Bus Rev. 5, 99−115.

Lean, H.H., Smyth, R., 2010a. On the dynamics of aggregate output, electricity consumption and exports in Malaysia: evidence from multivariate Granger causality tests. Appl. Energy. 87, 1963−1971.

Lean, H.H., Smyth, R., 2010b. Multivariate granger causality between electricity generation, exports, prices and GDP in Malaysia. Energy. 35, 3640−3648.

Lemoine, F., Ünal-Kezenci, D., 2004. Assembly trade and technology transfer: the case of China. World Dev. 32 (5), 829−850.

Liao, W., et al., 2012. Vertical trade and China's export dynamics. China Econ. Rev. 23, 763−775.

Lixin Sun, J.L., Ford, David, G., Dickinson, 2010. Bank loans and the effects of monetary policy in China: VAR/VECM approach. China Econ. Rev. 21, 65−97.

Lo Turco, A., Maggioni, D., 2013. Does trade foster employment growth in emerging markets? Evidence from Turkey. World Dev. 52, 1−18, http://dx.doi.org/10.1016/j.worlddev.2013.06.003.

Long, C., Yang, J., Zhang, J., 2015. Institutional impact of foreign direct investment in China. World Dev. 66, 31−48, http://dx.doi.org/10.1016/j.worlddev.2014.08.001.

Ma, A.C., et al., 2009. Global production networks and China's processing trade. J. Asian Econ. 20, 640−654.

Ma, H., et al., 2015. Domestic content in China's exports and its distribution by firm ownership. J. Comp. Econ. 43 (2015), 3−18.

Mah, J.S., 2013. Globalization, decentralization and income inequality: the case of China. Econ. Model. 31, 653−658.

Markusen, J., Venables, A., 1999. Foreign direct investment as a catalyst for industrial development. Eur. Econ. Rev. 43 (20), 335−356.

Michaely, M., 1962. Concentration in international trade. North-Holland Publishing Company, Amsterdam.

Michieka, N.M., Fletcher, J., Burnett, W., 2013. An empirical analysis of the role of China's exports on CO_2 emissions. Appl. Energy. 104, 258−267.

Milberg, W., Winkler, D., 2011. Economic and social upgrading in global value chains: problems of theory and measurement. Int. Labour Rev. 150 (3−4), 341−365.

Narula, R., 2003. Globalization and Technology: Interdependence, Innovation Systems and Industrial Policy. Polity Press, Cambridge, UK.

OECD, 2008. OECD Reviews of Innovation Policy: China. Organization for Economic Cooperation and Development, Paris.

Patanakul, P., Pinto, J.K., 2014. Examining the roles of government policy on innovation. J. High Technol. Manage. Res. 25, 97−107.

Pomfret, R., 1997. Growth and transition: why has China's performance been so different? J. Comp. Econ. 25, 422−440.

Rajan, R.G., 2010. Fault Lines: How Hidden Fractures Still Threaten the World Economy. Princeton University Press, New Jersey.

Ranieri, R., Almeida Ramos, R., 2013. Inclusive Growth: Building Up a Concept. Working Paper 104. International Policy Centre for Inclusive Growth, Brazil. ISSN 1812-108X. Retrieved 13 January 2015.

Rauniyar, G., Kanbur, R., 2010. Inclusive Development: Two Papers on Conceptualization, Application, and the ADB Perspective. Asian Development Bank, Mandaluyong City, Philippines.

Romer, P.M., 1990. Endogenous technological change. J. Polit. Econ. 98, S71−S102.

Sadorsky, P., 2011. Trade and energy consumption in the middle East. Energy Econ. 33, 739e49.

Sadorsky, P., 2012. Energy consumption, output and trade in South America. Energy Econ. 34, 476e88.

Schaaper, M., 2009. Measuring China's Innovation System National Specificities and International Comparisons. STI Working Paper 2009/1. <http://www.oecd.org/sti/working-papers>.

Shahbaz, M., et al., 2013. The dynamic links between energy consumption, economic growth, financial development and trade in China: fresh evidence from multivariate framework analysis. Energy Econ. 40, 8−21.

Shen, L., 2007. The changes of China's foreign trade structure are harmful to energy saving and consumption reducing. Manage. World. 10, 43−50.

Shepherd, B., 2013. Global Value Chains and Developing Country Employment: A Literature Review. OECD Trade Policy Papers, No. 156. OECD Publishing. <http://dx. doi.org/10.1787/5k46j0qw3z7k-en>.

Sims, C.A., 1980. Macroeconomics and reality. Econometrica. 48, 1−48.

Spilimbergo, A., 2000. Growth and trade: the north can lose. J. Econ. Growth. 5, 131−146.

Stolper, W., Samuelson, P., 1941. Protection and real wages. Rev. Econ. Stud. 9, 58−73.

Sun, L., Ford, J.L., Dickinson, D.G., 2010. Bank loans and the effects of monetary policy in China: VAR/VECM approach. China Econ. Rev. 21, 65−97.

Tang, M., Hussler, C., 2011. Betting on indigenous innovation or relying on FDI: the Chinese strategy for catching-up. Technol. Soc. 33, 23−35, Journal home page <www. elsevier.com/locate/techsoc>.

Taylor, M.S., 1993. 'Quality ladders' and Ricardian trade. J. Int. Econ. 34 (3−4), 225−243.

Taylor, S.M., 1994. TRIPs, trade and growth. Int. Econ. Rev. 35.

Tekin, R.B., 2012a. Development aid, openness to trade and economic growth in Least Developed Countries: bootstrap panel Granger causality analysis. Procedia Soc. Behav. Sci. 62 (2012), 716–721, <www.sciencedirect.com>.

Tekin, R.B., 2012b. Economic growth, exports and foreign direct investment in Least Developed Countries: a panel Granger causality analysis. Econ. Model. Available from: http://dx.doi.org/10.1016/j.econmod.2011.10.013.

Tong, S., Zheng, Y., 2008. China's trade acceleration and the deepening of an East Asian regional production network. China World Econ. 16 (1), 66–81.

Topel, R.H., 1997. Factor propotions and relative wages:the supply-side determinents of wage inequlity. J. Econ. Perspectives. 11 (2), 55–74.

Trejos, S., Barboza, G., 2015. Dynamic estimation of the relationship between trade openness and output growth in Asia. J. Asian Econ. 36 (2015), 110–125.

Wagner, J., 2007. Exports and productivity: a survey of the evidence from firm-level data. World Econ. 30, 60–82.

Wagner, J., 2012. International trade and firm performance: a survey of empirical studies since 2006. Rev. World Econ. (Weltwirtschaftliches Archiv.). 148, 235–267.

Wei, S.-J., Wu, Y., 2001. Globalization and Inequality: Evidence from within China. NBER Working Paper, 8611 (November).

Xu, B., Lu, J., 2009. Foreign direct investment, processing trade, and the sophistication of China's exports. China Econ. Rev. 20, 425–439.

Xu, B., Li, W., 2008. Trade, technology, and China's rising skill demand. Econ. Transit. 16 (1), 59–84.

Yang, Y., Cai, W., Wang, C., 2014. Industrial CO_2 intensity, indigenous innovation and R&D spillovers in China's provinces. Appl. Energy. 131, 117–127.

Index

Printed in the United States
By Bookmasters